Parks and Rec

Also by Jennifer Keishin Armstrong

So Fetch

When Women Invented Television

Pop Star Goddesses

"Sex and the City" and Us

Seinfeldia

Mary and Lou and Rhoda and Ted

Sexy Feminism,
with Heather Wood Rudúlph

Why? Because We Still Like You

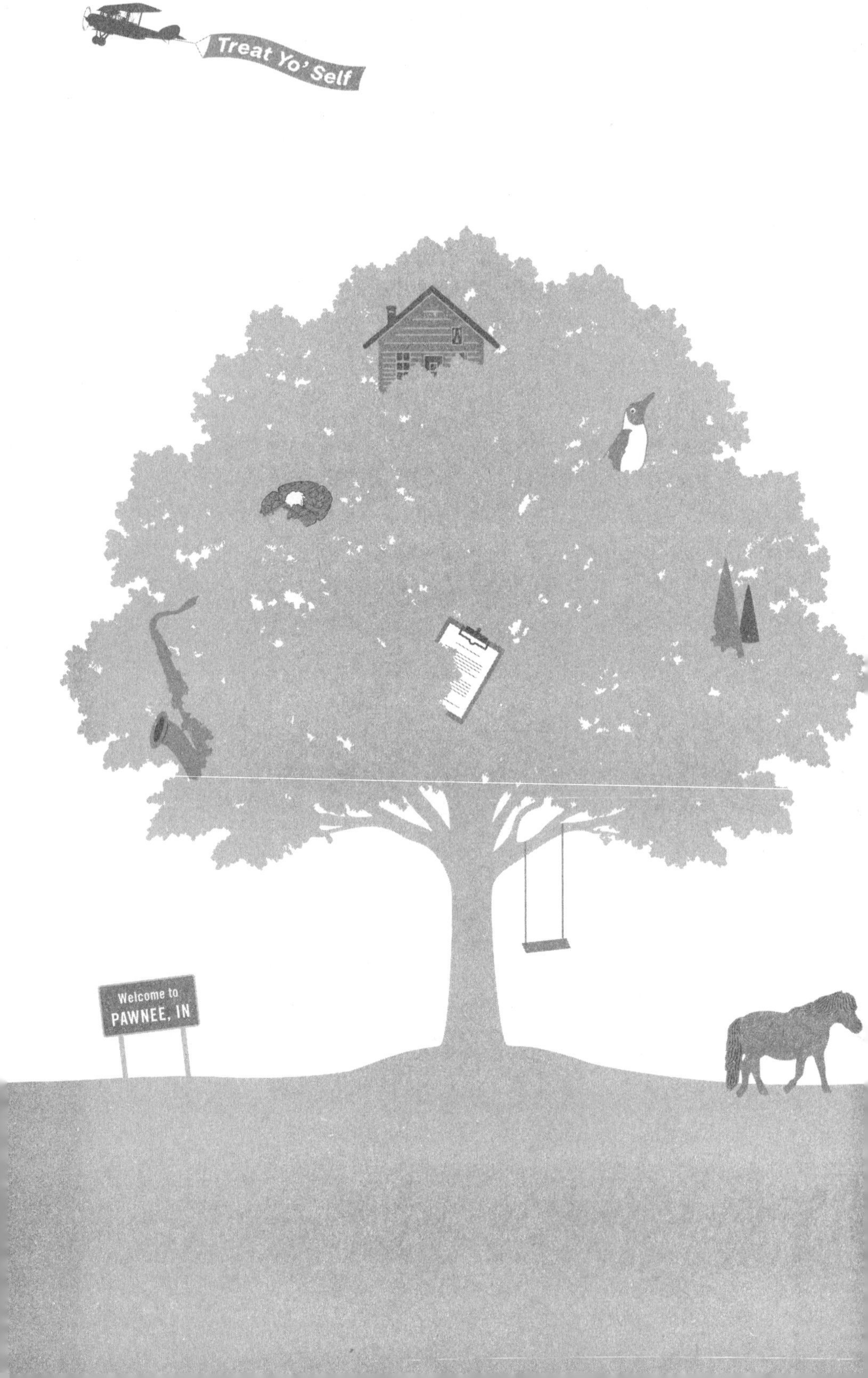
Treat Yo' Self
Welcome to
PAWNEE, IN

Parks and Rec

The Underdog TV Show That Lit'rally Inspired a Vision for a Better America

Jennifer Keishin Armstrong

DUTTON

DUTTON
An imprint of Penguin Random House LLC
1745 Broadway, New York, NY 10019
penguinrandomhouse.com

Title page art: biplane silhouette © vadimmmus/Shutterstock; clipboard illustration © yume_minol/Shutterstock; log cabin illustration © Limolida Design Studio/Shutterstock; penguin silhouette © Zeroeight.Studio/Shutterstock; pony silhouette © OryPhotograph/Shutterstock; saxophone silhouette © KR image/Shutterstock; tree silhouette © Freelancer Abdur Rahim/Shutterstock; waffle illustration © Moriz/Shutterstock

Book design by Laura K. Corless

LIBRARY OF CONGRESS CATALOGING-IN-PUBLICATION DATA

Names: Armstrong, Jennifer Keishin author
Title: Parks and rec: the underdog tv show that lit'rally inspired a vision for a better America / Jennifer Keishin Armstrong.
Description: New York, NY : Dutton, 2026. | Includes bibliographical references and index.
Identifiers: LCCN 2025036694 (print) | LCCN 2025036695 (ebook) |
ISBN 9780593854518 hardcover | ISBN 9780593854525 ebook
Subjects: LCSH: Parks and recreation (Television program) |
LCGFT: Television criticism and reviews
Classification: LCC PN1992.77.P2655 A76 2026 (print) | LCC PN1992.77.P2655 (ebook)
LC record available at https://lccn.loc.gov/2025036694
LC ebook record available at https://lccn.loc.gov/2025036695

Printed in the United States of America
1st Printing

The authorized representative in the EU for product safety and compliance is Penguin Random House Ireland, Morrison Chambers, 32 Nassau Street, Dublin D02 YH68, Ireland, https://eu-contact.penguin.ie.

To everyone working,
with the drive of Leslie Knope,
to sincerely make their communities better

CONTENTS

A group of individuals who have learned how to communicate honestly with each other, whose relationships go deeper than their masks of composure, and who have developed some significant commitment to "rejoice together, mourn together," and to delight in each other, making each other's conditions our own.

—M. Scott Peck's definition of "community"

FOREWORD BY NICK OFFERMAN

Where do I begin? How can I possibly introduce you to the life event that, excepting my marriage/salvation, was the most monumental, consequential moment of my life? Where do I begin to introduce you to this glorious tome on such an impossibly charismatic subject? It's too daunting. I might have an easier time introducing something more quantifiable, like the individual droplets of the Ohio River or the favorite sausages of my lifetime. *Parks and Recreation* changed my life so profoundly, I cannot even consider this conversation without a powerful swelling of emotion in my ursine heart. I mean, imagine you're just this guy with a mustache, a husband and woodworker and actor who happens to have a compulsion for grilling and eating meat, and then some really talented writers come along and turn all of that into Ron Swanson. Utterly life-changing. As it turns out, the show has changed a great many other lives as well, in both big and small ways, and I'm not just talking about Li'l Sebastian.

(Pauses to regain composure.)

Damn it.

At the time of this writing, this is a show that people have been finding, watching, watching again, and loving for sixteen years. That's how long people have been laughing and crying along with Leslie Knope and her team of protagonists, while shaking their fists at the (total butthole) citizens of Eagleton, the Sweetums corporation, and the infectious crapulence of Councilman Jeremy Jamm and the Saperstein family. For sixteen years, viewers having been quaking in erotic fear at the merest sexy whisper of the name Tammy II. Or is that just me? Since the advent of streaming services, more fans seem to watch the show now than at any time in its lifespan, because, as I'm given to understand, it's become a "comfort show." This checks out.

I've worked on a great many film and TV sets in my career, and I have found they're generally fueled by one ethos or another. In some instances, as you might imagine, ambition and greed will drive a production, which can breed fear and unrest among the cast and crew. Fear that you might mess up and get yelled at, or worse, fired. These sets are not fun to work on, because even if the show succeeds, the cast and crew don't want to go to work because nobody wants to be with mean people or "assholes."

It may sound corny, but the other kind of set is powered by love, laughter, farting, and joy (not necessarily in that order), which, despite sounding like a self-help book, is exactly what I found when *Parks and Recreation* began. Our top producers Mike Schur, Morgan Sackett, and Amy Poehler are the best I've ever seen at using this wonderful tradition, that of the serialized narrative television series, to manifest a show that was truly so amazing, you yourself are now beginning to consume an actual book about its history. Throughout each of the seven seasons, they treated every one of us with affection, respect, creativity, and a sense of humor. They stirred that alchemy on the set where we embroidered and delivered the most medicinal and good-hearted pack of storytelling I've ever seen; thanks in no small part to a literal "no assholes" rule. If you were a jerk to anyone, or yelled at somebody, you were excused from our show . . . forever.

In this splendid book, Jennifer Keishin Armstrong has done a magnificent job of chronicling the unlikely beginnings of the show—the way that Greg Daniels and Mike Schur conceived of the premise and the world, and then the ragtag way they put the cast together. She shares the story of how we set off slightly in the wrong direction with a sort of six-episode pilot, which everyone agreed was almost good. Good in a lot of ways, but the cornerstone of the show, Leslie Knope, still needed something that we weren't seeing a lot of on television at that time—what she needed was optimism. Ebullience. Mike and Greg and Amy determined that they didn't want our leader to be cynical in any way. She was meant to be an unflappable female leader in a world where that's a difficult thing to be. Once we wrapped our heads around that, the world said, "Please do this for six more years and 120 more episodes. Line up a murderer's row of Pawnee, Indiana's absolute all-stars, a buttload of waffles, and a daunting number of rib-eye steaks, then pick up some dozens of three-ring binders on wholesale, because we got us an old-fashioned doozy of a must-see-TV comedy joint."

One thing I love about this book is that it delivers so much more than just the names you now know. I love to lionize Mike Schur, Greg Daniels, Dean Holland, and Amy Poehler for their leadership. But I'm also always quick to give some special attention to Morgan Sackett for his quietly midwestern frugality and his ability to move money around, thereby cleverly delegating our different departmental budgets in a strategic fashion, which allowed us, without getting any extra money from the studio, to take *Parks and Recreation*, our small-town

Indiana sitcom, all over the world (some people, in crime novels, call this "cooking the books"). Thanks to Morgan's genius, we were able to take the production from its home base in Los Angeles to Indiana, New York City, Washington, DC, Wrigley Field in Chicago, San Francisco and the California redwoods, London, the Lagavulin distillery on the Isle of Islay in Scotland, and, oh, Paris—they just nipped over to Paris for a quick Leslie and Ben scene!

You'll be treated within to all manner of winning anecdotes about the adorable and talented team of champions that made up our cast, as well as the actor Jim O'Heir. For every plucky thespian that graced the screen, there were many more behind the scenes concocting every detail of this damn fine comedy program, and quite often doing it with a smile. That's because for a show that's as stupid as ours was—"First in friendship, fourth in obesity," or like anything to do with Entertainment 720, or every word out of Bobby Newport's mouth, or Jerry Gergich's fart attack, or "Stop! Pooping!," or the number of patties in a Paunch Burger, or "if we put a tax on soda, I mean, what's next, income?"—it's a world like the Simpsons' Springfield, where the ridiculous is commonplace, which means there are jokes everywhere you look. That's just a stupidly fun place to get to work, and that's why we were so damn happy making this show for you.

Then, on top of that, to fabricate and inhabit a world like that, yet still have the emotional stories sneak up on you to strike the right notes and actually make the viewers cry? That's why the writers of our show should have won every award there is. Nobody could do it like them. April and Andy's wedding. Ben and Leslie's wedding. Li'l Damn Sebastian. I'm literally crying just making this list. When Ben gave Leslie the box with her campaign button. When Ann tells Leslie she won the race. Ron waiting at JJ's for Leslie to ask her for a job. Leslie giving Ron the job of superintendent of Pawnee National Park. Ron being proud of anyone or listening to Willie Nelson sing "Buddy."

I'm afraid this list is leaning a little Ron-ward but, hey, I'm only human over here.

I'm sitting in the laundry room of an RV park in Oregon, doing our laundry because I'm a good spouse, and I'm openly weeping warm tears of gratitude and love, and laughing just thinking about our show. That's all I ever wanted to be part of. The kind of TV that made me both laugh and cry, and feel so powerfully, deliciously human. That's what made me love shows like *Cheers* and *M*A*S*H* and *Six Feet Under* and, of course, *The Office* (both versions)—the relationships make me care about these people, who thereby help me want to be a good and generous participant with the people I love, and to laugh and cry with them. I want them to find a great deal of eggs and bacon—really, *all the bacon and eggs* and other breakfast delights to boot. Because, please say it with me, "there has never been a sadness that can't be cured by breakfast food." I can't really tell you in words how special this show was to all of us, but I think we do a pretty good job of telling you in the episodes themselves. Now please enjoy this excellent book.

INTRODUCTION

"American Normality"

When I worked as a local newspaper reporter in the late 1990s, my first job out of the prestigious and expensive Northwestern University's Medill School of Journalism paid $15,000 a year, much less than Medill's annual tuition. The publication that hired me, *The Hemet News*, sat out in the middle of the desert, eighty-seven miles southeast of Los Angeles and, spiritually, not even on the same planet as Los Angeles. After I escaped that nadir months later, I landed in Newport Beach, an ultra-wealthy community in conservative Orange County, California, at the *Daily Pilot*, where I made only $50 more per week. I qualified for government assistance on my phone bills even as I met with city council members on their yachts. My go-to black dress cost about $25 at Target, but it was a simple cut and flattering shape. One of the council members admired it and asked, "Is that Calvin?" As in Klein. I made a noncommittal noise. How could I explain to this woman that some dresses come from Target?

To a girl who grew up in a small Midwestern town, this felt like the heights of glamour. I wrote three stories a day and competed with the *Los Angeles Times*' local bureau for scoops. It was so stressful that I had my first panic attacks and an ulcer. The local residents made the job both exciting and exhausting; rich people are vocal with their complaints, as they worry about property values around their multimillion-dollar homes, and they feel entitled to things being the way they prefer them. But working in local news for five years provided the best journalistic training I could ask for—in fact, when I got my dream job at *Entertainment Weekly* magazine, which led to two decades–plus of pop culture writing, the editor who hired me said he chose me out of dozens of applicants because of my news training. I have appreciated local government ever since. Being a reporter requires dedication and perseverance, and a commitment to being underpaid, just like being a public servant does—all in the name of the greater good.

Recently I moved from New York City to the small upstate town of New Paltz, New York, and my interest in local government has been reinvigorated. Debates over whether to allow a new pizza place, cannabis dispensary, or hotel in town get intense because they affect everyday lives in tangible ways. And as my partner, Jesse, and I have been building a new house in town, I've found myself back at planning board meetings, to my nerdy delight. *Here* was the real room where it happened, where the tiny details of people's lives were scrutinized and negotiated, where people fought their way through infuriating bureaucracy, and where colorful locals could air any and all grievances and be, at least briefly, heard.

And yet, though I spent hundreds of hours attending city council and planning board meetings in person during my newspaper career, what my visits to town hall make me think of most is the NBC television show *Parks and Recreation*. Running from 2009 to 2015, and cocreated by *The Office* producers Greg Daniels and Michael Schur, it follows ambitious deputy parks director Leslie Knope, played by Amy Poehler, as she tries to make her midsize town of Pawnee, Indiana, just a little better, one action at a time, with the help of quirky department staffers—and, occasionally, her obstructionist boss, Ron Swanson, a proud anti-government libertarian played by Nick Offerman.

Local officials know their territory, and often know many of their constituents, which makes the job personal to them (and means they answer to folks they see at the grocery store). I have witnessed this, first as an intern and summer reporter during high school and college, and then for my five years at the *Daily Pilot*, as well as covering Seventh-day Adventist–dominated Loma Linda, California, and mall-dominated Orland Park, Illinois, for other local papers. I reported on sewage-management meetings, planning board meetings, and city council meetings. I got scoops on hospital expansion plans and investigated police overspending on lap dances at a strip club that they were supposedly trying to shut down. (My god, the amount of time I spent in the parking lot of the Mermaid, Newport Beach's version of Pawnee's Glitter Factory, trying to nab interviews with workers or witness police officers exiting.) I monitored strife over airport plans, bay dredging, and lights from a new Mercedes dealership bouncing off the waterfront and disturbing residents of those multimillion-dollar homes. I interviewed many Leslies, Rons, and Councilman Jamms in my time. Some of them proved corrupt or incompetent. But the ones I remember most were working hard to do their jobs, often for very little recognition or pay.

Parks and Rec goes several steps beyond depicting the truth that many local officials have good intentions. It creates a world of its own—as all good sitcoms do—and in that world, local government officials like Leslie and her crew are truly beacons of hope. It makes small-town government into a font of optimism, of faith in institutions. Government isn't perfect, it says, but it helps people, no matter who they are or whether they deserve it. While many denizens of Pawnee are dim, vapid, wacky, infuriating, and sometimes all of these at once, *Parks and Rec* shows us that many bureaucrats are working for us despite all our flaws.

Writer David Foster Wallace argued that television is a good barometer for Americans' fondest desires: "If we want to know what American normality is—what Americans want to regard as normal—we can trust television. For television's whole raison is reflecting what people want to see. It's a mirror. Not the Stendhalian mirror reflecting the blue sky and mud puddle. More like the overlit bathroom mirror before which the teenager monitors his biceps and determines his better profile."

Indeed, *Parks and Rec* creates the kind of world in which I want to live. Like millions of other streaming viewers, for the past few tumultuous years, I have found solace in its vision of can-do optimism, of government officials who care, of people who have different beliefs moving past their opposing views to make others' lives better. I can feel the good intentions of its creative team and its cast emanating through the screen. Talking to cocreator Schur and stars Poehler and Offerman confirms this; they speak of this show as something like a spiritual experience.

This book is meant to share the joy and light that *Parks and Rec* continues to bring to the world, at a time when we need it more than when it was on the air. While it's lighthearted, it's hardly lightweight, especially in an era when democracy is under threat and faith in government is at all-time lows. TV has a unique ability to change people's attitudes and lives as a medium that comes into homes regularly and allows us to know characters more intimately than we know some of our closest friends. *Parks and Rec*'s characters feel like good friends, and can also restore our faith in institutions as well as in humanity as we watch Leslie passionately lead the Pawnee Goddesses, a feminist version of the Girl Scouts; put everything she has into saving the parks department with a killer Harvest Festival; or scrape together a last-minute children's concert despite budget cuts.

Schur, a nerd about both politics and philosophy, and a huge Wallace fan, wanted to impart a specific message. "*Parks and Rec* was explicitly designed to be about the Obama era and about the idea that Obama was an incrementalist," he tells me. "Leslie Knope was an incrementalist. It was about, 'Let's make this town one percent better than it was yesterday.' Obama was less about enormous revolutionary change than he was about saying, 'Let's grind it out and make everything a little better than it was before.' He was always a guy who preferred to do things in concert [with Republican opponents], and in a sober and reasoned way." This recalls a quote from sociologist Max Weber: "Politics is a strong and slow boring of hard boards. It takes both passion and perspective."

Governing, Schur says, is "difficult work, and you're often not rewarded for it, and you're not going to be lifted up on people's shoulders and carried off in a triumphant parade. You're going to probably get nothing but grief and pain and misery for your work. But that's not the point. The point is that your job is to try to improve the place where you live."

Poehler saw this in her character immediately. She says, "Leslie was coming off of the 'Yes, We Can' Obama years of 'you can make a difference.'"

Schur, however, didn't regard the show as a deeply political statement in the moment. "We were more trying to reflect back what the vibe was that we felt from the country," he says. "It was a show very much made for the era in which it was made. You couldn't make the show now with the same themes because things have gone so sideways that it would seem naive."

Parks and Rec constructs a deliberate fantasy, a vision to aspire to, as Wallace wrote. While politics gave *Parks and Rec* its bite, relationships became its strength and its secret to selling its satire. Fans seized upon its sunny celebration of friendship, whether it was Leslie's with local nurse Ann—as Leslie says, "She's my best friend, and anyone who would hurt her is someone I would murder, probably"—or the self-care-worshipping duo of Tom and Donna, who preach the gospel of "Treat yo' self." The show invented "Galentine's Day," a female friendship–based alternative to Valentine's Day that women continue to celebrate. It depicted enviable romances between Leslie and fellow bureaucrat Ben, and between deadpan April and goofball Andy. April's wedding vow: "I guess I kind of hate most things, but I never really seem to hate you."

Parks and Rec gave itself a difficult assignment, balancing sharp political commentary with heart, optimism, and top-notch comedy. And, in fact, it struggled to stay on the air for most of its 2009–2015 run. But it became the show we needed in 2016 and beyond, as the political landscape morphed from Obama-era hope and change to the fearmongering and extreme polarization of Trump eras one and two, and the mass trauma of the 2020 pandemic in between. During this period, *Parks and Rec* emerged as one of the most streamed shows in the country, and touchstones like Galentine's Day gained cultural momentum. Fan service projects proliferated: Andy's fictional band got a real album release; star Rob Lowe and executive producer Alan Yang launched a podcast called *Parks and Recollection*.

The people behind *Parks and Rec* constructed a unique blend of civic lesson, rom-com, love letter to local government, and comedy. This book traces their journey together from their origins in more optimistic political times to their efforts to make *Parks and Rec* great and keep it on the air, and to their postshow transformation into a symbol of a better America.

The cast members have all talked glowingly of their time on the show and remain close to this day, which is a tribute to Schur's careful selection of his colleagues. (In short: a strict "no assholes" policy.) They banded together to achieve something special, and they appreciate that this is a rare occurrence. Their all-for-one spirit comes through in the work itself, which is, at its core, about what can be accomplished when people who are good work together to make the world a better place. *Parks and Rec* shows us that caring people in local government can make lives better; this book will show how caring people in television can make lives better, too.

Television is a unique medium, particularly the traditional broadcast model under which *Parks and Rec* operated, because it allows for a show to find itself, right before viewers' eyes. A television series, as it airs, is a work in progress that we watch unfold. *Parks and Rec* was a striking version of this, because it was allowed extra leeway as an outgrowth of the successful show *The Office*. It clicks into place to some extent at the end of its first season, and even more at the end of its second, in palpable ways. This book tells the story of a group of brilliant and well-intentioned people who worked together to find that vision, following their hearts to clarify the show's voice and trusting that their vision would eventually find its way to viewers who would appreciate it. These good people followed their instincts and were rewarded, but those rewards were hard-won and took time.

Television has at least as much potential to do harm as good, to spread fear and darkness as much as optimism and light. The ascension and domination of Donald Trump, a very effective TV star, represented the equal and opposite reaction to *Parks and Rec*.

When Trump won the 2024 election, securing a second term of office with his defeat of Vice President Kamala Harris, CNN.com called it "the most momentous comeback in political history that will hand him massive, disruptive power at home and will send shockwaves around the world." Despite several criminal trials, indictments, a conviction, and a civil court holding him liable for sexual assault, he won not just the electoral college but, for the first time, the popular vote. Emboldened by the decisive victory, Trump and his henchman, billionaire businessman Elon Musk, began dismantling government institutions built over the nation's 250-year history.

Pete Buttigieg, the previous administration's transportation secretary and a former Indiana mayor, spoke soon afterward at a forum held by his alma mater, Harvard. "In moments like this, our salvation really will come from the local and the state bodies," Buttigieg said. "We would like a little more consistency in federalism, but a lot of the answers are going to come from mayors, from communities, from states that aren't captive to some wacky ideological project."

It would come, in other words, from real-life people like Leslie Knope.

One of those people is Ric Offerman, the father of *Parks and Rec* star Nick Offerman and the mayor of Minooka, Illinois, where Nick grew up, and a few towns over from where I grew up in Lockport, Illinois. Minooka has faced major challenges in recent years due to its growth. A new transportation hub there threatened to bring increased truck traffic and concerns about water supply; think of the gentrified Pawnee in *Parks and Rec*'s final season. (Minooka has about 13,000 residents now; when Nick was in high school, there were 1,000; and when Ric was in high school, there were 360.)

Minooka has also maintained an ongoing rivalry with the wealthier neighboring town of Channahon—not unlike Pawnee's with Eagleton—which Ric found extra complicated because he taught in Channahon for thirty-four years. At one point, the mayors of both towns made news by giving each other the finger, he says, which is the kind of thing you can imagine happening on *Parks and Rec*.

"I wasn't involved," Ric clarifies.

Has he ever encountered anyone like Ron Swanson in his time in local government?

"Listen, now, I got to be careful," he says. But he adds, "Nick's uncle is kind of like this. No matter what the subject is, it's almost an automatic null and sometimes he gets emotional, but he's not always wrong."

For example, he says, "Our public works wanted to buy a new small snowblower for our downtown area because we've just developed a number of nice restaurants and we want to keep it clean for the people coming to eat. And he didn't think the taxpayers should have to pay for that."

In Kingston, New York, a town of twenty-three thousand near where I live now, Mayor Steve Noble has followed a career path remarkably similar to that of Leslie Knope. He began as the second-in-command in the town's parks and recreation department, where he worked for a decade that included the span of the show. He even worked with his future spouse there.

"My spouse and I shared a desk for the first couple of years that we worked full-time for the department," he says, "and we would talk about the fact that we felt like we were living episodes of *Parks and Recreation* because we were dealing with all of the different cast of characters, people that were so vehement about how they felt about our city and about things that they wanted to see changed."

He appreciates the show because of the many details it gets right, like its focus on incremental progress and the challenges of getting things done in local government—and, more than anything, the impossibility of keeping constituents happy. "What we do is very visible," he says of the parks department. "So if we don't mow the grass in a park, someone is going to call us and complain. The show was able to make light of some of those things, that level of dedication that the public has about their parks and how much they care."

He thinks *Parks and Rec*'s depiction of the department itself as close-knit isn't merely a sitcom trope. "It's a stressful work environment, but at the same time, we know the work that we're doing is improving [things for] everyone," he says. "And you then have a better willingness to work with your colleagues, to then get to know them as people and bring out the best in people."

He adds: "In our department, we do act like a family. We still bake a turkey together for Thanksgiving."

When Noble became mayor in 2016, he hired a secretary who worked for him for four years. She decided to take the civil service test for the parks department. In 2020, the department's director retired and she took the job. She still invites Noble back for the department's holiday parties, and she has a Ron Swanson photo on the wall in her office.

Schur and his team had reflected what went on in local city halls across the country, using that as a microcosm for national politics. And they had anticipated what was to come in American politics. Before the final season, Schur said, "It was like, we're going to create people with completely polar opposite viewpoints and show that they can disagree strenuously on every single aspect of the way the world should function and still like each other, speak to each other in a respectful manner, collaborate on certain issues, teach each other certain things about the other's point of view that are actually real and logical and make sense and are practical and function. Really, that was it. It was, can we function as a country when we're heading toward these opposite ends of the spectrum?"

According to the world of *Parks and Rec*, the answer was yes. The real world was another story, but we could dream.

CHAPTER 1

"The Nobility of Working Really Hard for Your Little Tiny Slice of America"

Creating the Show

Mike Schur rushed into Greg Daniels's office on the set of *The Office*. The entire space was like a set of office nesting dolls: offices in offices from *The Office*, offices pretending to be offices, offices that actually were offices. Because of this, you can imagine Daniels's office fairly accurately by picturing Michael Scott's office on *The Office*, with its blinds and cheap particleboard furniture. Here, real life and fiction blended easily.

Schur couldn't wait to tell Daniels the news he'd just heard: Amy Poehler was leaving the cast of *Saturday Night Live*. Schur and Daniels had continued to brainstorm concepts for their *Office* spin-off, but the idea they felt momentum behind was *not* an *Office* spin-off: a show that would focus on a small-town government official. NBC was waiting for their big *Office* follow-up, ready to rush whatever Schur and Daniels came up with straight into production for a post–Super Bowl premiere set for January 2009. But the producers had yet to hit upon a galvanizing moment, the feeling that they were onto something ready to present to the network.

They continued to brainstorm on the government idea, a show that, in Daniels's mind, would center a "gullible, optimistic" bureaucrat: "She's really into the power of government, and I thought it would be funny to contrast her with a libertarian who didn't believe in government at all," he says. This concept could match well with Poehler, with whom Schur had worked at *SNL*.

Poehler as a sitcom star made a lot of sense to Daniels. Both Steve Carell and Tina Fey had become major stars in NBC's strong comedy lineup, on *The Office* and *30 Rock*, respectively, and Poehler had also come out of the Second City improv troupe around the same time.

"Carell had proven to be such an amazing leader, partly because he had all these years of improv experience," Daniels says. "Amy seemed like somebody who had the same heft as Carell, who could lead the show."

Hearing about Poehler's sudden availability felt like the glimmer of a real vision for Schur. He had started as a writer at *SNL* in 1998 and met Poehler when she joined the show in 2001. Poehler, a petite blonde who was now thirty-six, had become one of *Saturday Night Live*'s standouts over her seven seasons, known for her impressive range. She could play a Boston teenager; pop stars Avril Lavigne, Madonna, and even Michael Jackson; conservative commentator Ann Coulter or, on the other side of the political spectrum, presidential candidate Hillary Clinton. She became part of the series' first all-female team to host its faux-news segment, "Weekend Update," with Fey, her frequent comedy collaborator. Now, at the end of *SNL*'s 2007–2008 season, Poehler was planning to leave the legendary sketch comedy show that had made her famous (though she'd stay on for the fall of 2008 for the impending presidential election).

Like Daniels, Schur thought she would make a stellar sitcom lead. That is, if they could get her. As far as Schur was concerned, Daniels ranked as the No. 1 reason *The Office* was so successful, but No. 2 was Carell. As cringeworthy boss Michael Scott, Carell carried the show with his underlying intelligence and his comedic talent, but behind the scenes, his grounded personality, work ethic, and dedication were also key. "He's just a very, very sturdy, load-bearing wall on a TV show," Schur recalls. "And those people are very rare. There aren't that many people who can be at the center of a giant ensemble comedy like that."

Parks and Recreation grew from seeds cultivated at *The Office* and cross-pollinated with Obama-era spirit.

Its existence became a foregone conclusion when, in 2007, NBC hired a successful agent-turned-producer named Ben Silverman as cochair of its entertainment division. He would be taking over for Kevin Reilly, who hadn't managed to reverse the network's downward trajectory. The thirty-six-year-old wunderkind's expertise became widely coveted after he, as an agent, shepherded hits such as *Ugly Betty* and *The Office* to television, translating other countries' shows for American audiences.

As one of Silverman's first acts in his new job, he had asked Daniels, who had adapted the British *Office* for American audiences, to make a spin-off of the breakout show for the 2008–2009 television season. As talks progressed, the offer crystallized: thirteen episodes in the second half of the season, starting with a premiere in the hottest slot on TV, after the Super Bowl in January 2009.

Optimism was taking hold at NBC and in America. The nation was on its way to electing its first Black president, the handsome and charismatic Barack Obama (a man who literally espoused "relentless optimism" in a 2017 speech). The Great Recession remained many months in the future. And *The Office*, a show about mundane office workers with regular-person problems, was hitting new heights in its third season on NBC, a bright spot on an otherwise struggling network. The network had ordered six "supersize" forty-minute episodes of the season's total of twenty-five, one of their latest promotional gambits and a major vote of confidence. Surely the guy who had brought *The Office* to America could turn things around for NBC.

The Office's American life began with a six-episode first season in 2005. Along with the British series' cocreators, Ricky Gervais and Stephen Merchant, Silverman—who had secured the American rights while an agent in England—had chosen Daniels, cocreator of the animated series *King of the Hill*, to make it for US television. Daniels cut a professorial figure, standing six feet two, with dark, slightly graying hair, a light beard, and, often, dark-framed glasses.

The American version employed a mockumentary style, like the British version, this time to chronicle the workday lives of the employees at the Dunder Mifflin paper company branch in Scranton, Pennsylvania. The first season, largely a remake of the first UK season, struggled tonally, and landed with a thud, ranking No. 102 of 156 network shows that year. The cast and the creative team did not believe they had a hit on their hands before it aired. "There was a moment when we were shooting the last episode [of the first season], where the cast was sort of huddled outside, and everyone was a little bit glum because it was our last week of shooting," remembered Schur, who was writing for the show at the time. "Even though the show wouldn't air for months, everyone kind of felt like, there's no way this ever works."

Schur, then twenty-nine years old, was six feet tall and had a thicket of dark hair, a boyish face, and an impish smile; he was prone to wearing Converse sneakers, jeans, and fleece jackets. He was one of three junior writers who supported Daniels, along with Mindy Kaling and B. J. Novak, both of whom also appeared on the show. Schur had a different vibe, coming from *Saturday Night Live* as a writer, just as Daniels had. "We hit it off pretty early," Daniels recalls of Schur.

By the third and fourth seasons, *The Office* had found its own voice and steadily grew to become one of the biggest and best comedies on television at the time. Its focus on regular characters at regular jobs resonated with viewers, and the mockumentary format, with characters often talking to the camera as if being interviewed by an unseen producer, rhymed with the zeitgeist as reality TV invaded airwaves using a similar technique. Thus Silverman's excitement over the possibility of a spin-off, though Daniels felt too overwhelmed by *The Office*'s speeding train to think it through much and generally resisted the idea of trying to clone success.

But after twelve episodes of the fourth season of *The Office* had been shot, the Writers Guild of America decided to go on strike, shutting down productions across Hollywood. During the strike, as Daniels had more downtime to think, he widened his view. He realized that any show, any kind of sitcom that had existed in the past, "you could do a mockumentary treatment of it and refresh. So I got open to doing another mockumentary." He adds, "And Ben was begging for a spin-off."

He didn't want to do the project alone while running *The Office*, so he looked around his writers room for people he could develop with. His most senior writers were Jen Celotta, Mindy Kaling, Paul Lieberstein, B. J. Novak, and Mike Schur. Kaling, Lieberstein, and Novak appeared as series regulars on-screen, so they couldn't leave. He decided to start with Schur, who had gotten to the show a year before Celotta. Schur, he says, "felt to me like he was ready to run a show."

As Daniels and Schur walked the picket line together one day in the fall of 2007, Daniels said, "Hey, NBC wants me to do a new show. Would you want to do it with me?"

Schur, then thirty-two, couldn't believe that his idol, the man he regarded as the best in the sitcom business, was asking him to collaborate. And on a show with the rare privilege of getting directly on the air, in the prime spot after *The Office*, rather than having to go through a laborious pilot process. Daniels would step down from day-to-day showrunning at *The Office* to devote more time to the project, leaving Celotta and Lieberstein in charge; Daniels would then mentor Schur toward becoming the new series' showrunner and its driving creative force. They would develop the show over the next year, and then it would debut after the 2009 Super Bowl.

Though Schur was nervous, he said yes. "You'd have to be an idiot to say no," he says. That decision would change his life and recalibrate TV's appetite for unflinchingly empathetic comedy not undercut by the cringe factor that *The Office* had made so popular.

Their considerable mission: an unspoken request to live up to the network's biggest recent hit. They needed to reproduce the magic of *The Office*, capturing a setting that people related to and filling it with charismatic actors playing amiable but flawed characters. They had to find another Steve Carell to be at the center, no small feat; Carell imbued *The Office*'s boss character, Michael Scott, with pathos despite his bigotry and buffoonery.

When the writers' strike ended, Daniels and Schur began meeting for breakfast a few times a week at Daniels's favorite restaurant in Van Nuys, California—NORMS—pitching each other idea after idea.

Schur took notes as they worked together and still refers to them to this day: "Greg understands that you have to generate dozens and dozens and dozens of ideas just to get to the ones that are good," Schur says. "It requires a tremendous amount of generating ideas, throwing them away, revising them, coming back to them, remembering little bits of them that are worth pursuing."

Raised in West Hartford, Connecticut, Schur graduated in 1997 from Harvard University, where he was president of *The Harvard Lampoon*. (Daniels had served on the same staff in the eighties alongside future late-night host Conan O'Brien.) Like many *Lampoon* grads, Schur landed on the writing team at *Saturday Night Live*. In 2001, he became the producer of the show's trademark "Weekend Update" faux-news segments. He won his first Emmy in 2002 as part of the writing team and left the show in 2004 to move to Los Angeles with his then-girlfriend, J. J. Philbin, a fellow TV writer who was working on the teen drama sensation *The O.C.* at the time. After interviewing with several shows, he secured a position at *The Office*.

Now, as he and Daniels pondered what could be Schur's biggest career move so far, they felt stymied by the concept of a spin-off. Still, they dutifully came up with a few spin-off ideas, the most promising being a series that centered Ed Helms's character, Andy, from *The Office* with a new, quirky family living in the suburbs, inspired by the progenitor of the reality genre, the 1970s PBS documentary *An American Family*. It would, like *The Office*, use the mockumentary format, and they envisioned calling it *American Family*. They would make Andy's family the most average family in America—with the most common number of kids, living in the most average city, with the most average income.

Other ideas included a show about Jim and Pam's family, a show about Dwight on his beet farm, or a show about Craig Robinson's rule-following warehouse foreman Darryl. None seemed quite right to Daniels and Schur. For starters, they could not take Jim and Pam, played by John Krasinski and Jenna Fischer, or even Dwight, played by Rainn Wilson, off *The Office*. And the other ideas just didn't feel inspiring. They worried, in fact, that with any of these ideas, they would be "robbing the mother ship" of colorful characters who might not hold up as leads, Schur says.

The bit about the average family, however, came closer to something that would inspire them: What if the show were about an average town instead? So many shows were set in exceptional cities like Los Angeles and New York, but that wasn't where most Americans lived. What if they could see their own town reflected on a major network series?

From there the producers riffed on doing something about local government. Daniels thought there were two kinds of government narrative: the politician and the small bureaucrat. Since the politician had been done plenty, Daniels liked the idea of focusing on a small bureaucrat. "We were trying to build the character of a very government-believing, optimistic bureaucrat who was taking herself very seriously," he says. "And in order not to repeat a lot of the real estate that *The Office* was taking up, we thought it would be good to center it around a female character."

Daniels still liked the family idea. But Schur latched on to the government idea, particularly as a fan of *The West Wing* and of Robert Caro's *The Power Broker*, a behemoth biography of Robert Moses, the urban planner who shaped mid-century New York City to extreme degrees while never holding elected office. That was fine, Daniels figured. He could do the family one with Celotta next.

The stage was set. It was time to move forward. In the early spring of 2008, Schur called Poehler from his office to tell her about the new show he was working on, with only the vaguest idea of what it might be about. He wanted to know: Did she maybe want to star in a sitcom? One that was made by the people behind *The Office*?

Poehler, for her part, had been preparing to leave *SNL* for a while. That was not only because she had been on it for seven years but also because she was starting a family with her then-husband, actor Will Arnett. She knew she would have to abandon the weekly grind of a live sketch-comedy show that airs at 11:30 p.m. Eastern time to become a mother.

Schur told her that he and Greg Daniels, *The Office* guy, were making . . . something together. They hadn't settled on an idea yet. "We're working on a new show," he remembers saying to her. "We understand that you're leaving *SNL* at the end of the season, and we want to just sort of see if you'd be interested."

She said yes, to his delight. They would keep in touch as plans developed.

Soon afterward, however, she demolished those plans by revealing that she was pregnant and due to give birth in October, exactly at the time when the show would already need to be shooting to make the Super Bowl date. They were back to the beginning again.

At first, Schur felt hopeless. Would their show ever happen?

For the next few months, Daniels and Schur kept brainstorming ideas for both shows and stars, but nothing jelled.

Then it occurred to them: They were too focused on the Super Bowl of it all. Poehler was the key to the project, the most important part. Would she do it if they started shooting in February instead and gave up seven of their thirteen episodes as well as the Super Bowl slot to do so? To them, there was only one choice in the end. "Airing after the Super Bowl is a short-term decision, a decision that has the most impact now," Schur explains. "But getting Amy Poehler on your show is a long-term decision."

They agreed: Their priority was making a show with Poehler at the center.

Schur called Poehler from the balcony of his house to tell her this, and to get into the nitty-gritty of the concept a bit more. As he chain-smoked, Schur mentioned that they'd been considering a family-centered idea and something on local government. Poehler still liked the idea of doing a show with them, but she knew she didn't want to play a mom, like so many sitcom moms before her. Sunny and agreeable when it was warranted, she also had clear boundaries and was quick to express them. So that eliminated the family concept for good.

Schur switched gears, offering the faintest outline of the idea: an average American town and its government. She would play some kind of city hall wonk. They had some folks in mind for supporting roles, funny people they'd seen on TV, in improv shows, who were friends of friends. They hadn't yet determined a title, or even a strong premise; they felt like her commitment could help them to start writing.

She liked the idea and responded to the small-town setting of this show in progress. She grew up in Burlington, Massachusetts, a not-large town (with a population of about twenty-one thousand around the time she was born). Though it's only sixteen miles from Boston, she says, it "seemed culturally very far away. We were a suburban town, very middle-class." Her parents taught in local public schools and were always attending school board and committee meetings. They would often have campaign signs on their lawn for candidates running for selectman, a New England term roughly equivalent to a city council member, with one called a "first selectman" equivalent to a mayor. She spent time at a local candidate's campaign headquarters when she was in fourth grade. She went door-to-door passing out pamphlets for Michael Dukakis around the time she was in junior high. She understood what it was like to feel connected to your town, your local government.

But more important, she had learned in the past decade or so of her career to follow one rule: She should always work with people whom she liked and cared about. From their time together on *Saturday Night Live*, she knew she loved both Schur and his writing. She understood "how he operated in the world," she says. "Mike and I spoke the same language comedically." She also admired that he knew every word to the song "Baby Got Back."

On top of that, she appreciated what Daniels had done with *The Office*. She had loved the original British *Office*, which she had watched with Schur and her castmate Seth Meyers on the set of *SNL*. She had followed the American adaptation because it starred Carell, a friend from Second City. Now, she liked what Schur told her about Daniels's improv-friendly approach. "It felt like a logical next step," she recalls, "this way of collaborating and working in real time on the set that didn't involve so much 'Lights, camera, action!' That felt really exciting to me."

Poehler wanted her own show, but the right project had yet to present itself. She had fielded some offers during her time at *SNL* that didn't appeal to her and had done several other TV pilots and table reads that hadn't amounted to anything.

She appreciated that Daniels and Schur were planning to shoot the series in the single-camera style, which mimicked movies instead of the way traditional sitcoms are shot, with a laugh track or a live audience. (Mockumentaries like *The Office* took this a step further, mimicking documentary film specifically.) She had liked the format when she was part of a pilot called *North Hollywood*, created in 2001 by future super-producer Judd Apatow. It featured Poehler alongside Kevin Hart and Jason Segel as a group of young people trying to make it in Hollywood. But ABC rejected the show; HBO considered it but found it too similar to another show it was weighing, *Entourage*, which would go on to become a sensation of the 2000s.

With all this in mind, Poehler told Schur that, yes, she wanted in. He was relieved. His show was finally coming together.

Poehler appreciated his and Daniels's display of faith, giving up the prime premiere spot and half their season just to work with her. And she felt that this show was *the one*, the sitcom she should star in. Her philosophy: "If you're working with the right people, you're a success. Whether or not it hits for other people, that's not really the point." She knew that no one could will it into popularity, much less into having a lasting impact. She and her castmates at *Saturday Night Live* used to joke about this kind of thing: "What are you going to work on tonight?" "Oh, I'm going to write a classic sketch." TV didn't work that way. You did your best work, showed it to the masses, and it was none of your business how they received it.

Now, however, Poehler had to make a gamble, to match the producers' ante with her own: She would have to move from New York to Los Angeles, at least for a few months. With a husband and a new baby. Mostly, she remained in denial: "I did not think a lot of it through, because if I had, I would have been overwhelmed," she says. "I just did that one-foot-in-front-of-the-other thing at the time. That is kind of how people get you to do projects, right?"

At the time, she concentrated on what Schur had told her: They would be in LA shooting for two months, would put together a few episodes, then they'd see what happened from there. Maybe no one would want them to make more. If someone told her that she was going to make seven years of a show and raise her children in Los Angeles, she might have thought twice. But at the time, she couldn't know, which was probably for the best.

Poehler did have a long talk with Arnett about moving to Los Angeles, at least while the show was filming, and they decided to give it a shot. "I was such a New Yorker," Poehler says of her hesitation to commit to the West Coast. "I didn't physically *and* emotionally move to LA for a long time."

While she was closing out her run as a full-time *SNL* cast member, she put in overtime the following fall for the 2008 election. She continued to play vanquished Democratic primary candidate Hillary Clinton as the presidential campaign season kicked into gear for the Democrats' Barack Obama versus the Republicans' John McCain. Poehler, while visibly pregnant, played Clinton in a memorable sketch in which she and Fey, as vice presidential candidate Sarah Palin, address the nation together about the "very ugly role that sexism is playing in the campaign." Poehler as Clinton follows up with "an issue which I am frankly surprised to hear people suddenly care about." Later in the sketch, she breaks down. "I didn't want a woman to be president," she says. "*I* wanted to be president." Though Poehler is perfection here, the sketch would be best remembered for Fey's quip as Palin: "I can see Russia from my house!"

Poehler would continue working through what the *SNL* cast called "the gauntlet," when they aired not only their weekly live shows on Saturdays but also Thursday-night editions of their "Weekend Update" segments, which Poehler was still coanchoring, now alongside Meyers. So in the final weeks of her first pregnancy, she was appearing in two live shows per week, including an astonishing performance of a rap from the perspective of Palin. (Palin was appearing as a guest but, perhaps wisely, declined to perform a rap written for her.) Poehler was so pregnant during this one that it was hard not to wonder if she was about to go into labor that second.

"It would be like if at the end of a seven-year marathon, the last mile was a sprint," she says.

She got as far as she could in the election season. On October 25,

2008, just hours before she was scheduled to appear on a Saturday edition of "Weekend Update," she gave birth to son Archie Arnett in New York.

Meanwhile, Daniels and Schur were getting somewhere on the new series. They understood that *The Office* succeeded because it was set in a familiar workplace. Viewers knew fluorescent lights and cubicles all too well. "It occurred to us that if we did a show about small-town government, we had the opportunity to do for the public sector what *The Office* had done for the private sector," Schur says. "The government is an abstract concept, but everyone uses it, right? If the trash doesn't get picked up, we sure blame someone. And we get parking tickets, and we have to go to traffic court, and we need to get a dog license or whatever. The government, as a concept, was a thing that had been demonized and continues to be by roughly half the country. Our feeling was the government is just a group of people that aren't very different from the people in *The Office*."

Schur thought about his hometown of West Hartford which was a smoothly functioning town with excellent schools and libraries and well-maintained parks. He appreciated the nice life the town had made for him and wanted to examine the kinds of people who might have made that happen behind the scenes.

He was always struck by the way that in a crisis, like a hurricane, the people who showed up to help were from the government. "They were handing out water and food and shelter and providing services for people," he says. And they delivered in everyday situations, too: "Your trash is picked up and your kids are educated and there are firefighters who come to your house if it's on fire."

But NBC was still pushing for an official *Office* spin-off. Newly installed *Office* co-showrunner Paul Lieberstein, who also played HR rep Toby, had a half-joking idea to link the new show to the old: On an episode of *The Office*, a copy machine would break. After a repairman tries to fix it, to no avail, it's shipped away to be fixed but still cannot be saved. It's loaded onto a truck that takes it to a small Midwestern town. This is the spin-off: Instead of a character who transfers from one show to another, it is a copy machine. Ultimately they would abandon the idea, but the spirit remained.

Daniels and Schur had bought some time by giving up the post–Super Bowl slot, which would go to *The Office* instead. They began to shape the new series while Poehler was finishing up *SNL* and then taking maternity time off. First, they decided that while the new show would not be an *Office* spin-off, they would use the same mockumentary style of filming to tie it to its successful predecessor.

As with Daniels, Schur also liked the approach; he told Poehler that once she shot this way, she'd never want to shoot any other way again. The loose method allowed for the improv that they, and Poehler, loved. It favored grit instead of polish.

"The way in which you could push story along by using talking heads was major," Poehler says. "You could tell the audience what you were feeling, and then the camera could tell the story that the actors weren't telling. The camera became subtext, like our own subconscious." For instance, the camera could catch a wince or a sigh or a facial expression when a character might not realize the camera was zooming in on them.

For Daniels, this show marked a victory lap after his hit American adaptation of *The Office*, but for Schur it was the highest-profile shot of his career.

"Greg hiring me on *The Office* changed my life," Schur says, "and then him asking me to create a show with him sealed the deal."

The new show would become Schur's to shepherd, with all the possibility and pressure that came with it. Though he'd had some of the best jobs in Hollywood so far, this show would give him his first chance to make his own statement with his work, to make something that uplifted and celebrated the best in humanity, rather than resorting to cynicism, like so many other popular shows of the time, including *The Office* in its early days. Still, Schur remained grateful to have Daniels helping to guide the project.

"There is not a single aspect of television production that Greg doesn't fully think through," Schur says. "He has a million little aphorisms and rules and ideas and theories."

With Poehler's commitment, the producers began to gather inspirations in current culture that would prove crucial to shaping their vision. The media was touting that year, 2008, as "the year of the woman" in American politics. There had been a few previous years of women—in 1984 with Geraldine Ferraro's historic run as the first female candidate for vice president on a major-party ticket, and 1992, when four women were elected to the Senate. But in 2008, Clinton was a major contender for the Democratic nomination for president, though she lost to Obama. And Palin, a former midsize-town mayor, became the second female major-party candidate for vice president. There were also many women running for the Senate and the House, including Susan Collins in Maine, Gabrielle Giffords in Arizona, and Elizabeth Dole in North Carolina.

Dole was the one current politico whom Daniels and Schur *didn't* want Poehler's character to emulate. "There was a kind of woman in politics at the time, and I suppose to some extent there still is, who is hyper-polished, very stiff, like Elizabeth Dole was," Schur says. "She doesn't read as an authentic human being; she reads as a person who, if you want to be generous, you might say in order to survive had to take on a certain affect in a world obviously dominated, then and now, by men."

Dole had just given a major speech at the 2008 Republican convention and became Daniels and Schur's avatar of everything Poehler's character would not be. Instead, they envisioned her as an optimistic workaholic who strives to improve her town, despite every possible bureaucratic impediment, and is often foiled. The character's name would be Leslie Knope, her last name a knowing pun on the obstacles she would face.

Many other big ideas were circulating at the time that made their way into the DNA of the new show. The blockbuster book *The Big Sort*, by Bill Bishop with Robert G. Cushing, explained how Americans were increasingly moving into areas full of like-minded individuals, resulting in polarization with groups who lived elsewhere and felt differently about political issues and values. Schur hoped to show how people of different political beliefs could live in the same community and, in fact, work together to make it better.

Schur also admired David Foster Wallace, the novelist and essayist best known for the encyclopedic novel *Infinite Jest*. He died by suicide at forty-six in September 2008, as the show's first script was being written. He, too, would inspire many ideas at the core of this new show.

For Schur, reading *Infinite Jest* had prompted an enlightenment moment. "It's not a stretch to say that it's influenced everything I've ever written," he once said. "It kind of rescrambled my brain." This happened when Schur was in college at Harvard, and he wrote his undergraduate thesis on the book. He also arranged for Wallace to receive an award from *The Harvard Lampoon*, which the author came to campus to accept. The two remained in touch afterward, and Schur, once he was established in Hollywood, bought the rights to adapt *Infinite Jest*. Nothing came of the adaptation, but Schur wrote a character named David Wallace into an *Office* script and later directed the video for the Decemberists' "Calamity Song," depicting *Infinite Jest*'s fictional game Eschaton.

In short, he was a fan.

At the time Schur was writing this new show, he remained so enamored of the 1,088-page novel—about an über-capitalist future where, for instance, each calendar year is sponsored by a corporation—that his wife banned him from discussing it at social gatherings. Wallace presents a singular vision, dystopian but funny, dense and smart, with details and footnotes upon footnotes that serve as serious nerd bait. "The creation of Leslie Knope would not have been possible," Schur said, "without me reading David Foster Wallace."

Schur's production would lean more utopian than dystopian but would be undergirded by this Wallace quote, which he kept on his office wall for inspiration: "In dark times, the definition of good art would seem to be art that locates and applies CPR to those elements of what's human and magical that still live and glow despite the times' darkness." Wallace's dystopia had sprung from the cynicism he saw seeping into American culture. He showed that humor and sincerity could coexist, at a time when irony was the ultimate in cool. He did not see irony as harmless. He saw it as leading to his dystopia. Schur had the chance here to do the opposite, to create characters who could make the world better, who saw the point in doing so, who applied that CPR that Wallace spoke of.

Schur regarded his new show as a chance to do something he learned from Wallace: "I think TV has, at some level, trained people to believe that the only noble choice in life is to be the biggest, best, fastest, strongest," Schur said in 2012. "One of the themes of this show is to celebrate the nobility of working really hard for your little tiny slice of America, and doing as well as you can for that part of it in a way that tangibly helps people."

Daniels and Schur began to think about ways that their new show could "reflect back the vibe that we felt from the country, which was that the country was in desperate need of this kind of gritted-teeth optimism," according to Schur. By the time they were writing the pilot episode in earnest, the 2008 presidential election was dominating news cycles, and the electrifying Obama had everyone's attention with his message of hope and change. As Poehler was bidding farewell to *SNL*, Daniels and Schur were writing Obama's message into their show.

On a more obvious level, the new show was a response to one of Schur's favorite TV series, *The West Wing*, the NBC political drama that had ended two years earlier. "*The West Wing* is federal, right? So it's the stakes," Schur says. "Every episode has enormous stakes. It's global safety and security. It's literally the West Wing, the center of all power in the world." This show would be the opposite: just as political, but the smallest of stakes.

Daniels and Schur started on their script, drawing inspiration from all these books, events, and shows, along with the acclaimed HBO drama *The Wire*, with which they were obsessed during their time on *The Office*. (So much so that they tried to hire anyone they saw on the show. They succeeded in nabbing Idris Elba and Amy Ryan.) The pitch: What if we mashed up *The Wire* and *The West Wing* and Obama . . . but made it funny?

With this, NBC finally gave them the go-ahead to make their show, even though it wasn't an *Office* spin-off. However, Ben Silverman would maintain, more than a decade later, that he still believed they should have made a true spin-off. "They could have aired together back-to-back," he told author Andy Greene for his book about the show, *The Office*. "This would be like the biggest thing. It would have been incredible. It was just shortsighted. Everyone would have loved it. It would have been better for both shows."

Daniels valued research for his fictional projects. When he ran *King of the Hill*, he would take his writing staff to Texas every year, armed with reporters' notebooks to interview locals and find story ideas related to the show's setting. He also visited paper companies in Los Angeles, interviewing people with his "documentary crew" in tow, for *The Office*.

For the new show, he and Schur began to research local California politics, attending Los Angeles city council meetings to get a feel for their subject. They talked to government employees to inform their pilot script, including a city planner who said, "I'm a libertarian. I don't really believe in government." They couldn't believe they had found a real-life version of their libertarian character, the one who would serve as a foil to Poehler's enthusiastic believer in the power of government. Forevermore, they'd have a rebuttal for skeptics who didn't believe a libertarian would choose to work in government.

They still hadn't picked a department for their characters to work in, but they wanted something "likable," Daniels says. "And parks are just likable, right?" Daniels had also grown a bit weary of *The Office*'s indoor, fluorescent-lit, beige world. "We did want to make it brighter and more optimistic and more colorful."

They refined their vision for the fictional town. They wanted a town that had a Native American name, as so many US towns do. But the history of the town wouldn't match up with any real American history. That avoided any comparisons to actual towns, but also, as Schur says, "That's very American, to co-opt something and then to not pay attention to the details of the history of what you're engaging in." Schur looked up Native American tribe names and noticed the Pawnee, who had become the namesake of several towns across the country.

The Pawnee tribe originated in Nebraska and northern Kansas, where they combined village living with seasonal hunting in a matrilineal political structure. In the 1820s, the Pawnee's Petalesharo (Generous Chief) and Sharitahrish (Wicked Chief) visited President James Monroe at the White House as part of the federal government's negotiations with major tribes; both men were painted by portrait artist Charles Bird King in a series of works meant to preserve, as Secretary of War James Barbour said, "the likenesses of some of the most distinguished among this extraordinary race of people" because "this race was about to become extinct." After years of wars with neighboring and encroaching tribes, and bouts with disease brought by white settlers, the Pawnee were forced to relocate to the Indian territory in Oklahoma, where they are still based. In 1906, the US government dissolved tribal governments, including the Pawnee's, as Oklahoma prepared to become a state. They have about 3,500 enrolled members (as of 2019 statistics), who operate casinos, smoke shops, and a travel plaza, among other businesses.

Daniels and Schur placed their Pawnee in southern Indiana, Schur says, "because it was a place that no one knew anything about." They considered Illinois but felt like Chicago was too much of a dominating force there. They thought about Michigan because it was in the news a lot at the time as both a swing state and the site of the auto industry bailouts. Then again, maybe being in the news that much would cause problems. So Indiana it was.

Their Pawnee, Indiana, would be no town and every town. Midsize towns across the country shared many similarities: Each has its gadflies, its oddball government officials, its operators, its antidevelopment granola types, its slick developers, its wacky religious cult, its local media celebrities, its rival snooty town. Eagleton, Pawnee's haughty neighbor, "was based on the fact that there was a town next to my town called Simsbury," Schur says. "And Simsbury was, like, one-sixth the size. And everyone was rich and fancy. West Hartford had a real inferiority complex." (And for the record, my Connecticut sources tell me West Hartford is the Eagleton to Hartford.)

Daniels and Schur began to draft a background document on Pawnee that would be for internal use and serve as a primer to future writers so that the town remained consistent. A kind of private Wikipedia page for the fictional place, it detailed statistics, demographics, and history. Among their first decisions was that Pawnee was smaller than Bloomington, Indiana—the home of Indiana University, which had about seventy thousand residents at the time—and, in fact, was smaller than the other well-known cities in the state such as Muncie and Lafayette. Pawnee might rank as the sixth-largest municipality in the state—not the biggest, not the smallest. Maybe around forty thousand people. "It is a medium-sized town in a medium-sized state in the middle of the country," Schur concludes.

Pawnee, Indiana, was coming into its own.

As Pawnee took shape, so did Daniels and Schur's team for the new show. They had already hired Dan Goor, a writer for *Late Night with Conan O'Brien* for the previous five years, before Poehler was on board. He had been looking for a job in scripted episodic television. He wrote a spec script, an example script meant not to be produced but to show a writer's ability to mimic a specific show's style, for *The Office*. Two slots, he was told, were open: one on *The Office* itself, and one on a new show. He interviewed for both.

He got the slot at the new show, and, by coincidence, his old writing partner from *The Daily Show*, Charlie Grandy, got the *Office* job. Goor wasted no time moving from New York to Los Angeles for the chance to work with Daniels and Schur. His wife, a lawyer, even quit her job to come with him. But since the show's first season was delayed for Poehler's pregnancy, he began working in *The Office* writers' room, waiting for the new series to come together.

Goor had also written for the Grammys, and late-night talk shows such as *Last Call with Carson Daly* in addition to *Late Night with Conan O'Brien*. But he wanted to transition to scripted comedy, particularly after writing and producing sketches for O'Brien, which often involved assembling scenes and working with other departments like props and costumes. Coming to a sitcom was "not as difficult as I thought it was going to be," he says, thanks to the coordination skills he'd learned in late-night television.

Goor had come from a family in the Washington, DC, suburb of Bethesda, Maryland, which gave him a particular connection to the fictional government that Daniels and Schur were creating. His parents and grandparents had worked for the federal government, and he had interned at the National Institutes of Health in high school. His family identified as "New Deal Democrats who moved to DC to make the world a better place in the thirties," he says, referencing President Franklin D. Roosevelt's public works projects and reforms conceived to counteract the Great Depression after the Wall Street crash of 1929. This sensibility fit right in with Schur's vision for an Obama-inflected, optimistic take on governing, which, Goor recalls, was "very much Leslie Knope's vibe."

When Goor signed on, the project was called *Untitled Daniels–Schur Show*. Goor knew it was going to be in a government setting but that was about it. He attended occasional status meetings with Daniels and Schur as they worked out the pilot, but for the moment he was working on *The Office*. On the upside, he was getting credits on one of TV's biggest comedies, rather than an unclear series with an uncertain future.

Dean Holland went one step further: He asked to be sent from the very successful *Office* to this unnamed new show. Holland served as an editor on *The Office* and often found himself editing the episodes Schur had written. Schur, an editing nerd, would frequently join Holland in the editing room instead of Daniels, so the two developed a rapport.

One day, when the *Untitled Daniels–Schur Show* was in development, Holland came out with it. "I want to come with you," he told Schur.

When the two took the request to Daniels, he refused: "I told everybody I wasn't going to take anyone to the new show," Daniels said. That is, anyone who worked for *The Office*.

"Fine," Holland said, "what if I quit?"

Daniels's response: "Dammit, Dean!" What did Holland want, then?

Holland now pushed his luck: "I want to be at *The Office* and then go to the new show," he said. "And if the new show fails, I want to come back to *The Office*. And on the new show, I want to be a producer-director."

To Holland's surprise, Daniels agreed.

"Even to this day, I'm like, those guys might be dumber than I think if they really wanted to hire me," Holland says with a laugh, obviously indicating a joke.

As the growing team rushed toward their new April 9, 2009, premiere date, they considered titles. The network rejected their original idea, *Public Service*, out of concern that it seemed sarcastic, as if it were mocking the idea of public service. (No one yet knew how very earnest this show would be.) Instead, they settled on the name of Leslie's department, *Parks and Recreation.* Now they needed a cast to match their vision and Poehler's talent.

They were starting, as Poehler says, "at the bottom of Show Mountain." *Parks and Recreation* could be great, or it could be terrible. It could run for seven years or not last more than a few episodes. Every idea represented possibility, and each one could make or destroy the show. The team was now searching for the right mix of elements that would make it great—first and foremost, a cast.

CHAPTER 2

"That's My Fucking Part"

Casting the Show

Aubrey Plaza sat in Mike Schur's office on the set of *The Office*, starstruck. At twenty-four years old, she had served as an NBC page not long before. Schur thought she was fascinating—"weird" is a word that comes up a lot in descriptions of this meeting—but that may have just been her lack of artifice, simply because she had no idea what she was supposed to act like at this kind of meeting. She had a Daria-like deadpan humor, long dark hair, and huge dark eyes that could convey unflinching judgment.

Casting director Allison Jones, who had assembled *The Office*'s now-admired lineup of mostly unknowns, was working to fill up *Parks and Recreation*'s call sheet. Because *Parks and Recreation* was coming together in such an unusual way as the non-*Office*-spin-off everyone was waiting for, the casting process was taking on a unique form. While Greg Daniels and Schur were still working on the pilot script, they were already collaborating with Jones to fill roles that, in many cases, they hadn't written yet. The people they cast would help to determine the characters themselves.

Thus they ended up meeting Plaza before they were sure they had a role for her. Jones was casting a Judd Apatow film called *Funny People*, starring Adam Sandler, and for the supporting role of a young female stand-up comedian, she was interested in Plaza. Apatow had envisioned casting an actual working stand-up, but Jones insisted on this young improv-er from Upright Citizens Brigade (UCB), the improv troupe Amy Poehler cofounded. She had seen Plaza in a web series called *The Jeannie Tate Show*, created by Maggie Carey and Liz Cackowski. Cackowski played Jeannie, a soccer mom who hosts a talk show from her minivan. Plaza portrayed a deadpan delinquent teenage daughter named Tina. Guest stars included Bill Hader, Rashida Jones, and Jason Mantzoukas.

Donald Glover, whom Plaza knew from the New York comedy scene, helped her put together an audition tape for *Funny People*. The production asked Plaza for some footage of a stand-up set, which she didn't have. So she wrote a fictional one in the voice of what she imagined a comedian like Janeane Garofalo might do. Allison Jones loved it, and so did Apatow. They flew her to Los Angeles to do a chemistry read with actor Seth Rogen, who was already cast in the film.

Since Plaza was flying in, Jones also set up this meeting with Daniels and Schur, though Plaza didn't have an agent yet. Jones told Schur, "I just met the weirdest girl I've ever met in my life. You have to meet her and put her on your show."

The actress, new to the business, reveled in seeing the likes of Jenna Fischer and John Krasinski—Jim and Pam!—bustling about on the set of this hit TV show. In fact, Plaza took in every detail of the entire operation—the cameras, the monitors, the crew—because she had never been on a TV set like that before. She was thinking much more about this behind-the-scenes view than she was about the meeting itself. In fact, she didn't fully grasp that she could come out of it with a breakthrough role.

Daniels and Schur explained the basics of *Parks and Recreation* to Plaza and told her they were considering giving Leslie Knope, Poehler's character, an assistant whom Plaza might be able to play. As an improv trouper, she knew how to brainstorm. She offered her own idea: What if she was really good at her job but hated everyone and everything? "In some ways the character of Tina Tate was an early version of April Ludgate," Plaza says, referring to her part on *The Jeannie Tate Show*. "It was the beginnings of me messing around with that kind of character."

Daniels loved this idea, which worked better than Plaza may have realized when she casually pitched it. "Considering how ebullient and optimistic the Leslie Knope character was, Aubrey sounded like somebody that would be funny to play off that," he recalls. "You have Leslie, who's super energetic and trying to get everything accomplished, and her immediate boss doesn't believe in government. And then Aubrey is this very resistant kind of intern who has no affect."

Plaza didn't know if anything would result from the meeting, but the next thing she heard, she had been written into the script. They had even named the character Aubrey at first.

But because she hadn't been on television before, she would still have to audition for the role, at the network's request. Which meant that Plaza was all but auditioning to play herself. "If I don't get this part," she thought, "there's, like, something really wrong with me."

She did get the part—and with both a regular part on a network television show and a role in a Judd Apatow film booked from that one trip, she also got an agent, the agent she had wanted. Plaza had worked as actress Marcia Gay Harden's assistant a few years earlier, and had admired Harden's agent, Chris Andrews. Now she had signed with him. Soon she also snagged a role in the upcoming film *Scott Pilgrim vs. the World*. She was on her way in Hollywood.

Plaza's backward process demonstrates one of the many ways the *Parks and Recreation* casting proceeded unusually. While Hollywood neophyte Plaza stumbled into playing a character based on herself, a veteran character actor named Nick Offerman would torture himself for months and multiple auditions, hoping to land the role of Leslie Knope's boss. If this entire chaotic process resulted in a hit show, everyone would later talk about how brilliantly intuitive Daniels and Schur had been. If the show failed, everyone would point to this as one of the earliest warning signs.

Poehler, now *Parks and Recreation*'s star, would take part in auditioning and casting, at least once she was ready to transition from maternity leave back to work mode. For starters, she enthusiastically supported the fact that Daniels and Schur were bringing Rashida Jones over from *The Office*, where Jones had just finished her pivotal guest stint as Karen. Jones and Poehler had met a few years earlier in New York through their many mutual friends. Fast friends, the two would go clubbing in New York City in the early 2000s with Poehler's *Saturday Night Live* castmates Rachel Dratch and Seth Meyers, at a time when Jones worked as a club promoter to support herself between acting jobs. They would jokingly call themselves "the new Brat Pack." Poehler wrote in her memoir, "Rashida is my old friend and chosen sister." On the new show, Jones would play Ann, a nurse who befriends Leslie, though Daniels and Schur were still working out the specifics of her character.

Daniels and Schur handed her the role for two reasons: (1) They loved her work and wanted to give her something juicy after her stint as Karen ended, and (2) her presence on the new show would be a strategic defense against further *Office* spin-off talk.

"I was worried about still getting pressure to say they were in the same universe and that there could be guest appearances and stuff," Daniels says. "So one of the benefits of having Rashida was that if Rashida plays a different person on *Parks*, then the universes are disconnected."

Meanwhile, Chris Pratt, best known at the time for his roles on teen dramas *Everwood* and *The O.C.*, nailed the part of Andy, Ann's slacker boyfriend who breaks both of his legs when he falls into a construction pit. (The pit drives the plot in the first episode.) Daniels remembers Pratt as surprisingly funny in his audition, given that his résumé was full of teen dramas. Though he read only a short scene, in which Andy objects to Ann going to a government meeting because he fell "in a big dumb hole," he hammered home Andy's man-child whininess perfectly. "He was hilarious in his audition," Daniels says. "He just took the part and put it in his pocket."

Poehler also knew and approved of another one of Daniels and Schur's early picks, Aziz Ansari, who had made his name doing comedy with UCB. He met with Daniels and Schur after finishing the second season of *Human Giant*, an MTV sketch show. Daniels had seen Ansari in a sketch called "Viral Videos." In it, a man has gone viral on YouTube for cutting off his own penis with a pair of garden shears, and he's being interviewed on a news show about it. He expresses no regrets, because the video made him famous. Then Ansari appears as a guy who's gotten even *more* views on YouTube . . . for making funny noises, which he proceeds to demonstrate.

"I thought it was a super funny, weird sketch," Daniels says. "And when I did some research into it, it turned out that Aziz had written it. We thought that we'd make a Machiavellian sidekick to the gullible bureaucrat, and that was what Aziz was hired to do."

Ansari grew up in Bennettsville, South Carolina, where he acquired a slight Southern drawl, with Tamil immigrant parents. His father worked as a gastroenterologist, and his mother worked in his father's office. He attended the South Carolina Governor's School for Science and Mathematics, a selective boarding school for ambitious students. He then graduated from New York University with a business degree in 2004. None of this telegraphed a forthcoming comedy career.

But after NYU, Ansari started hosting a weekly stand-up show, *Crash Test*, at UCB in New York. His shtick relied on pop culture and celebrity references, never letting on whether he was truly shallow or just pretending to be. This worked even better when he moved to Los Angeles shortly before his meeting with the *Parks and Recreation* team, and he began to break through not only on *Human Giant* but also with a Twitter feed in which he feigned run-ins with famous people, a perfect mash-up of newly emerging social media culture and the tabloids of the 2000s. He pretended to have brunched with R&B group Boyz II Men, had sushi with actor Djimon Hounsou, and won a push-up contest against WWE star John Cena. He'd since started acting, mostly in small roles as scammy operators, similar to the part that Daniels and Schur were envisioning for him. *Parks and Recreation* would become the twenty-five-year-old's biggest break so far.

Daniels and Schur began to write their script in earnest, their casting inspiring their character choices. For Jones, who was arrestingly beautiful yet relatable, they dreamed up local nurse Ann Perkins, who's good at her job but has terrible relationship instincts. For Ansari, they created the character of Tom Haverford, whom Schur describes as "a young striver who was in government to make contacts and develop his own business interests." The character's Anglo name plays on his drive to conquer a racist American society at any cost; he explains that he changed it from Darwish Sabir Ishmael Ghani. Both Jones and Ansari agreed to be part of the show before seeing a script.

Rounding out the cast playing Leslie's staff in the parks and recreation department in a supporting role was Jim O'Heir, who was raised in the south suburbs of Chicago and came up through the Chicago theater scene. He became a go-to character actor on TV series such as *3rd Rock from the Sun*, *Malcolm in the Middle*, and *ER*. His *Parks and Recreation* role would be his biggest so far, though it would be thankless; he'd play Jerry Gergich, a bumbling but sincere longtime Pawnee staffer who's often made fun of by his coworkers. He'd also be joined by Retta, a stand-up comedian and actress from New Jersey who worked as a chemist before moving to Los Angeles to pursue comedy. Her *Parks and Recreation* character would be nearly the opposite of Jerry; Donna Meagle was self-assured, self-sufficient, direct, and largely uninterested in what her colleagues thought of her.

Around the same time, actors Nick Offerman and Adam Scott auditioned for a nebulous role on *Parks and Recreation*, a love interest for Ann who was, at the time, named Josh. The actors, who had known each other for years, both read for the part opposite Jones, checking for chemistry.

"If you're ever reading for something, especially if the words 'romantic interest' are involved, one person you don't want to see coming through the door is Adam Scott, the cutest otter of a leading man," Offerman says.

Indeed, Scott could play a quintessential charming, unthreatening TV boyfriend, with his slight build, dark hair, angular features, and friendly dark eyes. Offerman, on the other hand, came off quite differently—not traditionally cute but manly, a solid Midwesterner with a round face, hangdog blue eyes, a slow and deep voice, and the ability to grow facial hair nearly on demand.

Scott recalls auditioning with script pages that were possibly from *The Office*. "I'm sure part of why my audition wasn't very good is because I wanted it so badly," he says. He had heard about the show in progress while he was in Connecticut in the deep of winter shooting an independent film called *The Vicious Kind*. He read online that Daniels and Schur were working on an *Office* spin-off. He was waiting to return to the HBO drama *Tell Me You Love Me*, "which was a good show," he says, "but it was taking a year between seasons, and it was a deadly serious show, and nothing sounded like more fun" than working on an *Office*-adjacent project.

He called his agent and asked if he could get an audition for the project. He did, but he left the reading feeling insecure about his performance. "I knew I had kind of missed the bull's-eye," he says. "Part of the challenge when you're auditioning is you want it, but you can't let that seep into the audition, or it feels desperate." Though he was sad that it hadn't worked out, three weeks later he ended up on *Party Down*, a cable comedy about a group of struggling actors working for a catering company, cocreated and written by his longtime friend actor Paul Rudd. So he presumed his journey was over with this spin-off project, or whatever it was.

Offerman hadn't had much luck with Josh, either, but he had a harder time letting it go. Not long afterward, he was pulling into the Big 5 Sporting Goods at Wilshire and San Vicente in Los Angeles, planning to buy a couple of jockstraps, when he got the call. He parked and picked up.

"It's not going forward with Josh," his agent said. "They showed your tape, your chemistry reads with Rashida, to NBC, and they said, 'You told us someone like Aaron Eckhart, and you hand us Nick Offerman?!'" At least, this is the self-deprecating way the emotional Offerman remembers it. In fact, he punctuates it aloud in the retelling: "Question mark, exclamation point?!"

In his head, Offerman heard his agent saying, "You expect us to watch him kiss Rashida Jones, or more to the point, her kiss him?"

He said goodbye, then went in and made his purchases. He came back out to his car, and his phone rang again: "Okay, Mike and Greg really want you on the show. There's this part of Amy's boss. There's no pilot script yet." They had already hired Plaza and Ansari, his agent explained. They wanted to put together what Offerman remembers as "a Bad News Bears–slash–Dream Team."

His agent explained that the producers had originally envisioned the character older than Offerman's thirty-eight years, but they had begun to shift their concept to suit Offerman. The actor shrugged. It sounded great, he thought, but not "like I should run out and buy a car just yet." He had been burned in this way a few times before: A writer would create a great part for him in a pilot, only for him to be rejected by the network executives. "No, he's weird," they'd say. "Get me Jim Belushi, or get me someone conventional."

When Offerman received a few pages of dialogue in this new character's voice, he grew a little bit more excited. Offerman began reading the pages aloud to his wife, *Will & Grace* actress Megan Mullally, and felt his hands shaking. The truth! The comedy! "I felt like Christopher Guest finally called and was like, 'I was thinking about putting you in one of my make-'em-up movies,'" Offerman says.

He had some things in common with this character, or at least his own initial vision of the character: "Without even having much knowledge of what a parks and recreation department was, I just immediately envisioned a guy in a pickup wearing a lot of flannel, and he may even have some shotgun on a rack over his truck seat, like an outdoorsman." This didn't *exactly* match Offerman himself, but he did enjoy the outdoors and working with wood, and he knew a lot of guys like that from growing up in the rural outskirts of the Chicago suburbs. His family had even spent some time in local government there.

But he would have to gain network approval before the part was his.

Meanwhile, that blurry character of "Josh" became Mark Brendanawicz and began to come into focus. He would serve as something of a love interest for Leslie Knope, a man she'd once had a one-night stand with and for whom she'd continued to carry a torch. His job as a city planner had turned him into a cynic with its rules and regulations. "City planning jobs can kill even the most optimistic person's optimism very quickly," Schur explains. "Because a lot of it is like: Is this up to code? Is this median on this road the correct width? Have you accurately leveled the hedges around your house to a height of two feet six inches, which is the maximum allowable by the city code? It's just a lot of drudgery."

The character would counter Leslie's enthusiasm whenever she got worked up about a new project. Over the course of the show, however, perhaps some of her optimism would infect him, and he'd change for the better. Schur envisioned him as handsome and charming, a "Sam Malone type," he says, referencing Ted Danson's character on *Cheers*, and perhaps explaining why neither Offerman nor Scott ended up in the role. The part went instead to Paul Schneider, a tall actor with dark hair, dark eyes, and strong brows, who very much looked the part.

Ron Swanson, the role that Offerman was now up for, would run defense against Leslie's efforts from another angle, as a strict libertarian and obstructionist. Offerman had often thought that if he were to get a big break, it would be in an idiosyncratic role like *The*

Office's Dwight Schrute. Or Jim Ignatowski on *Taxi*, if you want to go further back. This seemed like that chance.

Born in Joliet, Illinois, about forty-five miles southwest of Chicago, Offerman grew up in the nearby small town of Minooka on what he calls a "three-acre homestead out in a cornfield" with three siblings. "My mom and dad are storybook parents and, looking back on it, I had an idyllic childhood," he said. "It was a very frugal environment; we provided a lot of things for ourselves."

He learned basic woodworking skills from his father, grandfathers, and uncles Dan and Don of Roberts Brothers Farms. As he wrote: "A baseball bat of Ash. A footbridge of Redwood. A trebuchet of English Oak. A dining table of Mahogany. A Cherry toothpick. The list of useful implements that can be crafted from wood is infinite and amazing, and I am spellbound by the ancient practice of woodworking, fueled by the ingenuity of men and women to cleverly alter this natural material into items of use and beauty."

He went to theater school at the University of Illinois at Urbana-Champaign, which, as he says, "sounds funny, and if you look at it on a map, it looks funny, that you would aspire to the boards and the Bard" from there. "But it's actually a particularly fine preparatory conservatory for a life in the regional theater. I learned all the things that you do as a serious actor, including creating a backstory for your characters, and analyzing scripts, and scrutinizing the emotional journey of these people you're trying to inhabit." He found his place there among the theater kids, even as the rest of his family stayed in Minooka: His three siblings ended up in homes within one block of their parents. But he maintained his woodworking practice, honing his craft in the theater scene shop on campus.

In his twenties, he began to realize the value of the community-centered lives his family lived and vowed to match their standards, even while attempting to work in entertainment, "taking their value system and incorporating it into what I create," he says. In fact, his family remained involved with the community there, with his dad now the mayor, as his father was before him. The Offerman family continues to be a major part of the Lions Club, the school board, and the volunteer fire department.

"I'm the black sheep that's not part of this incredible family and tight-knit community," Offerman says, "so I go back as much as I can. At first it seemed like a hell of a row to hoe: In the horrible, superficial world of Hollywood, how does one get that kind of work ethic and morality across?"

He made his way to Los Angeles in his late twenties with the intention of becoming a working actor. But he wasn't making a living at it at first, so in 2001, he opened the Offerman Woodshop in East LA to take on projects for pay. He translated his talent for building scenery into building decks and cabins inspired by Frank Lloyd Wright and the Greene brothers, masters of the California Arts and Crafts style. He also studied fine-woodworking magazines and taught himself how to make furniture.

But he never stopped acting or auditioning. As his career progressed, he landed memorable supporting parts on *Deadwood*, *ER*, *The King of Queens*, *24*, *George Lopez*, and *The West Wing*.

He had first encountered Daniels when he auditioned for the lead role on *The Office*, Michael Scott. At the time, he didn't know Daniels's work on *King of the Hill*. But he didn't hesitate to audition for Michael. He loved the British *Office*, and, he says, "When they started *The Office*, there was a real ambivalence because all of us that loved the original British *Office*, naturally, said, 'Please don't mess with this, America.'" But, he says, when he got the audition, "my fealty to Ricky Gervais ended quickly and I said, 'Okay, I would love that.'"

That role ultimately went to Steve Carell, but Offerman continued to read for guest parts on the show, including one for an episode that

Schur had written three years before, which was about Michael meeting several fellow regional managers at a gathering in New York City. Offerman would have played the one who "was a bigger moron than Michael Scott," Schur says. But the scheduling didn't work out. Disappointed, Schur wrote Offerman's name on a Post-it that he stuck to his computer to remind himself to write a part for the actor.

Now, the time had finally arrived.

Schur crafted the role of Leslie's libertarian boss, Ron Swanson, into Offerman's image. Offerman came back to read some early Ron dialogue for Daniels and Schur in the fall of 2008, while they were still writing. Yet his casting remained an open question. He had to wait while the script came together and Poehler finished her maternity time off.

Offerman had known Poehler since 1997, when they met at a Halloween party thrown by mutual friends who lived together in a house in Chicago. He was appearing in a production of *A Clockwork Orange* at the Steppenwolf theater, so he had a big, bushy beard and hair that was dyed orange, on top of which he dressed like a devil as his costume for the party. Poehler would not forget meeting him that night.

As Offerman chatted with her about improv comedy, he couldn't imagine doing what she did: "You make shit up in a bar? Good luck with that!" He thought, "I perform works of literature! Or, actually, at the moment, I build scenery for people who perform works of literature." He and Poehler formed a familiar bond, a mutual admiration.

Since then, Offerman had seen Poehler a handful of times, like when Mullally hosted *Saturday Night Live* while Poehler was part of the cast. Still, he didn't feel like it made sense to call Poehler to make a plea for the *Parks and Recreation* job. He was, indeed, very Midwestern about it: "I could get a hold of her and say 'hi,'" he says, "but any of that would be self-serving."

This role seemed to Offerman like a long-awaited gift in a career that had so far kept him in dull supporting roles, often skewing older than his age. But he hadn't locked down the role yet. Though Daniels, and especially Schur, wanted Offerman, network executives had to approve every casting choice, and they hadn't signed off on Offerman. After he auditioned in the fall, months then went by while, he says, "NBC made them audition every breathing mammal in North America, and probably some other continents."

When he took part in a winter improv show at the UCB theater in Los Angeles, several of his castmates, including Matt Walsh, Seth Morris, Jason Mantzoukas, and David Koechner, mentioned that they'd read for the role of Amy's boss. Offerman's role. It was, they said, *the* role to get that season. Some of them remember reading for "Josh," too, so there may have been some confusion, but the emotion was real for Offerman in the moment.

"That's *my* fucking part," Offerman seethed to himself. He had to step out of the theater for a moment alone and some fresh air to calm down, tears forming in his eyes.

He called his agent the next day to ask what was going on.

Offerman didn't get an answer until about a month later, when they heard: The show was on, Poehler was ending her maternity leave, and things were moving forward. Poehler was coming to Los Angeles. They wanted him to come in and audition with her for the role of parks and recreation department director Ron Swanson, rather than the standard casting directors and producers with whom earlier auditions would have taken place. They would make their final decision based on that. Daniels, Schur, and the network would be watching, and they would make a choice then.

Offerman prepped for the audition with his wife. He calls her "my teacher" for good reason: She gave him some precious advice this time, and many times before and after. He wanted this role so badly now that he was tempted to push himself, to *try hard* in the audition to make it happen. He could feel his desperation. "I hadn't learned fully yet to stop acting."

He thought, "I'm gonna do something really fucking cool. Like Daniel Day-Lewis or Anthony Hopkins."

Mullally said, "Honey, please, just stop. What's that? What are you doing? Stop. Just talk."

Offerman showed up at the audition, at long last, excited to see Poehler. But when he got off the elevator at the Norvet Building at Radford Studio Center and stepped into the foyer, he saw Mike O'Malley lounging on the love seat there. O'Malley, a well-liked character actor, had recently finished a six-year run on a successful network sitcom called *Yes, Dear*. He was in his early forties, with a round, friendly face and close-cropped hair often covered with a hat—ball cap, fedora, or newsboy.

Motherfucker, Offerman thought. If it were someone else sitting there, someone very different from Offerman—Owen Wilson on one end of a spectrum, Sean Bean on the other—he might have been able to tolerate that. If someone like that got the gig, Offerman thought, "then they weren't looking for my particular toolbox." Even those guys at UCB who'd said they read for the part—Offerman loved them, he thought they were some of the most talented guys he'd ever seen, but they were so different from him that in the end, he couldn't let them worry him too much.

O'Malley, on the other hand, stood smack in the middle of his general type range, and was a little closer to the appropriate age, and was a known quantity, and was *good*. Offerman hadn't counted on O'Malley showing up at the same final audition. The two knew each other from the Los Angeles theater world, Offerman says, "and he'd always been really generous to me, and he's famously a great guy. I was just like, 'Ah, fuck.'"

But he held it together as he entered the audition room. He greeted them all as if nothing were rattling him. Everyone acknowledged that this was it, the final audition.

Daniels and Schur had set up a table representing Ron's desk. Offerman and Poehler would do a scene together with a fair amount of improvisation. Leslie would ask Ron for something, and Ron would say no. It was that simple. "That was the moment it was born, in that room, where Amy is a dynamo, Amy is a just ridiculous unstoppable comedy machine," Offerman recalls. "She has charisma, more charisma shooting out one ear than the entire cast of most sitcoms."

When Offerman and Poehler faced off as Ron and Leslie over that desk, Offerman concentrated on one main strategy: "I basically had the good sense to let her fulminate and bluster and blister and blow and then say no," he says. "I'd learned enough to simply be complementary to Amy. And that means hold still, shut the fuck up, and say something pithy. And thankfully I was right and the room was like, *Bingo*. Laughing their asses off."

Poehler had been in a lot of audition rooms, some of them where she was auditioning and some of them where someone else was. She had come to believe that the right part finds the right person. Poehler, watching him work, noticed that Offerman "has a stillness that Ron really needed. Nick has this weird thing where he has a very kind and scary face at the same time." She could see that Ron was a difficult character to get just right: "If he tips over to the wrong side, you don't like him. You're just like, 'Who's this asshole?' There has to be a warmth, as there is with Nick, underneath him."

Offerman, as Ron, "treated her with ambivalence or low-key annoyance" as he describes it; he could feel that it was, maybe, going well. As someone who was not a trained improviser, he says, "I was pretty damn scared."

The next day, Offerman got a call from his agents: Schur wanted to call him.

When the two spoke, Schur made an almost rom-com-perfect confession: "It was only you." Well, actually: "It was only you and Mike O'Malley. We taped both of your improvs. And then we only gave yours to NBC."

Offerman had been waiting fifteen years to hear this kind of offer. "Listen, Mike, I'm going to start openly sobbing," Offerman remembers saying, "but please just keep talking to me."

What Schur said next only induced more sobs. Schur told Offerman about the stray Post-it that he'd written Offerman's name on. (The piece of paper also contained the enigmatic code "57XW12," its significance lost to time. Dimensions for a bookshelf? A license plate number?) As to the impact of that story, that Post-it, on his life, Offerman says, "It might as well be Thor's hammer."

And he learned a valuable lesson from the experience: "Me getting to taste any success in my life has everything to do with learning, on an ever-extending matriculation across my life, that my authentic self is the most valuable thing I can bring to the service of any effort, whether it's a show or a marriage or woodshop." Sixteen years later, Offerman still gets choked up when speaking about the moment he heard the part was his.

Once he got the role, Offerman, who leans liberal in real life but had an understanding of middle-American conservative politics given his Illinois upbringing, began reading about libertarianism and digging into Ayn Rand's *The Fountainhead*, a novel credited with helping to launch the modern American libertarian movement, with strong ties to the Tea Party of the late 2000s. Offerman talked with Schur about the ideology, which they agreed is fantastic on paper and makes a lot of sense in its purest form. "The problem is, then you mix human beings into the goulash," Offerman says, "and you realize, oh, this can never work, this can only lead to anarchy."

These ideas came into more focus for Daniels and Schur as the cast formed and the creators developed and refined the show. The Tea Party versus the newly elected Obama, who believed hope and change came from the government, would become a defining dynamic of this time in America. A remarkable schism opened up, between people who were thrilled at his historic election and people who thought it was the downfall of America.

"The nation's divide was getting worse every day," Schur said in a 2015 interview. Leslie and Ron personified this divide: Leslie worked hard to make government a crucial part of citizens' everyday lives, and an effective one at that. Ron wanted the government out of his and everyone's business. Their on-screen relationship sought to answer whether two people with such opposing views could work together. Or, perhaps more specifically, it sought to show that they *could*, because Schur is an idealist.

Daniels and Schur had managed to get their dream cast approved by the network, and their first script was close to done with that cast in mind. *Parks and Recreation* rushed into production to make its April 9, 2009, premiere on NBC. That dream cast now had to deliver.

CHAPTER 3

"Surrounded by Negativity"

Planning the First Season

Amy Poehler and Aubrey Plaza first met at a swing set, before they knew much about the show they were soon to shoot together. They had to film a promo for *Parks and Recreation* to run during the 2008 Olympics—even though the show barely existed. Greg Daniels and Mike Schur were still working out the concept and the script, and they hadn't filled out the cast yet.

This made Plaza understandably nervous. Here she'd just landed her first network television show, and now she had to play a character she knew almost nothing about. And she had to do it in front of Amy Poehler.

They swung on the swing set together while the cameras rolled, trying to play characters who weren't fully created. They had no idea what plots might befall these characters. In fact, perhaps the only thing they knew for sure was that this show was *not* a spin-off of *The Office*.

This fact would be surprisingly hard to communicate to the audience throughout the promotion of the new show, a failure that would prove nearly fatal for *Parks and Recreation*.

As the cast's de facto leader, Poehler felt the weight of this problem and a responsibility to get the show through its fledgling stages. When she had first signed on, she was looking forward to the chance to concentrate on and live in one character for a while, as opposed to the sketch grind of *Saturday Night Live*. Now, she was beginning to feel the consequences of that decision. While Daniels and Schur were in charge of making and running the show, she would set the tone as the series' lead and the cast's most famous member. Plaza, for one, immediately looked up to her. Poehler would also serve as the public face of the project, its lead and its only famous name.

But the show, and Poehler, faced unusual pressure as filming began. Another promo spot was running during the Super Bowl's 2009 broadcast, a high-profile ad placement. The show would have been premiering after this Super Bowl, if the producers had chosen that coveted slot and related marketing instead of waiting for Poehler. In its place, the network had run a special one-hour episode of—what else?—*The Office*. The *Parks* promo that ran the same night, highlighting its connection to *The Office*, would weld the two together in viewers' minds, which would prove largely to *Parks and Recreation*'s detriment.

At that point, five months after the swing set promo, the new series was fully cast and preparing to shoot its six-episode season, shortened because of Poehler's pregnancy, rather than the thirteen the network had wanted. Poehler called it a "seasonette." Going into shooting, Poehler felt "dumpy and exhausted," she later wrote. Her first child, Archie, had just turned three months old. Now she had to recenter herself in her own body and identity, and she had to find her character. She was coming off a defining run playing Hillary Clinton on *SNL*, but she could see that her new character, Leslie Knope, was very different from primary candidate Clinton, even if Leslie admired her. "Leslie was this Energizer Bunny, who I think is outside of the system," Poehler says. "And just from a performance standpoint, Hillary is a lot more grounded."

Leslie, a neurotic try-hard, had plastered her office with photos of Hillary and other real-life female politicians. As Poehler would describe Leslie to *The Advocate* as the show began, "She's this deluded, somewhat fragile person who doesn't have any real power but wants to change the world." She presented a touching, if a bit cringe-inducing, image of a small-town bureaucrat with big dreams, a woman who wants to be Ruth Bader Ginsburg but who right now needs to moderate a raucous community meeting about a pit in the center of town.

With so much of the show's DNA entwined with that of *The Office*, the creative team would struggle to figure out how Leslie Knope differentiated herself from Michael Scott while also being funny, which was important to Poehler. She didn't want to be Kermit the Frog, the sane center always haranguing everyone else to get back to work.

"People talk about how it's hard for the main character to be funny," she says. "But I'm always like, 'Take a look at what they did with Leslie.' Because Leslie is the engine of that show, and they make her deeply funny. She has crazy shit she gets to do."

Still, Poehler had no idea at the time how much work she and the rest of the team would have to put into cutting ties with Michael Scott and *The Office*.

The behind-the-scenes team was beginning to assemble as well. Editor and producer Dean Holland had gotten himself to *Parks and Recreation* by threatening to quit *The Office* if Daniels and Schur didn't take him with them. He would use his editing expertise on the very first episode, and he was a self-deprecating perfectionist. He developed a rating scale for episodes that his colleagues began to recognize: "Good" is not as good as "pretty good." "Pretty good" is the highest, because he would never say that anything he had done was "great."

And yet, he wanted everything he worked on to be great. "I would spiral, but I think part of it motivates," he says. "If I constantly kick myself and kick myself, I do think I make episodes better. And so you never stop."

He talked notoriously loudly. Everyone on *The Office* knew it, and now everyone on *Parks and Recreation* was learning it. When he'd walk into the writers' room, they'd hit a button that played the song "Shout." He had been trying for years not to be the loud talker. But he had not succeeded. He just got too excited about things, and then he'd find himself yelling. "I give myself headaches," he says.

Holland had learned from Daniels to listen to himself—that is, internally. Not necessarily to trust his gut but to at least give voice to it. Crew members should offer their expertise and opinions, even if it meant arguing with the creators and showrunners. Daniels and Schur reinforced this on their sets.

"Whether I was right or wrong," Holland says, "I was passionate about it and I fought for it." Holland mostly lost to Schur, which he didn't mind. And Schur would always remind Holland of the few times Schur had gone with Holland's ideas: "Remember when I gave that to you?" Schur would say.

Production designer Dan Bishop joined the show for only these first six episodes, because he already had a steady gig with the prestigious drama *Mad Men*, which was not a position one carelessly tossed aside. He had a unique idea for the *Parks and Recreation* set layout as the show took residence at Stage 21 on the CBS Radford lot: Normally, a crew would build the first sets in one corner of the soundstage so that they could methodically maximize the rest of the space as the show progressed. Bishop suggested instead building the "bullpen"—the main office of the parks and recreation department—in the middle. Then, he said, you could expand around it to essentially make an almost-workable city hall with hallways that at least made a little bit of sense, that felt real as characters walked from one office to another. At the time, the producers envisioned incorporating "walk and talk" scenes like those made famous by *The West Wing*. They quickly learned, however, that "walk-and-talks aren't as good in comedy," producer Morgan Sackett remembers. "You want to deliver a joke and not be walking."

Of course, they couldn't entirely build out a city hall full of distinct hallways. So Bishop created something he called the "zone of confusion." The crew would change out the art hanging on the walls in this section to make it seem like it was a different part of the building. If characters walked the halls at length, they might just circle back around to the same section they'd already been in, but different murals would be hanging there, so it would feel real. (While a technical real-life mural would be painted onto a wall, *Parks and Recreation*'s were acrylic paint on canvas that could be switched in and out easily.)

The murals would become a running visual joke on the series. The beautiful, Works Progress Administration–style paintings depicted, if you looked closely, harrowingly racist scenes from Pawnee's history: Native Americans are run over by a train barreling through town as stereotyped Chinese laugh at them on one side of the tracks, and, on the other side, teetotaler suffragettes yell at Irish immigrants who look like leprechauns; two American soldiers prepare to blast an

Indian chief tied to a nearby tree with a cannon at close range; settler Emily Lagana marries the Wamapoke's Chief Kuruk, just before the forbidden 1867 wedding turns into a bloodbath once the word gets out.

Ian Phillips, who would take over for Bishop when he returned to *Mad Men*, joined the production after parting ways with the *Twilight* franchise. He had worked on the first 2008 film in the teen vampire saga but quit because he wanted to stay in Los Angeles instead of moving to Canada for the second one.

"Definitely a mood shift," he says with a laugh.

He explains that the *Parks and Recreation* team began by thinking through what government buildings are like. "The show itself is very character-driven, and it was not necessarily about the place that they worked, but the place that they worked needed to feel real," he says. "When you saw the show, you knew exactly where you were. You knew that you were at city hall, and that could be any city hall anywhere in America."

Daniels had attended a wedding in Bartlesville, Oklahoma, where, he says, he was "struck by these incredibly racist murals that were in the public buildings. The depiction of the Native Americans is really not cool. They're like, yeah, these are our beautiful murals from the Works Progress Administration."

The *Parks* crew researched public buildings constructed around the time that Pawnee would have been founded, near the turn of the century. WPA murals had become a common sight in government buildings across the country in the 1930s and '40s, so the city could have conceivably commissioned them during that time not long after being built.

To make the Pawnee murals, the production design staff had to consult with the writers to come up with the jokes that would form their basis. Then the production designers and the artists they hired figured out how to render the joke. "How do you very quickly sell in a mural that there are terrible atrocities?" Phillips says. "Now, of course, today, everybody can pause, and they can go back and look, but when you're airing and you have twenty-one minutes, you have to sell that stuff really fast. So that's always a challenge."

The insanity of these mural scenes set a standard for *Parks and Recreation*'s future and how far the creative team felt they could go in constructing this world.

"It's a crazy fictional universe," Schur says. "We were creating a little bit of a cartoon universe, and we're gonna stretch the boundaries of what's possible."

Daniels was directing the pilot and spent a lot of time obsessing over the set with the production design team. He wanted to make sure the show looked as different from *The Office* as possible, to the point where he insisted that none of the windows would have blinds. To him, blinds meant *The Office*, and no blinds felt like a distinct visual difference. He had other ideas, too, about how to make the show seem so obviously separate from its predecessor.

"I had all these thoughts about the long interior hallways and the courtyard," he says. "I was very proud of the courtyard having pigeons. There was a whole line item for pigeon wrangling."

But his ideas presented their own downsides. The courtyard just outside Leslie's window allowed for some outdoor scenes but was difficult to light. The set lights never looked like real daylight. On the other hand, Daniels and Schur had planned it for maximum story potential: Leslie's office window looked across to where Mark, her crush, worked in his office. Building the initial relationship into the set design came from *The Office*, where the characters' desks were arranged with an eye toward who could see whom. Most important, the layout allowed the central couple, Jim and Pam, to stare longingly at each other or catch each other's eyes for a flirtatious moment.

"One of the great things about *The Office* was on our little, tiny lot, we were able to use the exteriors whenever we wanted to, because the outside of our writers' building *was* the outside of Dunder Mifflin," Daniels says. "And so whenever we wanted to, we could shoot in the parking lot, and we could have people walk in and walk down the hall and come around, come up the street, and the exterior played." On the other hand, *Parks and Recreation* was shot on a soundstage, so the production couldn't move outside without it becoming a location day.

"I was really concerned with not feeling cramped inside," Daniels says, "and I wanted to have different types of environments."

Daniels determined that *Parks and Recreation* would also shoot its talking-head shots differently from *The Office*'s, using two cameras instead of just one. This would provide both side and front angles, whereas *The Office* used only front angles. "I thought I was doing all these things that were super different from *The Office*," Daniels says. "But you're so familiar with what you're doing that you see all these differences." These would not be as apparent to critics and viewers as he had hoped.

But for now, *Parks and Recreation* needed a true producer, a logistical mastermind of the type that every successful show has but who rarely gets the recognition they deserve. *Parks and Recreation*'s secret weapon would turn out to be Morgan Sackett, who knew how to work miracles on a small budget.

Sackett grew up in a small town in Iowa with parents who were both attorneys. He watched them in the courthouse and, for a while, planned to follow the same career path. Pawnee brought him back to that Midwestern upbringing. Its civic buildings reminded him of those in his hometown of Spencer, which even had WPA murals lining their hallways. "A lot of that stuff felt very real to somebody who grew up in a small town in the Midwest," he says.

He moved to Los Angeles and got a job with Castle Rock Entertainment in the mailroom. He soon got promoted to a production assistant on *Seinfeld*, where he interviewed cast and crew for the DVD extras. From there, he got jobs behind the scenes on *The Single Guy*; *Zoe, Duncan, Jack & Jane*; and *Watching Ellie*. Burnt out on network television, he then produced a 2008 documentary about a sailing competition called *Morning Light*, a pet project of Disney heir Roy E. Disney.

He was lured back into television when a friend who'd worked on the *Seinfeld* extras with him ended up editing and directing at *The Office*. The friend recommended Sackett to Daniels, and Sackett's combination of comedy experience and documentary experience—both with the *Seinfeld* DVD extras and *Morning Light*—gave him a unique angle to land the job with *Parks and Recreation*. Sackett could also size up a budget quickly—*Parks and Recreation*'s, he remembers, was in the "mid-twos," i.e., around $2 million per episode—and know roughly what they would get for that amount.

In a typical moment, he talks like this about the first season: "Also, we did six episodes, which were more expensive, because the amort budget is higher, because you're not dividing all the prep over more episodes." Translation: The total budget for the production starts with baseline preparation for *all* the episodes, and that cost is divided by a smaller number in shorter seasons, resulting in a higher per-episode amount.

His first assignment: producing a lot-size hole in the ground, in the middle of a suburban neighborhood, that they could potentially continue filming for up to seven years. Daniels appreciated how unfazed Sackett seemed by this request. But in all honesty, Sackett didn't believe in it. He thought, "Somebody's going to talk them out of this. This isn't going to really happen."

He admits that when he realized the pit *was* happening, it was hard to find. He lucked out when he discovered a lot in the Valley where an apartment building had been torn down to make way for new condos, but the project had stalled because the economy was crashing. He rented the lot for the production. At this point, Ian Phillips and the production design team took over to get the pit dug. "I feel really, really proud of the hole that I dug in the ground behind Ann's house," he says with a laugh. "The whole show would not exist without that one hole in the ground. A very large hole."

As crews began digging there, bank representatives showed up with notices to repossess the property. The owner they were renting from hadn't been paying the mortgage. So Sackett had to make a special deal with the bank to continue renting. They also rented a nearby home as the exterior of Ann's house.

Costume designer Kirston Mann had worked on *United States of Tara*, a buzzy Showtime drama created by *Juno* screenwriter Diablo Cody and starring Toni Collette as an artist and mom dealing with dissociative identity disorder. While that series' showy costume challenge was distinguishing among Tara's different personalities, *Parks and Recreation* shifted her work closer to the "regular." Mann says, "It's not New York or LA. So it's fun to do, because the character's wardrobe gets to say so much more about the person. It's not generic or ordinary; it's character-based."

She began building the characters alongside the actors. "These people, they love their characters," Mann says. "Everybody was game to play along."

For starters, Leslie was, as Mann says, "Suit Woman. We plowed through women's suits, nothing fancy." She used many patterned blouses from Equipment, a brand that specializes in feminine, work-appropriate pieces. "We were so grateful every time they made a new one," she says. "I think we had every single one, plus some vintage." Mann's staff made some similar blouses as well.

Ron began the series in suits, given that he was the boss, and this would remain the case until the show made a major overall shift at the end of the first season when he adopted his standard look of polo shirts and khakis.

Though Ron was in charge, Aziz Ansari's Tom Haverford would get the pricier wardrobe, because he cares more about style. "Aziz himself is a big fashion plate," Mann says. "He knows everything that's going on, and he loves all that stuff. So it was fun to do it with Aziz because he's into it." For instance: "He knows more, like, Adidas is doing a collab with so and so, and wouldn't that be cool if he was wearing those sneakers? And my answer was always yes."

Each character would have a closet, from which they could mix and match pieces throughout the season. "We repeated all the time," Mann says, "because we wanted to make it look as real as possible."

Mann found the *Parks and Recreation* set to be welcoming, enthusiastic, and full of heart, without much ego to battle. "There was not a lot of preciousness," Mann says. "Everybody was a joy. It was all about the character and not about personal fears or insecurities. It was very free."

Furthermore, she noticed, the *Parks and Recreation* producers did not try to test her the way some others might. Often, costume designers would encounter a producer who would reject their initial idea and then make them run around, trying to find some other item the producer had requested, and then when they found it, the producer would go back to the original idea. Schur, on the other hand, proved quite decisive, an underappreciated quality in a showrunner. If Mann gave him a choice, he picked one and never questioned it again. He didn't ask to see twenty more. "He knows I'm giving him the two best options," Mann says. "He trusts me. And then we are able to go forward full steam and make something really good."

Both Holland and Mann admired how kind, and calm, Schur was in his new role of cocreator and showrunner. He never seemed to lose his cool. While this was mainly due to his temperament, it was also a joint decision he made with Poehler: "I'm proud that Schur and I rejected the idea that creativity needs to come from chaos," Poehler later wrote.

The show favored collaboration from the beginning. Case in point: Aubrey Plaza helping to create her character before she was cast. She would continue to contribute to her character and help April to grow throughout the series. At the beginning of the show, April has a boyfriend who has a boyfriend, another idea that Plaza pitched: "I thought that was a really funny plotline and ahead of its time." Her friend Blake Lee was cast for the part.

She based her portrayal of April, particularly her eye-rolling, over-it attitude, on her sisters: Natalie, who is seven years younger than her, and Renee, who is twelve years younger. Plaza, as an actor, looked forward to chipping away this facade: "It's really fun to show the tiny little cracks of vulnerability and sensitivity that she has," Plaza says. "She doesn't really hate everything. It's a slightly performative thing for her. It's a defense mechanism."

Ansari, meanwhile, joined the show on an upswing in his career. He had just wrapped a role in the Seth Rogen film *Observe and Report* and had made an impression as a cocky intern on the final season of the hospital sitcom *Scrubs*. The star of that show, Zach Braff, praised Ansari's improv skills in *The Wall Street Journal*: "With Aziz, you really get a sense that he's just coming up with this crazy, random stuff off the top of his mind." Braff recalled "staring with wide eyes" while Ansari riffed about having a *Matrix* viewing party in a bit that was unscripted and unconnected to the scene they were filming.

Ansari had moved to LA a year prior to capitalize on his growing renown, which was partly fueled by his unique approach to Twitter, posting his wild, made-up plans with famous people he did not know. As *Parks and Recreation* readied to air, Ansari had a super-meta moment. While he was actually out partying with the actual Kanye West—in West's least-problematic time, before even the Taylor Swift VMAs moment—someone from the gossip site TMZ approached them. Ansari didn't let the moment slip away. "*Parks and Recreation*, April ninth at eight thirty, y'all!" he yelled in the background. "Keep an eye out!"

The group collaborating on the show in the writers' room had also grown. A small writing staff was now breaking and writing stories, even before the first episode was shot. They had come from some of the best comedy shows at the time: *Late Night with Conan O'Brien*, *SNL*, *The Sarah Silverman Program*, *Mad TV*, *King of the Hill*, *South Park*, *The Daily Show*, and, of course, *The Office*. The first season of *Parks and Recreation* would consist of six episodes that were guaranteed to air, so they barreled ahead through the entire short season.

Norm Hiscock was among that first small group of writers. After growing up in Montreal, he worked at *Saturday Night Live*. Daniels's wife had a job at Broadway Video, the company that produces *SNL*, and she recommended Hiscock to him when he was looking for writers for his animated series *King of the Hill*. At that time, though, Hiscock had recently started at *SNL* and didn't want to quit so soon, so he turned the job down. Two years later, he did decamp for *King of the Hill*, and Daniels eventually asked him to join *Parks and Recreation*. Hiscock had a gentle demeanor and a light Canadian accent and often wore baseball caps and rumpled plaid button-downs. He connected with the show, having lived in a number of smallish Canadian towns similar to Pawnee, particularly Swift Current, Saskatchewan, which has a population of about eighteen thousand. "There's a very tight community, everybody knows everybody," he says. "I lived on the main street, and that's where the parade went down."

The writing staff meetings did not yet occur regularly at this point in production. Hiscock remembers sometimes working on scripts with just fellow writer Alan Yang, a first-generation Taiwanese American with close-cropped dark hair. Dan Goor, a clean-shaven white guy with dark hair, who joined *Parks and Recreation* after six years at *Late Night with Conan O'Brien*, might be there sometimes as well, or he might be off working on his own episode.

Daniels and Schur had written the first episode, which established the main arc for the season: When Pawnee resident Ann Perkins requests that the construction pit near her home be filled in after her boyfriend, Andy, fell into it and broke his legs, Leslie Knope vows to make it into a park. The pit was meant to remain a driving force throughout the first season, and maybe even through the entire series.

"It was important to me that it was about a project," Daniels says. "We had this idea that what the documentary crew is there to look at is this project to fill in a pit and put a park on it. It was going to be about how slowly the government works and how this very energetic, optimistic person is having trouble getting anything accomplished."

Each of the five writers got one of the remaining episodes of the short season. Rachel Axler wrote the second one, "Canvassing," in which Leslie and her committee go door-to-door hoping to gain support for their park plan. Goor handled "The Reporter," when we first meet local newspaper staffer Shauna Malwae-Tweep (played by Alison Becker) as she writes a story about the pit. Yang wrote "Boys' Club," in which Leslie crashes an after-hours meeting full of male staffers in hopes of breaking up the male-dominated political ranks. Tucker Cawley got "The Banquet," in which an event honoring Leslie's mother's work in public service presents Leslie with the opportunity to blackmail an official into supporting her park project. And Hiscock took on the finale, "Rock Show," in which the season's plotlines come to a head at Andy's band's performance.

There in the writers' room, the world of Pawnee began to take shape, with strong direction from Daniels and Schur's vision research and pilot script. Pawnee would be a midsize town in Indiana that had once been occupied by Wamapoke Indians and eventually colonized in 1817 by a ne'er-do-well named Luther Howell, who'd been driven west from Connecticut by "several dozen death threats that had piled up after years of petty larceny, inveterate gambling, cuckolding, and running a crooked dog/cock/bear/goat/village idiot fight," according to the book about Pawnee that Leslie would later write.

These days, in the present-day Pawnee of the show, the town had around seventy thousand residents and was about 85 percent white, 9 percent African American, and 2 percent Native American. Its median income was $38,360.

It's known for its major raccoon problem, its "thousands, if not hundreds of thousands" of critters scurrying about its lawns and garbage cans. The government consists of a five-member elected city council headed by a mayor. "His job—and I say 'his' because Pawnee has never had a female mayor—is to be the public face of the government, listen to the people, and help the council figure out ways to improve the city," according to Leslie's book. "But really, the city manager's office does all the work, and the mayor just plays a lot of golf and gets his picture taken."

Goor remembers feeling like every tiny decision mattered in these early scripts. Once, he was sitting at the computer keyboard with Axler, watching her pour copious amounts of sugar into her coffee. He typed in a stage direction commanding Leslie to put excessive amounts of sugar into her coffee. "That kind of thing becomes bible, becomes part of the lore of the show," he says. "The first writing staff on any show ends up being responsible for creating the world, because everything you've come up with is new."

This is where Leslie's love of sweets, and particularly waffles with whipped cream, began. Food, in fact, would become a major theme for many of the characters, including Ron's passion for a number of meat forms, such as bacon, turkey legs, bacon-wrapped turkey legs, steaks, burgers, and meat tornadoes. Leslie and Ron shared a love for JJ's Diner, which specialized in both waffles and breakfast meats in particular. Because of that, JJ's, which Leslie's book tells us is located between TrampStamp Tattoos and the ChloroTech Cadmium Refinery, would host many of the scenes that took place outside city hall. "Pawnee's premier waffle location opened in 1976, forever changing the lives of me and everyone else who likes things that are amazing," the book says. "Grab the best seat in the house before Kyle snags it—the corner booth near the rotating pie display. Gaze out at the hustle and bustle of Sunrise in Pawnee and sip on the morning brew, being careful not to spill anything, because I swear to God I love the place, but it's like pulling teeth to get extra napkins."

Daniels and Schur were co-showrunning for the first season, and they had plenty of challenges to overcome. They hadn't faced the traditional arduous pilot process, making one episode and then awaiting NBC's judgment. Because of *The Office*'s success, the series went straight into production. "But the downside of that is that you learn a lot from a pilot," Daniels says. "Television is like doing a Broadway comedy or something—you don't necessarily start in New York. You usually start in Boston or Philadelphia. And then you make your changes, and you refine it, and *then* you bring it to Broadway. And that was often what a pilot did."

The first episode opens on Leslie explaining why she believes in the power of government to help people, a thesis that would remain consistent throughout the run of the show, even as it shifted creatively. The episode follows Leslie's relationships with her friends and coworkers in Pawnee as they figure out what to do about the pit. Far-flung locations in the Los Angeles suburbs played Pawnee on camera, their surrounding palm trees often digitally removed. The Pasadena City Hall at 100 N. Garfield Avenue stood in for Pawnee's. Later, the Harvest Festival would take place at the Pierce College Farm Center in Woodland Hills, and Leslie would work to save a mini-golf course that was actually Golf N' Stuff in Norwalk. Interiors for Leslie's favorite restaurant, JJ's Diner, would take place on location at Kountry Folks HomeStyle Restaurant in North Hills. And the posh neighboring town of Eagleton, Indiana, would, in fact, be the equally posh Arcadia, California.

In the first script, a scene depicting a community meeting about the park stands out from the rest. Daniels and Schur had found some inspiration from watching televised city council meetings, and by observing towns in both Indiana and California, and this is where it shows. Leslie, always trying to see the best in people, says the residents are "caring loudly," i.e., complaining. The script describes the crowd in vivid detail. "The front row is mostly old people and weirdos," the stage directions say. "The old people stare impassively like cows." One speaker is "a 50-ish weirdo . . . very animated and inexplicably super sarcastic." He's the one who says, "The head of the police is a ninth-degree Mason," and also, "One day there was a fire. That's what killed my snake."

Daniels loved to come up with writing tricks and name them, and one of those was a "killing field." It came from him reading a book on Vietnam that described how soldiers would set up an ambush, ready to shoot at the enemy from two sides. On *The Office*, a killing field might be a scene in the conference room where all the characters are assembled, firing off their strong, opposing points of view. "You wouldn't need to do a lot of clumsy stagecraft and have somebody walk in," Daniels says. "They were all there. They were all dug in to just fire jokes one at a time into the room."

The public meeting worked as a killing field for *Parks and Recreation*. "Part of that was from us going to the LA City Council and being shocked at how the council people had to listen to everybody for their two minutes," Daniels says. "They listened to the most insane bullshit from people who just wanted to hear themselves talk. They very patiently listened, because that was part of their job."

And while the first episode contained the seeds of romantic entanglement with Leslie pining for Mark, Daniels wanted to avoid hitting that too hard and seeming too similar to Jim and Pam on *The Office*. So the episode ends on the note of the budding friendship between Ann and Leslie. "She's surrounded by negativity," Daniels says, "so having this female friend was important."

Poehler, a newcomer to the mockumentary format, loved it as a cast member. "That form provides this incredible way in which you can have your mask, your presenting self, and your feeling self happening at the same time," she says. In other words, the camera can show the audience the facade a character is putting up—whatever she says during her talking head—and her real feelings in a close-up later. The best moments come from contradictions.

The camera operators became almost like cast members because of this. They often shot from "hidden" locations, as if they were documentarians trying to capture a candid moment. And they were almost always shooting, which meant the actors had to stay in character. "In those early episodes, when we were all sitting around, and all of us were on set, we discovered a lot about our characters," Poehler says. "There was nothing off camera."

Even during the first week of rehearsals for the first episode, the cameras were rolling. Daniels had Poehler lead a tour of the office while talking to the camera and to her castmates in character. She remembers interacting with Retta, who played staffer Donna Meagle, while Donna was at her desk. The art department had tacked a leaf up on the corkboard next to her.

"Whoa, where did you get that leaf?" Poehler remembers saying, as Leslie.

"Outside," Retta deadpanned as Donna.

Oh, okay, Poehler thought, *Donna is going to be the kind of person that doesn't enjoy these tours.*

While the cast was having fun getting to know one another and their characters, the outside world was developing its own opinions about this much-hyped sibling to *The Office*. Mostly, no one could comprehend that it wasn't a spin-off. "*Parks* was not a spin-off in any way," Poehler says. "So once I was told it wasn't, I didn't worry about it. It was everybody else that had to get used to it."

NBC's marketing did not strive to disabuse audiences of the idea that *Parks and Recreation* was closely related to *The Office*, a strategy that would backfire. I recall seeing promos at the time, and even though I was reporting on the television industry for *Entertainment Weekly*, I still found myself wondering what Poehler standing in front of a pit had to do with Dunder Mifflin.

"It was terribly launched," Poehler says. "It seemed like a crossover. And then everyone was like, 'What is this?'"

The network did a test screening of the first episode, and this confusion permeated the results. NBC reps called Daniels and Schur during a thirty-minute break from shooting to deliver the news: "People did not really go for this. They did not enjoy it that much." In Hollywood, where everything is sugarcoated, this was bad.

The series was already in this metaphorical hole before it premiered. Then the hole got deeper: The industry publication *Deadline* published the pilot episode's less-than-stellar test results. The March 23, 2009, article came with the headline, "Problems with NBC's 'Parks & Recreation.'" "NBC's upcoming Universal Media Studios sitcom *Parks And Recreation* was supposed to be a real winner since the mockumentary comes from Greg Daniels and Michael Schur of *The Office* and stars Amy Poehler," Nikki Finke wrote. "I say 'supposed' because there are problems galore in the rough-cut pilot, according to a March 18th-dated 'Consumer And Market Intelligence Research Summary' which I saw this weekend. Considering the show starts airing April 9th, can *Parks And Recreation* get fixed in time?"

Bullet points included:

- "PARKS AND RECREATION's overwhelming resemblance to THE OFFICE caused many viewers to simply see it as a 'carbon copy' of a successful show. The pilot was seen as 'predictable' and lacking in character development, even for a pilot."

- "Expectations for this show are very high, especially among OFFICE viewers. Many had seen the promos and were expecting an 'OFFICE-type mockumentary' with the same tone, but felt the pilot was too close and similar to the OFFICE." *(Author's note: Well, this is confusing.)*

- "Focus needs to evolve away from the pit—consider showing Leslie [*Amy Poehler*] and her team dealing with various parks and recreation duties. There is a lot of interest in exploring the comedy potential in a government office." *(Author's note: That's nice, actually!)*

- "Although many saw her as the 'Michael Scott character [from *The Office*]', Amy Poehler was well liked. SNL fans felt her character Leslie was a bit 'too serious' and 'too low-key' and many expected her to have more energy and enthusiasm, especially when she is getting drunk at the end of the show." *(Author's note: More enthusiastic drinking, please!)*

- "The show could use a genuinely likeable male lead. The lack of quality male characters was evident in both the Dial Test and Focus Groups. . . . Because there are no 'datable' men in the cast, there is little 'romantic tension' or 'interesting relationship potential' in the show." *(Author's note: Sorry, Mark Brendanawicz.)*

- "Good positive spikes in the opening scenes and during the classroom open forum session but positive spikes flatten during the scenes in Leslie's office and when she meets Mark out on the patio (Approx Mins 8:30-9:30)." *(Author's note: Mark is getting hammered here.)*

- "Highest positive spike comes from Leslie falling into the pit." *(Author's note: Fair.)*

- "The last 6:30 (approx) suffer from lower positives and higher negatives as 'slower' and 'more tedious' scenes are featured. Ron's opinion on the role of government and his discussion with Mark received low positives throughout." *(Author's note: Oof.)*

Parks and Recreation looked close to dead before it began, with two weeks to go before it started airing.

Nights of insomnia followed for Schur, who couldn't stop thinking that he was going to be responsible for ruining Poehler's career. She doesn't recall feeling quite as dire. "My job was, frankly, to bond with the cast," she says, "to figure out how to make this character funny and pay service to the writing. I think the writers, Schur especially, had a much harder job in the beginning. They had to create a world. They had to make us care. They had to fight against a lot of preconceived notions about what the show should be." She adds good-naturedly, "I'm glad he was up all night. He should have been."

Nonetheless, they had to barrel through the episodes that remained to be filmed, regardless of outside expectations. They would, for the most part, have to keep going as they started airing, getting feedback from audiences and doing their best to adjust when they saw fit.

For Poehler, much of it also felt like a blur: Just months before, she'd left a life-defining job at *SNL*, where she'd been for seven years and which had made her famous. Then she'd given birth to her first child, who was now a few months old. She had little bandwidth left for worrying about what people thought of her new show before it had even aired.

However, some of the points raised by the test audience rang true, like the problems with the Mark Brendanawicz character, which would be tabled for now, and the more pressing issue of building an entire show around an empty pit. Daniels said they even considered calling the show *The Pit*, but now it was becoming clear that perhaps the hole could not remain a major focus for the entire run of the show. These first six episodes felt like perhaps the natural lifespan of a pit-based plotline.

The writers were still, in all honesty, struggling to hit the right tone in those first few episodes. Poehler, meanwhile, was finding her "groove" with Leslie. "I love people and process," she says. "That's what turns me on, and that's what Leslie was about, too." In fact, Poehler felt energized by Leslie: "She would push me and remind me to stay connected." Poehler loved that Leslie "didn't hide her enthusiasm" and was "not embarrassed by caring out loud."

Not all was lost. Plenty of good had come through in the episodes they'd completed so far. Poehler also loved that Leslie forges an enviable friendship with Ann, the woman complaining about the pit. "The female friendship on the show is one of the things I'm most proud of, and it certainly came naturally because Rashida Jones and I had been friends for a long time," Poehler said. "My female friendships are very important to me, and it was nice to play a consistent relationship."

I personally responded to Leslie, even this early version of her. I had never seen a character quite like her on television, type A and proud of it. As a lifelong type A girl who had worked relentlessly since high school to get myself from the Midwest to where I now was, on staff at *Entertainment Weekly* magazine in New York City, I relished not only her presence but also her lack of apology. I did what a lot of women are taught to do, which is to be very ambitious and then pretend you're not whenever you're caught. Leslie did not mind being caught, and I loved it, even if I wasn't totally sold on the show just yet. Like all the other fans of *The Office*, I came in with high expectations and found *Parks and Recreation*'s execution a bit messy in the early days. But I loved Leslie's bravado. Poehler was touched by this, too, that Leslie didn't care about looking cool or being cool. "She had an urgency and a sense of humor," Poehler says admiringly. "She had a lack of preciousness."

Meanwhile, Leslie and Ron—along with the actors who played them, Poehler and Offerman—were starting to jell as the series' central (platonic) relationship. "We had a very mommy-daddy energy on that set," Poehler says. Offerman was an "incredibly loving, collaborative actor. I just felt so supported by him all the time."

This came as a relief, because if a movie is a fling, a TV show *might* be a long-term relationship. "Like if this goes right, I'm going to see you every day for seven years," Poehler says. "You need somebody that is consistent, who is someone you can depend on, who is open to new ideas but wants other people to shine. I couldn't have found a better partner than Nick for that."

Their characters, of course, were meant to gently oppose each other. Ron believes, he says, that "the entire government should be privatized." Leslie believes in nothing more than the power of government to do good. This opposition worked because "there was a personal warmth and respect," Offerman says. "These people can absolutely butt heads in the office to the point of hilarity. But then as soon as they punch out, they say, 'I admire you and respect you, and

I'll go to great lengths to defend your rights, even though I disagree with your insane liberal leanings.'"

They were getting attached to each other and to their characters, and they wanted this show to last. But they knew that the negative test results contained some good points. Now the cast and crew had to figure out how to respond: Push ahead without worrying about the criticism, or retool at the last second to pull off a turnaround?

CHAPTER 4

"Deluded, Vain, and Completely Out of Her Depth"

Season 1

Despite the bad reviews, the cast and crew had to press forward in developing Pawnee's world as they churned out episodes. The third episode, "The Reporter," began to build out the local media, introducing Shauna Malwae-Tweep of *The Pawnee Journal*, who's assigned to interview Leslie about the pit project.

"We were also looking at local government as an analog to national government, and you obviously need to have interactions with the press," says Dan Goor, who wrote the episode. "Leslie wanted to be a more public-facing figure and she was kind of inept at it."

Goor can't remember where Shauna's extremely specific name came from: "That could have been a combo where there were two alts, Shauna Malwae or Shauna Tweep, and then we made it Shauna Malwae-Tweep," he says. "Who knows." He hazards a guess: "Bob Tweep married Martha Shauna Malwae. And then they had Shauna Malwae-Tweep."

The episode would become the first in a series of small and large turning points for the show.

Dean Holland sat in the edit room, feeling a little frustrated as he worked with one of Shauna's big scenes, a face-off with Leslie, who has turned defensive and combative during an interview at JJ's Diner, which, as a leading waffle establishment, would become a go-to location as the series went on. The editing room was a stale and boring place. "Nothing on the walls because as soon as you get settled in, they cancel your show," he says. "It's a bit superstitious. I had an enormous leather couch with a leather ottoman, which we used to play card games and dice games on when we should have been working."

The scene as currently edited was still missing something; it felt as boring as the room. It was playing by the rules that Greg Daniels, Mike Schur, and Holland had agreed on when they began making the show. In fact, it was playing by *The Office* rules, strictly imitating what a real documentary might look like. But did this show always have to be like *The Office*? Didn't the test audience already feel it was too much like *The Office*?

Schur and director Jeffrey Blitz had asked Alison Becker, who played Shauna, to fire off a number of quotes her character had gotten in her reporting, all versions of people saying the park would never happen. Amy Poehler improvised responses, rapid-fire. They planned to choose just one for the final cut, but wanted to have plenty of options.

Shauna: "You should write an article on the pope getting married, because that's more likely to happen than this park."

Leslie: There are some countries where the pope can be married.

Shauna: "You should write an article on talking monkeys."

Leslie: Really, have you seen *The Wizard of Oz*?

Shauna: "You should write an article about the sun falling out of the sky."

Leslie: Why would you write an article about that?

Holland strung them all together, jump-cutting between each one, to show the team the options. Or maybe it could run just like this, with the jump cuts.

"It was really funny," Schur recalls. "And we were like, 'What if we just did that? What if we jump-cut all these things?' *The Office* was so hyperrealistic that we never did anything experimental like that."

Most viewers wouldn't have noticed, but that marked *Parks and Recreation*'s first act of independence from *The Office*. It still had a ways to go.

Becker, an Upright Citizens Brigade grad, loved doing the scene with Poehler. On other jobs, she would try to improvise and the script coordinator would correct her down to the tiniest details: "It should be 'the,' not 'an.'" What she remembers most about working with Poehler was the feeling of having fun. "It is like being a dork at school and hanging out with the coolest cheerleader in the world," she says, "and then she also happens to be amazingly kind."

Becker had just moved to Los Angeles from New York when she got the part. In fact, she was still sleeping on the couch at the apartment of her friend Nick Kroll, who would eventually play a very different member of the Pawnee media, shock jock Howard "the Douche" Tuttleman. "There was kind of a mass exodus of New York comedians, and we all helped each other out when we got to LA," she says.

When she got the call telling her she'd booked the gig, she still thought it was a spin-off of *The Office*. Even when she shot the episode, she couldn't quite tell, because nothing had aired yet. Nonetheless, she loved working on it, mainly because of Poehler. "Amy has not lost the joy of comedy, and she will give you the biggest belly laugh for a silly joke," Becker says. "She's so giving."

Becker also understood Pawnee on a visceral level. She'd grown up in a much smaller community, one that didn't even have a stoplight, called Allamuchy Township, New Jersey. It was mostly farmland that was formerly Lenape Indian territory until Quakers and descendants of American Revolution veterans moved in. Nearby was a place called Lake Shawnee. "So when I saw Pawnee," she says, "I was like, I got this."

To make things more interesting in the first Shauna episode, the writers threw in a personal-life conflict between her and Leslie: It turns out Shauna slept with Mark, Leslie's crush. This set the course for Shauna's disastrous dating life to come. For now, though, "We liked the idea that this woman whom Leslie had to impress had 'stolen' the love of her life," Goor says. "That just felt like such a juicy situation to put her in."

In Becker's audition, the producers had asked her to try delivering her lines a different way, a little . . . less innocently. That was her first clue that Shauna might have more going on than just setting up Poehler's improvs. "They were so brilliant for thinking about a guest star's character that far in advance," Becker says, adding that they eventually went with the more innocent version of her character.

Outside the safe walls of the production, *Parks and Recreation* was soon rolling out into a world that had already become a bit hostile to it. The cast and crew would have to prove to that world that they were better than they seemed—and that they were *not* a spin-off of *The Office*—once and for all. Oh, and they also had to save their network: NBC now ranked fourth among the major networks, and Ben Silverman, the wunderkind executive who'd been hired to rescue it and had pushed to make *Parks* happen, was now on the ropes. Former late-night host Jay Leno had been given five hours of prime time each week, which was not a good sign for regular programming. Reboots of *American Gladiators* and *Knight Rider*, both Silverman picks seen as lowest-common-denominator attempts, had tanked, which looked all the worse on the network known for quality programming like the old "Must See TV" comedies, *ER* (which was just ending, though the zeitgeist had long since passed it by), and *The West Wing* (which had ended three years prior).

Meanwhile, Silverman had also become infamous for a party he threw featuring women in bikinis and white tigers in cages, and he'd alienated the industry by insulting rival TV executives in an *Esquire* interview, calling ABC Entertainment president Steve McPherson a "moron," claiming that McPherson never liked Silverman's show, *Ugly Betty*, that became a hit on his network, and calling him a "sad man, a miserable guy."

He also took a swipe at both McPherson and Fox Entertainment president Kevin Reilly, his predecessor at NBC. "Traditionally, development executives rise through a specific subsection of the TV business—prime time, network, scripted programming. They're basically D-girls," Silverman said, using a derogatory term for young, attractive women at the lowest levels of the business. "That's what Steve McPherson is, that's what Kevin Reilly is. That's bad vernacular, but they're all D-girls."

Suddenly the industry saw *Parks and Recreation* as his, and the network's, last chance at redemption. It would likely take more than a few surprising jump cuts in the third episode to get there.

And yet, the *Parks* set, led by Poehler's example, looked at the shrapnel coming their way and made a radical choice: to have fun. First of all, even if they failed, at least they'd do it while having a good time. Second, fun was infectious. It charmed audiences into going along for the ride. This philosophy would serve them well both now and into the future.

As Becker had learned, improvisation helped. The standard *Parks* process included time for "fun runs." After the producers had gotten all the takes they needed, they'd encourage the cast to do a few fun runs—fearless, no-holds-barred, don't-worry-about-it improvs. Aubrey Plaza loved the feeling of being in the moment for a fun run and seeing what came up. She wanted to take advantage of every second of this creative challenge. "A lot of the fun run stuff made it onto the show," Plaza says. "That was the time when we all got to try to make each other laugh or try something that was insane."

This also sometimes had the effect of making the scene more conversational. "There's more of a natural feel when they're just living in it for a while," writer Norm Hiscock says.

Daniels also introduced the "candy bag," an idea he conceived on the set of *The Office*, where every solid joke option that was pitched but didn't get into an episode would be put into a bag. If there was a little extra time after nailing a scene, they might pick a few of the other options from the candy bag and try those, too.

Some TV productions might have responded to the kind of scrutiny *Parks* was facing with stress and tyranny, but *Parks* countered with fun and candy.

The show premiered on NBC on April 9, 2009, airing at 8:30 p.m. Eastern time on Thursdays as part of NBC's "Comedy Night Done Right" lineup with *My Name Is Earl*, *The Office*, and *30 Rock*.

The initial reviews provided little comfort for the *Parks* team. "After a spin through the debut episode of *Saturday Night Live* alum Amy Poehler's new NBC comedy, *Parks and Recreation*, one question stuck in my brain like a glass splinter: If NBC was going to make a carbon copy of *The Office*, why didn't they just stick with their original plan to create an actual spin-off series?" wrote *St. Petersburg Times* television critic Eric Deggans.

Critics did not like Leslie. She was "deluded" and "ditzy." It was hard to tell whether this was a compliment or a pan when it came from *The New York Times*'s Alessandra Stanley: "Leslie is a classic ditz, which is to say that she is ridiculous and endearingly obtuse," Stanley wrote. "What makes Ms. Poehler's star turn a milestone is that ditzes are traditionally supporting characters, like Jenna on '30 Rock' and Karen on 'Will & Grace' or, reaching back, Edith on 'All in the Family' and Georgette on 'The Mary Tyler Moore Show.'"

She continued, "The show looks a lot like 'The Office,' but there aren't many female leads on television quite like Leslie. The closest ones are women who volunteer to look foolish on reality shows like Bravo's 'Real Housewives of New York' or TV Land's coming, self-explanatory dating show, 'The Cougar.'"

But hey, as Leslie would say in season 6, "One person's annoying is another's inspiring and heroic."

For other critics, it felt *too much* like *The Office*, but not as good as *The Office*, and also, why was Leslie so much like Michael Scott, but not as funny?

New York magazine described Leslie in unflattering terms: "Knope is an idealistic, hopeful, and endlessly optimistic do-gooder who honestly believes that government can make the world a better place. Of course, because her show is 'from the people who bring you *The Office*' (as you might have heard 80 times if you've been watching NBC at any point in the last two months), she's also deluded, kind of vain, and completely out of her depth."

Even *Rolling Stone*, *Parks and Recreation*'s greatest apologist, said, as if with a shrug, "*The Office* started slow too."

For what it's worth, some parks and recreation officials from around the country liked it. They appreciated the details of the town meeting full of residents "caring loudly," a product of Daniels and Schur's research. "I thought that scene had it down perfectly," said Brian Taylor, a recreation manager for Pasco County in Florida, speaking to the *St. Petersburg Times*. "For anyone who has worked in local government, I think they can relate to that forum where there are many issues raised that are important, and a few that aren't. We listen to them all, just like they did in the scene."

If the park plans for the pit were, as Schur had once implied, the determinant of how long this show would run, Harry Johnson, the recreation manager in Hernando, Florida, had an answer. "Something like getting a park there in that spot would take at least four to five years," Johnson said. "I mean, that would be a mind-boggling process, what she wants to do."

That said, they could see that all the characters were a bit . . . bumbling. They felt that everyone, even Leslie, was unprofessional, though they could see she was better than the others. "It does seem like she's the only one who does care," Taylor said. "She might have been trying too hard, but her heart is in the right place. I like to think that that's what I do, but I plan on watching the show to see what happens." He was looking forward to seeing the next episode, when Leslie would deal with some graffiti.

Schur had lost sleep over what *Parks and Recreation*'s struggles might do to Poehler's career. But he pulled himself out of his funk enough to take the feedback in, just in time to rethink the final episode of the six, "Rock Show," which has Leslie confronting her crush on Mark Brendanawicz, Ann and Andy breaking up, and everything culminating at Andy's band's show, where they play a rousing ode to the pit he fell into, called "The Pit." Directed by Schur, the episode would become the biggest turning point to date for the series.

For starters, he determined, the episode needed to focus more on the ensemble, bringing everyone together in the same room. And it had to conclude the pit story. The pit and Leslie's relationship with Mark had become untenable, and Schur knew he needed to move on from them. He didn't know how he'd do it, or if it would be in this episode, but he needed an exit strategy for both.

Next, Schur wanted to add some real music, something funny and rousing. Writer Norm Hiscock came up with the first verse of "The Pit" in his outline for the episode. He thought that *Parks and Recreation* could pull this off, because there were several people working on the show who were musicians. Chris Pratt could play guitar and sing. Writer Alan Yang could play bass. This could really happen, instead of just being an offhand joke about Andy being in a band.

"I wrote the dumbest lyrics I could about a pit," Hiscock says. Most of the verses are variations on this: "The Pit / I was in the pit / You were in the pit / We all fell in the pit." There's not even a rhyme scheme, just repetition.

The music in this episode would prove a major addition to the show's toolbox. Aziz Ansari recommended composer Mark Rivers, who'd worked on *Human Giant*, to write "The Pit" and the other songs performed by Andy's band, ostensibly "written by Andy."

"They needed a guy to write some stupid songs," Rivers says, "so my name came up." Rivers would also serve as the band's on-screen drummer.

Rivers took Hiscock's ideas and then, Hiscock says, "continued writing the dumb lyrics. I use Spinal Tap as an influence." He also thought about nineties sensation Hootie and the Blowfish ("Hold My Hand," "Let Her Cry," "Only Wanna Be with You") as a reference, and

Andy himself in the episode describes their music as "like Matchbox 20 meets the Fray"—i.e., middling 2000s radio rock. Rivers remembers the show's producers telling him that "it didn't have to go very far musically. It's very repetitive."

Pratt could not only play and sing competently, he could also perform onstage. "You could see why he would be fronting a band," Hiscock says of Pratt's charisma. But Rivers barely considered that when writing the songs. "We weren't trying to write bad music, just music by people with bad taste," he explains. "I had to resist urges to be clever or to not repeat myself, all those things that Andy wouldn't do." The chords are as simple as possible: three major chords, in the key of C, repeated over and over: G, C, F, a standard 1-4-5 structure.

However, Rivers maintains some admiration for that song's lyrical conceit: "'The Pit' was obviously about his having fallen in the pit," he says. "Metaphorically, it's about all of us. Which, in hindsight, is probably the smartest songwriting moment Andy really ever had, to see that there was a metaphorical pit that we've all fallen into."

The mood at the read-through of the episode was elevated; it was the first time a script got laughs from beginning to end. Just in time, they'd found the show. "That episode probably saved us," Schur says. "Right at the very last possible second, we figured out how to showcase the cast and make them shine. In a weird way, the fact that someone obnoxiously leaked our testing results to *Deadline* probably saved us in the end."

This episode marks one other milestone: the first time Ron Swanson switches from wearing suits and ties to what would become his uniform, a long-sleeve polo shirt tucked into polyester pants. "It's so funny because Nick is not actually Ron Swanson," costume designer Kirston Mann says. "He is very styley in real life. But he was so into it. You would never know he wasn't Ron Swanson."

In one of the episode's funniest scenes, Andy, in a talking-head segment, enumerates the many names his band had gone through; some of the names were scripted, but Schur encouraged Pratt to improvise, too. Options included the Andy Andy Andies, Crackfinger, Department of Homeland Obscurity, Fiveskin, Fleetwood Mac Sexpants, Just the Tip, Malice in Chains, Penis Pendulum, Possum Pendulum, Teddy Bear Suicide, Two Doors Down, and Mouse Rat. The decision to edit this scene similarly to Poehler's answers to park criticisms in "The Reporter," as a long series of jump cuts, established this technique as a hallmark of *Parks and Recreation.*

The edit that Holland prepared included many more than originally intended: twenty-nine in all. (In the episode, the band is called Scarecrow Boat, but will soon return to Mouse Rat.) "It was one of those things, like, you just try it, and you see how everybody reacts to it," Holland says. "If they react well to it, then, great. If they don't, then that was a stupid idea, and we move on and go do another thing. I feel very comfortable in the edit room. I will try just about anything."

He adds, "The goal of an editor is you don't just cut something one way and go, 'There it is!' I cut it thirty-seven different ways until I'm happy."

Pratt's joyous and appealing turn as a frontman, meanwhile, opened up another new possibility for the next season: Perhaps Andy, once intended to be a guest character for a limited time, should stick around somehow.

"He was so wonderful that we started changing course to figure out how to keep him," Daniels says.

Though the episode notched the series' smallest audience so far at 4.29 million viewers, critics noticed the uptick in quality: "I'm not saying 'Rock Show' was a masterpiece, or the series' Rosetta Stone," Alan Sepinwall wrote, "but at the very least it's a signpost on the way to it becoming the kind of comedy I believe it can be with the talent in front of and behind the camera."

Parks and Recreation's season 1 signed off on May 14, 2009, ending up at No. 96 for the network television season with an average of 5.97 million viewers. But NBC's loyalty to *The Office*'s creative team, and the glimmering promise evinced by the sixth episode, pushed them toward giving *Parks and Recreation* one more chance. Executives green-lit another half a season to see where it would go. The changes to come in the second season would determine the fate of the show.

Daniels and Schur had made it to the end of their first season, and they had, they thought, fixed some problems with the solid season finale. But they also felt they still had some major reworking to do as they went into season 2 to fully resolve all the issues. They met with NBC executives to discuss their direction for the future.

When thinking of ways to pivot, Daniels remembered the 1960s sitcom *Green Acres*, on which Eddie Albert plays a New York City lawyer who yearns for a simpler life. He impulse-buys a farm and drags his socialite wife, played by Eva Gabor, to live there with him. While it was hardly a brilliant piece of television, Daniels recalled how the small town where the characters lived was full of oddballs who contrasted with Albert's more grounded nature. Leslie, he thought, should no longer play the fool. She should be trying her best to make things better while the fools around her scuttle her efforts.

Perhaps more urgently, they needed to do away with the pit. One can see how it seemed brilliant, philosophically, in its conception: an entire show chasing the question of filling in this pit. The phrase "*Godot*-ian" came up in the *New York* piece. Schur had found in his research of local government in suburban Claremont, California, that this could be realistic. When he asked employees there about this conceit, they explained that they were about to break ground on a new park that had been in the works for eighteen years. "We thought, *Okay, that'll work,*" Schur told the magazine. "If our show's on for eighteen years, we'll be pretty happy."

But after the pit became an apparent pitfall, the network instead wanted the show to shoot on location more, get the audience out into Pawnee—aside from the pit. Daniels and Schur would work toward Leslie negotiating to fill in the pit early in season 2, when it would become an empty lot that could host events such as the Winter Wonderland and Pawnee Summer Kick-Off. In addition, they decided, they needed a character who was a match for Leslie "both in terms of personality and in terms of worldview," Schur says. That is, Leslie deserved a love interest who was *not* Mark Brendanawicz. Not only was the chemistry lacking but also their backstory—that they'd slept together once and it had meant something to her but not him—was bringing things down.

"We thought of it as just a funny joke," Schur says. "And the reality was that it didn't play that way. It played as, she's a weirdo who was obsessed with this guy." Worse, he says, "it was sad, and that was the one thing we never wanted the show to be. So I started dreaming of a character who had a certain amount of skepticism of what is really possible, but also his soul is much more like Leslie's soul."

We'd have to wait a little longer for him, but for now, *Parks and Recreation* was righting its course for season 2.

CHAPTER 5

"That Extra Realness"

Season 2

Katie Dippold couldn't believe her luck: She had landed in a network television writers' room in Los Angeles, on one of NBC's Thursday-night sitcoms. Just a few years earlier, she had been struggling to pay rent in New York City, working as an intern at *Late Night with Conan O'Brien*, and living for the times when the staff would order lunch in. At that time, she'd thought, "My god, this is a dream realized. It's all I ever wanted." Free food *and* a TV job!

She joined *Parks and Recreation* at the beginning of the show's second season, and she was intimidated. An Upright Citizens Brigade alum, she had worked for the past three years at the sketch show *Mad TV*, which she describes as "mayhem. It was just nonsense, because you didn't have to worry about a story. There was less pressure. We were not winning any awards, were not being discussed in any way. So it was just a bunch of silly geese in a writers' room together."

She had watched and liked *Parks and Recreation*'s first season.

Then she walked into the *Parks and Recreation* writers' room on the second floor of a building at the CBS Radford lot in Studio City, where canonical series like *The Mary Tyler Moore Show* filmed. Four couches surrounded two coffee tables, with bulletin boards and whiteboards lining the walls and a writer's assistant desk in the corner. The most basic of conference rooms. There she saw Norm Hiscock from *The Kids in the Hall*, Rachel Axler from *The Daily Show*, and Dan Goor, who had worked at *Conan* as a full-fledged writer. Axler had written her a nice email the day before welcoming her, which had "meant the world" to Dippold, given how nervous she was. She'd gotten the *Parks* job when her manager, Greg Walter, slipped her sample script to Mike Schur, whose manager worked at the same firm. Getting the gig had thrilled her, but now she wasn't sure what to do in the face of these brilliant writers. She had no idea how to pitch a story.

Soon, though, she learned that in many ways, the staff would all be starting over together. Major changes were coming to the series, with an eye toward differentiating it from its predecessor, *The Office*, and distinguishing its own comedic tone. And they had to work even harder to keep *Parks and Recreation* on the air now that their network benefactor, Ben Silverman, had been replaced by a new chairman of NBC Universal Entertainment, Jeff Gaspin. He would keep *Parks and Recreation* for now, but he was watching for changes—particularly shifts in Amy Poehler's character and the possibility of bringing in a love interest for her who wasn't Mark Brendanawicz.

When Greg Daniels and Schur convened the writers at the beginning of the second season, they laid down some new rules. Schur told them, as Dippold recalls, "that he wanted less pipe. There's so much government jargon in season one." He wanted them to bring him "more relatable" pitches, "rather than focusing on what motion was going to pass."

Also, as Daniels had been pondering, Leslie needed to display more smarts while "not having the main ensemble undermine her constantly."

But perhaps the most critical thing that happened in the second season was that the production began to move as one, connected by a force that is unusual in Hollywood: goodwill. *Parks and Recreation* ran on the cast and crew's genuine affection and respect for one another. People were nice to one another. Not fake-Hollywood nice, not people-pleasing nice, but thoughtful and caring. They played basketball together during breaks. The show was built, Offerman wrote in his memoir, on a "foundation of mutual love" that felt familial.

Everyone wanted to make this thing work so that they could keep seeing one another every day. And everyone understood what a privilege it was to get to try.

"We were so lucky to be surrounded by really good people," Aubrey Plaza says. "Not jaded. And grounded. That's really hard to come by when you're in this industry. People have horror stories about being on a television show for ten years with people that they hated or complete assholes or toxic working environments, and I feel so incredibly lucky that my first big experience was so positive."

Plaza credits this largely to Poehler, whom she calls "the absolute number one boss in Hollywood. She has got it all going on. She's, first of all, always the funniest in the room. And she knows how to be a leader. She knows how to treat people with respect. I learned from her how to produce, I learned how to treat the crew."

Nick Offerman, too, became a guiding force for Plaza on set, like when she began to get a little too used to the ways that the crew tended to the actors. "They treat you almost like a baby when you're an actor," she says. "They're constantly catering to you, and they're asking you what you need. And it's this really weird vibe. Some people are like, 'I could get used to this.'"

Though it made her uncomfortable at first, she would sometimes let them bring her a coffee. Offerman would clock it, mosey on over to her, and say, "The coffee machine is right over there. You could just get up and get your own coffee. Sometimes I think that's a better thing to do."

This interaction would stick with her, prodding her not to fall into the babied-actor trap.

"He was always a good reminder of, like, this is all not real, don't drink the Kool-Aid," she says. "Be a real person at all times. I took that to heart."

If you find Offerman blending into Ron Swanson in your mind when you read that anecdote, that's no accident. In the second season, the writers got bolder about incorporating elements of the actors themselves into their characters.

"When you start a show, both the performers and the writers are often feeling their way toward each other in the dark," Offerman says. "And they say, 'Oh, you're a meat-eating woodworker? Do you mind if we use that in the show? Because that's hilarious.' And I said, 'Sure, please, milk me.'"

He adds, "The backstory is one of the delightful things that you, together with the writers, get to discover and create and embroider."

Schur had the writers tour Offerman's real-life woodshop in Los Angeles to see him in his element and understand his work, which would become a major part of Ron Swanson's character. Offerman had been debating what to do with the shop—which had recently been his main occupation—now that the show was continuing. For the moment, he had decided to keep it going.

As the season progressed, the actors and their characters began to meld more. Aziz Ansari told the *Daily Beast*, "For example, me, I really am into suits. I like hip-hop music and songs. . . . Nick Offerman really does have a woodshop. Nick Offerman makes canoes. That canoe he paddles in *Parks*, that episode where Ron is in a canoe, Nick Offerman built that canoe, for real!"

April's sister on the show, Natalie, was named after Plaza's real-life sister, and Plaza cops to the fact that "the lines between us and our characters were very blurry. I think that's why the show's so good. The writers really paid attention to who we were and infused that into the show to give it that extra realness. It was hard not to get lost in it."

Perhaps not coincidentally, the show began to work. As a *Variety* headline on a piece that included *Parks and Recreation* said, "Winning characters keep sitcoms alive while they figure out what's funny."

The producers and network agreed that keeping Chris Pratt on as Andy Dwyer, and making him a regular, was the right move. But it made no sense that Ann's ex, a layabout with a garage band, would start working in the parks department. Schur discussed the dilemma with production designer Ian Phillips.

"I want Andy to be around in city hall more," Phillips remembers Schur saying to him, "but he can't work in the parks department because he's not qualified. He's just kind of a doofus."

"Well, you know, in a lot of places like the state houses, city halls, there's a shoeshine guy," Phillips replied. He had, after all, researched quite a few such buildings when helping to design the set. "Why don't we make him a shoeshine guy?"

Schur agreed that that made sense, so Phillips was charged with making Andy a shoeshine station that looked increasingly lived-in, decorated with many, many photos of Ann at one point, and Mouse Rat band merch, photos of him at gigs, and newspaper clippings as things progressed.

"We generated all of that stuff," Phillips says. "We tried to give as much character as we could to these people, because when you go to work, people collect stuff in their cubicles. That's where you live in the middle of the day."

Daniels and Schur also embraced a network directive to tackle more issues on the series to move away from the pit. Not every episode—they didn't want to become a modern *All in the Family*, or date the episodes so much that they wouldn't make sense to future audiences in reruns—but there was a way to lightly satirize national debates by bringing them down to the Pawnee level. This would serve as yet another method of separating *Parks and Recreation* from *The Office*.

Parks and Recreation's second-season premiere put this into practice, tackling gay marriage. Several states had legalized same-sex marriage, while others had faced ballot initiatives seeking to ban it. The writers came up with the idea of a gay penguin couple, which had actually been in the news. Scientists had observed same-sex coupling among penguins in field research and at zoos in Berlin, Toronto, and New York, which inspired the 2005 children's book about two male penguins who raise a chick together, *And Tango Makes Three*. Writer Norm Hiscock liked the idea of Leslie trying to do "a cute thing to promote the zoo, but then it gets out of hand."

In the script, Leslie holds a local-media photo op, performing a marriage ceremony for two penguins at the zoo. Only afterward do the assembled journalists notice that both penguins are male, and turn the stunt into a politicized statement on gay marriage. Leslie at first fights this characterization—until she discovers she's a hero at the local gay bar, the Bulge.

"That, for me, was an eye-opener in terms of, like, she has to watch her step as she's in the public eye and represents the town, and she has to represent everybody," Hiscock says. He thought it was interesting for the series to show her "navigating those waters." This would mark Leslie moving away from that Michael Scott–like incompetence and toward, Hiscock says, "trying to be savvier in politics."

The second-season writers' room consisted of mostly the same people as the first season's, headed by co-showrunners Daniels and Schur. Dippold, Harris Wittels, who had just finished a stint at *The Sarah Silverman Program*, and Aisha Muharrar, a Harvard grad, joined as new hires. Dippold began to find her place in the room by relying on her improv background.

"It just gives you more of a curiosity, wanting to lean into jokes more," she says. "It's a playful mentality." Even so, she had never been in a room with this many funny people, and she felt the pressure, even as she laughed the hardest she'd ever laughed. One minute, she couldn't stop giggling, and the next minute she felt the most stress she'd ever felt as they tried to figure out an episode.

The *Parks and Recreation* writers' room worked in an unusually collaborative way, reflecting the spirit of the show. The writers pitched stories and jokes as a group, and broke storylines down into beats together. Only then would one writer take those notes and turn them into an initial outline. That would come back to the room to be discussed and elaborated, packed tighter with scenes and jokes. Finally, Daniels and Schur would assign the episode to one writer, which could be the same writer who did the outline or a different one. But by that time, there was a detailed outline to which everyone had contributed.

This made the *Parks and Recreation* writers seem almost maniacally communal and deferent to one another. They resist taking credit for any individual line or plot (including during interviews for this book). But they aren't just being nice; because their work was so mixed up together, they truly can't remember. On the other hand,

Dippold says, she can usually guess who wrote an episode when she sees it, so some distinctive voices were still coming through.

And ultimately, the show conformed to Schur's recognizable style. After a writer brought in an episode, Schur would put it up on the screen in "the room with the computers," as Dippold describes it. The brainstorming room was the one with the couches. The computers were where things got serious. Schur would pull the Final Draft script document up, and the whole writers' room would go through it, line by line, together, as Schur typed in his notes. The group would then pitch ways to address each of his notes, which they all worked together to execute.

At that point, Schur read it and made his final tweaks. But the assigned writer got the on-screen credit. "Shows are different about this," Dippold says, "but [Schur] is very gracious in how he wants writers to have credits for episodes, versus having his name on every episode." Writers got at least one episode per season, if not two or three, given that the season was twenty-four episodes long.

The writers' room remained mostly congenial, but fights could erupt, usually of a philosophical or pop cultural bent. The only time Schur ever yelled at someone in the *Parks and Recreation* writers' room was during an argument with Wittels about, as Schur said, "the loose ethics of reality TV, and while the details of the fight now seem impossibly unimportant, at the time I was truly upset. I don't remember the argument very well." But a few minutes later, Schur was hugging Wittels while Wittels drawled, "All right, well, I guess the argument is over."

Schur described Wittels as "a human teddy bear" who would then belie that image by picking such fights. Wittels, Schur said, would often try to "defend an indefensible position about something he hadn't thought through—at all—but had decided to argue anyway." For instance, Wittels once insisted that the band Silversun Pickups would have been as good as the Beatles if they had started, like the Beatles, in Liverpool in the 1960s. His argument: "Because, *think about it*."

Wittels also once tried to get out of work early to see a Phish concert in Long Beach by arguing that to not let him do so violated his freedom of religion. "It should be noted that: (A) He had seen more than seventy-five Phish concerts at that point, and (B) he asked me on the day he turned in an outline, meaning that the next step was for him to work all day with the entire writing staff," Schur recalled. "Which is hard to do when you're at a Phish concert."

Schur didn't often have to play the bummer boss. More often, he served as a benevolent mentor. As the writers were breaking the first few episodes of the season, Schur happened to have lunch with a film executive friend. This guy mentioned that he had a script idea he wanted to assign to a writer, a talking-baby movie perfect for a young go-getter. Did Mike have any recommendations? Schur mentioned his new writer, Dippold.

Just when Schur chose her to write the episode "Beauty Pageant," she also got word that she had landed that movie assignment, her first feature. She panicked: How was she going to do both and do a good job? But she didn't feel like she could pass up either opportunity, so she went for it. She had three weeks to write this talking-baby movie, which she would cram in late at night while writing her first *Parks and Recreation* episode at the same time.

She asked Schur how long her show script should be. "I don't know," he said. "Somewhere in the thirties."

"What's the *ideal* page count?" She wanted *something* about her script to be ideal. "Like thirty-four pages?" she said.

"Sure," he said, bemused by her precise question. "Thirty-four pages."

Later, he popped into her office to tell her, "Make sure to put *you* in this show. Get your sense of humor in the show, the kind of jokes you did in your sample. I want to see that here." That stuck with her. She was so tempted to focus on what she was *supposed* to do, but she needed to remember that she was hired for a reason.

"That was a really wonderful thing to hear before you go off and write your first episode," she says.

After she turned in her first draft, Daniels pulled her aside to talk about it. He brought up one scene in particular that they were going to cut, then patiently explained what makes a scene worth keeping. She thought very robotically and mathematically: *Okay, sure, then let's cut it*. Why was he talking to her so much about it? Later she appreciated the lesson he was trying to impart.

Somehow, she managed to get both that script and her talking-baby movie done; though the talking-baby movie did not get made, it began a feature-writing career that would blossom later.

The show returned to the air on September 17, 2009, with the episode "Pawnee Zoo." The penguin storyline lifted *Parks and Recreation* out of the pit of the previous season—literally—and launched it into the colorful surroundings of the town of Pawnee. This included the introduction of Pawnee media beyond newspaper reporter Shauna Malwae-Tweep. It would become clear that *Parks and Recreation* did not hold a high opinion of the fourth estate, though it did acknowledge the media's significant influence on Pawnee. And Shauna would emerge as the most serious reporter in town, despite her penchant for dating city staffers, and as a slightly more grounded character whom I related to as a former local newspaper reporter. (For the record, though, I dated only one local political staffer, a Ben Wyatt–like assistant to a county supervisor. The city halls I frequented were not brimming with datable young men.)

Here, we meet the larger-than-life host of television's *Pawnee To-*

day, Joan Callamezzo, with her perfectly done, flowing curls, tight-fitting dresses, and gotcha journalism. "It's not even that the writer has to write that Joan is in a leopard-print Diane von Furstenberg dress," costume designer Kirston Mann says. "It's that her character is so on the page that most people can just picture what that woman would be wearing."

Mad TV alum Mo Collins embodied Joan vividly. Joan's backstory would come to include a small part as a strip club waitress in the movie *Flashdance* and time as an aerobics instructor in Chicago before pivoting to journalism as a host on Pawnee's cable-access Channel 46, according to Leslie's book about the town. But when Collins first signed on for the episode, the role was meant to be a one-time endeavor. Collins recalls being told in the audition that Joan was "this very green, local-access-television personality." She thought back to her upbringing in New Hope, Minnesota, a suburb of Minneapolis, watching public-access television, "and those personalities being very real, very imperfect but trying."

She could connect to the Midwestern-ness of Pawnee. "It's a tangible thing, the Midwest life," she says, her accent still peeking through. "If you grow up in it, it's ever present."

Soon we meet another major figure in Pawnee's TV media: Perd Hapley, whom Jay Jackson played with a fierce commitment to newsman cadence despite the character's total vacuity.

Jackson inhabited news-speak so easily because he was, in fact, an on-air reporter, not an actor. He'd done musical theater in high school and some church plays, but his professional training was in political science and journalism.

"People have a real craft as far as acting," he says. "I've never really considered myself that, and I don't have the energy to go out and develop that skill. So I just do what I know how to do."

Not only that, but the skill he had practiced for decades, delivering news on the air, proved far more in demand than general acting. "It's a world of difference when you see an actor trying to be a reporter versus a real reporter," he says, "because it takes years. All over the country, all over the world, it's similar news reporter behavior. You just know a real news reporter when you see one."

Believe it or not, the man who would become Perd Hapley spent a large portion of his career reporting the darkest of local news. "If I showed up, generally somebody was dead," Jackson says. "It was a terrible death, it was murder, or a flood or a plane crash. I was a hard-news reporter at CBS in LA, and, you know, it's a hard town. It's a dangerous city."

His Hollywood career had grown out of a side hustle, the Los Angeles Reporter's Clinic, which he launched to make demo reels for student journalists who were looking for jobs. He had realized that most colleges at the time were not helping students to make good reels, so he started one of the few companies to do so. The company expanded to the point that he couldn't work full-time as a reporter anymore. Then one day, one of the students who came in to make a demo was also an actor, and she explained that she would send this reel out to Hollywood casting directors as well as news stations. Many of the casting directors, she said, were looking for real news reporters to play fictional ones in movies and television. Jackson happened to appear in her reel as an anchor, talking to the student as she pretended to be reporting in the field. An agent spotted him and contacted him, asking if he'd be interested in going out for auditions to play fictional reporters, too.

He started "playing" a newscaster on the serial-vigilante-killer drama *Dexter*, where, he says, he "got bit by the bug of being on a Hollywood set."

He says, "In LA, maybe there's ten working reporters who are doing this on the side." He was reliable and easy to direct, so he was castable. "In Hollywood, everything is the path of least resistance."

When he signed on to appear in *Parks and Recreation*'s fourth episode of the second season, the role was, like Joan's, meant to be a one-time thing. Perd first reports on city councilman Bill Dexhart's sex scandal, in which the politician is revealed to have had four-way sex in a Brazilian cave while pretending to be "building houses for the underprivileged," a riff on South Carolina governor Mark Sanford's real-life 2009 scandal, when he claimed to have been hiking the Appalachian Trail but was actually conducting an affair in Argentina. Jackson decided to exaggerate the newscaster-ness of his delivery, and the *Parks and Recreation* team loved it.

They would bring him back whenever they could, including the twelfth and twenty-second episodes of that season, and many more to come. He appeared concurrently on the hit ABC drama *Scandal*, so he was often flipping back and forth between the absurdity of Perd and the intensity of presidential comas and hostage crises.

Soon, Perd had a distinctive look that Mann describes as "basic Midwestern. In the way that you'd mix paint colors, Perd could just pop right off his browns and tweeds." His shtick developed more: He would say lines nearly devoid of meaning but infuse them with gravitas using his newscaster voice. "I'm Perd Hapley, and I just realized I'm not holding my microphone." "Up next is my introduction to the next segment, and my introduction to the next segment is as follows: Here's the next segment."

As his time on *Parks and Recreation* progressed, he found himself learning a lot by observing Poehler's acting. Just the smallest things—a frustrated noise, a gesture, a way of responding to other actors. More than anything, he says, he learned from her "how to move the scene along." And he meant that both figuratively, in an actory way, and literally: "At the end of the day, we're all just people working on a set, trying to get the day over, get through traffic, and get home," he says. "The quicker you can get things done right, without having to retake the scene over and over again, the quicker you're going to get through traffic and get home."

Jackson, in other words, wanted to get to "Cut!" That meant they were moving to the next scene, he hadn't screwed up, and everybody was happy. For this reason, he tried his best to never break in the middle of the scene, never laugh, no matter how funny everyone around him was being. "If you laugh and mess up a scene, that means you have to reshoot the scene," he says. "That means you're on that set longer, and you're pissing everybody off."

The same second-season episode that first introduced Perd also revealed another new character of sorts: Duke Silver, Ron Swanson's saxophone-playing alter ego who has secret regular gigs in the neighboring town of Eagleton (and an enthusiastic middle-aged-woman fan base, obviously). Mark Rivers, who'd written the music for Andy's band, got to write some decent jazz riffs this time.

"Those were using your more typical composer-songwriter chops to do that stuff," Rivers says. "It helps that Nick Offerman plays a little bit of saxophone. So like Andy with the guitar, he did a good job of mimicking." Rivers did, however, bring in a saxophone ringer, Jay Work, to play the music we actually hear on-screen.

Within the first few episodes of the second season came another pivot away from the *Office* rules: Characters on *Parks and Recreation* would swear, goddammit. They would be bleeped, but they would swear.

It happened like this. In "The Stakeout," Ron is suffering from a hernia but doesn't want anyone to know. So he remains in his desk chair all day, until everyone leaves and the automatic lights turn out. April, suspecting the truth, returns to check on him. Their relationship is beginning to take on the same father/daughter vibe that Plaza and Offerman had in real life. She holds up her keys and asks if he's ready—to go to the hospital, that is.

Ron's line as scripted was, "I was born ready. I'm Ron Swanson." But on the eighth take or so, Offerman improvised, "I was born ready. I'm Ron fucking Swanson."

Schur decided: They would leave it in and bleep it. "We'd never bleep stuff on *The Office*," he recalls. "It was a very, very PG-rated show when it came to language." But, he says, "I think Leslie curses. I think Ron curses. I think they all do. And so that episode, shooting it and airing it, was a moment for me."

Next, *Parks and Recreation* began to level up its guest-star roster. Though the show was not a ratings smash, it had now been picked up for a full second season, and the people involved had major connections. *Saturday Night Live*'s Andy Samberg played a loud-talking park ranger (modeled on producer Dean Holland's loud talking), and Fred Armisen guested as the visiting vice director of the parks department in Boraqua, Venezuela, Pawnee's sister city. Poehler's then-husband Will Arnett appeared as a guy Leslie goes on a bad date with. Her dating luck turned around when Louis C.K. showed up as Dave, an insecure cop who courts her until he gets a job in another city, and she flirts with Justin Theroux, playing a slick lawyer who helps her when she's sued for trying to build a park.

One of the series' most impactful guest stars first appeared in the eighth episode, "Ron and Tammy." When Offerman and his wife, *Will & Grace* star Megan Mullally, first got the script, she immediately took him out to their backyard, he says, "to the lush grass, to practice violent kissing." Written by Mike Scully, this would mark the first episode featuring Mullally as Ron's ex-wife Tammy.

It introduces Tammy as an affront to Ron's heretofore unflappable presentation. He is, as Offerman says, "an impenetrable stoic." So what happens when he's confronted with an ex-wife who is, as he says, "ruinous to him" because she is an agent of chaos who lives to get under his skin? More important, who could play such a person? As the script was being written, Schur asked Offerman if he thought Mullally would do it.

"Yeah, I think so," Offerman remembers saying. "But let me ask my teacher. I would never presume."

She said yes. The couple loved working together, from the stage to a 2001 episode of *Will & Grace* in which he plays a hunky plumber whom Mullally's character, Karen, flirts with. The *Parks and Recreation* role would offer a similar opportunity, with Mullally playing Ron's ex-wife who, as Offerman says, "unmans him with her sexuality."

Mullally could literally do this like no one else. Not only was she an Emmy Award–winning comedic actress, she was also, as Offerman says, "the person who can, by definition, push my buttons most easily and [wield] her sexuality as a comedy weapon against me. She'd walk on set, and I'd just be fucked from the moment she made eye contact with me. My thing is stoicism. I will keep it together through anything. But she would just gently rub her boobs against my arms, and I was like, 'Man, this is just not fair.'" He adds: "She is the funniest person I've ever met. And I've met Mel Brooks."

Mullally would appear in nine episodes throughout the show's run as Tammy, the evil librarian and enemy of the entire parks and rec department. (We would eventually learn that she's actually Tammy II, the second Tammy to have a disastrous marriage with Ron Swanson. Tammy I, played by Patricia Clarkson, was even more chilling with her calm intensity.)

* * *

In defiance of those early test results, Ron Swanson was becoming the show's clear second lead as his identity merged more with Offerman himself. The "Hunting Trip" episode highlighted the twin poles of Ron and Leslie, and how well they played off each other.

It had begun in the parking lot after Offerman had recorded the season 1 DVD commentary. He ran into writer Dan Goor, who asked him, "Is there anything you want to do in season two?"

Offerman answered, "I want to shave my head."

Goor came up with the idea that Ron gets shot in the head. This could happen on a hunting trip that involved most of the gang. Schur liked it, and the writers started trying to break the story. But they got stuck. They couldn't figure out how this would happen. In the writers' room, Hiscock argued, given that this was a faux documentary, they could make it into a bit of a mystery: Maybe the documentary crew didn't catch who shot Ron. That could make it fun.

Everyone agreed.

Goor wrote the resulting episode. One of the moments that made Poehler laugh the hardest in her time making the series, she wrote in her memoir, was when she and Rashida Jones, as Leslie and Ann, "had to try to pin Nick Offerman down and feed him medicine in the 'Hunting Trip' episode."

Daniels contributed another key facet of the episode, that Leslie turns out to be great at hunting. "The temptation is going to be to make it that she's bad at it," Goor remembers Daniels saying. "But she grew up in the Midwest, and we should say that her dad took her out hunting." Goor loved one of her wildly misguided talking-head lines in particular: "If there's one thing I know about men, it's that they love it when a woman is better than them at something they love."

In the B plot of the same episode, April and Andy get stuck in city hall together alone. These scenes would deliberately test Plaza and Pratt's on-screen chemistry as a potential couple. The writers had been discussing the possibility for a while, with some writers loving the idea and others not sure, or still actively rooting for Andy and Ann. While the other characters were off-site, the two would show the writers whether they should get romantic in later episodes.

Early on, it became clear that they should, and thus began *Parks and Recreation*'s first major couple. "I remember that being a standout episode for me," Plaza says, "because I was really driving the idea that April and Andy could be a couple."

She continues, "It felt like there was magic going on in that episode."

The writers also began to appear in some episodes, none more memorably than Harris Wittels as an animal control officer who's always obviously high.

"Harris was one of the funniest performers," fellow writer Dave King says. "Hysterical improvs. Felt like a real weird guy that worked in your town."

Meanwhile, Leslie was taking a turn from her bumbling first-season persona to a more-than-competent local government official.

The Christmas episode, written by Schur, was, by his description, "very silly and fun," but also a revelatory moment for Leslie's character. In it, the tabloid-esque *Pawnee Sun* falsely accuses Leslie of seducing Councilman Dexhart, last seen having another sexual scandal exposed. At the same time, Pawnee is preparing for its annual Christmas village. Set designer Ian Phillips put together a plan for fake snow, large Santas, and colorful decorations. When Daniels read the script and saw the over-the-top plans for the Christmas village, he noted, as Schur recalls, "This is kind of insane. We're saying that these people have no money to build the park, and yet, this is clearly like a $100,000 Christmas spectacular."

Schur's fix: making it clear that Leslie, "by hook or crook, could get things done that made people happy." It took a team of eight people covering for her during her scandal, each of them doing an episode's worth of work, to do what Leslie normally would have done on her own without breaking a sweat, pulling in favors from various townspeople to make a beautiful Christmas on a budget. In just one example, they decide to skip one item on her to-do list: "Bring a case of beer to Sanitation." Why do that? Those guys should buy their own beer. But it turns out she had made a deal with the sanitation guys that they would clear out a dumpster on the Christmas village site if she brought them a case of beer. When they don't, Pawnee's famous raccoons swarm upon the location.

"It was basically like Leslie had rigged the whole town through sheer force of will, and doing favors for people and working tirelessly, eighteen hours a day," Schur says. "And her goal was not selfish. Her goal was, 'I want kids to come to this Christmas spectacular and have the best time of their life.'"

It may not have stood out as a turning point to a casual viewer, but it changed the essence of Leslie's character, and the series' core philosophy, going forward. *Parks and Recreation* no longer focused on a try-hard, inept government official. Now it shined a spotlight on a sincere and competent government official battling through a byzantine system to make life better for the people she serves. *This*, it said, is how wonderful things happen in your community. If you go to a Christmas spectacular, or a kids' concert in a park, or, say, a Harvest Festival, you likely have a Leslie to thank.

* * *

Holland, the editor who had changed the show with his innovative jump-cut talking heads, began to direct episodes during the second season and would become the show's most frequent director. With the second-season episode "Sweetums," he further broke the *Office* documentary mold. A subplot features Tom's "DJ Roomba," which is an MP3 player attached to the self-directing vacuum cleaner that bumps about a room on its own. After Jerry accidentally steps on DJ Roomba, Tom accuses him of murder. In the episode's ending tag, a rebuilt DJ Roomba is haunting Jerry at city hall while playing "I Gotta Feeling" by the Black Eyed Peas.

For this scene, Holland put a camera on the ground showing Jerry's legs and DJ Roomba coming around the corner. "Any idea of this being a documentary was thrown out the window," Schur said, "the moment you put a camera in between Jerry's legs."

"You're right," Holland said. "So no more mockumentary. Let's just shoot things to make it funny." This was the final major way they would distinguish themselves from their predecessor. "*The Office* had the cameraman and *Parks* had the audience" is how Holland describes the pivot in approach. "The looks and the talking heads, that's to the audience as opposed to the camera person or interviewer."

Rules and restrictions can, ironically, make for good comedy. The standards and practices departments of broadcast networks have often forced some of the best moments in sitcom history: 1970s single-woman Mary Richards of *The Mary Tyler Moore Show* left home at night for a date, then came home during daylight in the same dress, without ever acknowledging what happened overnight. *Seinfeld* dedicated an entire episode to an abstaining-from-masturbation contest in the nineties without ever using the word (only euphemisms like "master of my domain" and "queen of the castle" to indicate who was still in the game).

In the case of *The Office* and its self-imposed mockumentary dictates, Holland says, "There's something fun about sticking to the rules. It's a little bit of a challenge. Like, you could never cut to somewhere where there would have been a cameraman. You can't cut something and go to the complete reverse right away, because you're like, No, I would have seen the cameraman." And there certainly wouldn't have been a camera on the floor shooting through Jerry's legs to catch the Roomba coming around the corner. This time, they decided, breaking the rules made for the funniest approach.

Right around this time, Holland noticed that *The Office* copped *Parks and Recreation*'s signature move, the jump-cut talking head, this time with Ed Helms's character, Andy Bernard. "They probably, years later, got bored, saw that we did something like that on *Parks*, and they're like, 'Why can't we do it?'" Holland says.

Parks and Recreation had finally broken away from its predecessor so much that *The Office* was now imitating it.

Leslie had been pursuing some romances, most notably with Louis C.K.'s Dave character, but sparks didn't exactly jump off the screen between the two. "I think it was more played for comedy," Daniels says. Dave shipped off with a plotline about his National Guard unit being called up for duty. He asked Leslie to come to San Diego with him, but that was a hard no for many reasons.

Now Leslie—and by Leslie I mean the *Parks and Recreation* team—longed for more intense romance. Paul Schneider's Mark Brendanawicz had not worked out, either, even after the writers had tried to make a relationship between him and Ann work. The time had come to pull the plug on that one.

"I felt bad for Paul, because I don't think he did anything wrong," Schur says. "Our original conception of the shape of the show just didn't totally work and we had to make a change."

Parks and Recreation had transformed itself into an independent, unique entity worthy of love. And it was about to heat up with one of TV's greatest romances, just before the production faced what to do about Poehler's second pregnancy—and, once again, imminent cancellation.

CHAPTER 6

"A Game Changer"

Seasons 2 and 3

When Mike Schur thought about how to bring love into Leslie Knope's life, one face appeared in his mind, a heart-shaped thought bubble around it like the perfect Valentine: Adam Scott.

The actor—who had a malleable image and range and could play a total jerk, or a thoughtful and vulnerable softie, or a total dork, or some combination of any of those—had first entered the *Parks and Recreation* team's field of vision when he'd auditioned for the role of Jim on *The Office*, and had again read for them when they were casting the Josh part that eventually became Mark. Schur doesn't remember why they chose Paul Schneider over Scott for the role, but, Schur says, Scott was "really good. He claims to this day that he was bad in the audition. He's never bad. And so I was like, 'Man, if we could just swap Adam Scott in that role, that might be the answer to our problems.'"

They had tried pairing Ann with Mark, which, Schur says, "was an interesting story for his character growth and a little bit for Ann's character growth." But now the time had come for Mark to say goodbye. As Schur and Greg Daniels were transitioning Schneider's never-quite-right Mark Brendanawicz character off *Parks and Recreation*, they thought: What kind of character could be a real romantic possibility for Leslie now that she'd evolved from clueless to competent, with political dreams of her own that seemed closer to her grasp in her new iteration?

Scott had been watching the show from afar, not knowing he might soon be a part of it. He'd noticed more friends talking about it in the second season: "Have you started watching *Parks and Rec*? It's getting really, really good." (Fans had begun to shorten its name this way, and soon people would swear that "Recreation" had never been spelled out in full in the title.)

Right around this time, Schur called to ask if Scott would like to join them. Scott had been starring on the critically favored but ratings-challenged *Party Down*, a comedy about a group of Hollywood caterers on Starz. Production had just ended on its second season, and it was in danger of cancellation. Former HBO CEO Chris Albrecht had taken over at Starz and was clearing the decks for some new programming.

"We were starting to get a sinking feeling over there," Scott says. "I remember when we were shooting the last day of the last episode of season two, we were all sort of thinking: *This could be it*." In fact, Scott was holding back tears during filming "because we were all so connected and so in love with the show and each other."

Now Schur wanted Scott to join one of his favorite new shows. "It was the first time in my career where things were coming at me, rather than me going toward them," Scott says. "After fifteen years, or however long I'd been at it, it felt so good to have these people that I respected so much asking me if I wanted to come join them."

Scott visited the office for a meeting with Schur, who told the actor that he had a character in mind for him, a government official who had once been elected mayor of his town as a teen but was impeached when he overspent on a winter sports complex called Ice Town. They'd considered giving this backstory to Leslie when they were first conceiving the show. "We abandoned that in part because it seemed a little high-concept for the main character of the show," Schur says. "But I always liked it, so when I started conceiving of this new character, I thought, *I can give that backstory to this person*. And the story of this person is, because his sin was budgetary, he has spent the last however many years trying to dig himself out of that hole and to prove to himself and to everybody else that he is a fiscally responsible and adult person."

When we meet Ben Wyatt, he's working as a state auditor. "Here he is, twenty years later, and he really is interested in public service and is serious about it," Scott says. "But he was also this teen mayor who was a media sensation for a minute and destroyed his town because he was eighteen years old and stupid—like any eighteen-year-old. An eighteen-year-old should not be running a town. It was a terrific backstory with so many fun possibilities. And it was yet another thing I couldn't wait to dive into."

But Starz hadn't given a definitive answer on *Party Down*'s future, which made it impossible for Scott to commit to *Parks and Rec*. As it came time to write the episode in which Scott's character would debut, he had to get a final word from Starz one way or another. He called a Starz executive he knew and said, "You don't have to tell me, just stay silent on the line like Woodward and Bernstein," a reference to how the famous *Washington Post* reporters once tried to get an important confirmation from a major source on the Watergate story, as seen in the film *All the President's Men*. "If we're going to get canceled, just don't say anything." A long silence ensued. Scott had his answer.

Because there was not yet an official announcement of *Party*

Down's cancellation, but there *was* one about Scott joining *Parks*, it looked like his departure had caused *Party Down*'s demise. "It was just kind of messy," Scott says. "So it was a bummer, but I had the opportunity. And I couldn't wait to join the show."

He signed on as a guest star for the final two episodes of season 2; assuming all went well, he would be a regular starting with the following season.

Scott grew up in Santa Cruz, California, so he felt a connection to Pawnee as a "medium-size small town." When he moved to Los Angeles at eighteen, he realized how small his hometown really was. "Santa Cruz, like Pawnee, has its own characteristics, and it's almost like a living organism, in a way," he says. "There's nothing I find more annoying than, 'Oh, it's like Santa Cruz is the eighth character,' or 'Pawnee is a character,' 'New York City is the seventh character in our show,' or anything like that. I feel like that's overused." However, he adds, "Pawnee really does have the characteristics of a person in the story."

He visited the writers' room and was impressed. "We had the best, funniest people," he says. "Every single person in the writers' room could have been running their own incredible show. Every single writer was a comedy assassin." For so long, he had just been trying to get a job as an actor, auditioning for, say, every *CSI* show. But now things had changed. As Scott remembers, "I fell into doing things that I actually like. And that's where I excelled, is working on the things that I would be watching. And it's probably what I should have been focusing on in the first place, rather than trying to just work."

Schur hadn't quite yet figured out what to do about another looming logistical tangle: Amy Poehler had told him she was pregnant again. At the moment, the show seemed to be turning an important corner, and sometime soon he'd have to figure how to navigate both at the same time.

But for now, as the production was negotiating to bring Scott on, NBC executives pitched Daniels and Schur another idea. They loved the show, they said, and wanted more people to see it. Rob Lowe had managed an impressive second act after being an eighties heartthrob who had, for a time, descended into tabloid scandal and been off TV and film screens. Now he had emerged as a massive TV star thanks to his turn as deputy White House communications director Sam Seaborn on *The West Wing* and was planning to leave his subsequent show, the family drama *Brothers and Sisters*. Lowe had proven himself a reliable audience magnet; the industry regarded him as a surefire ratings weapon. People just loved looking at him on-screen, and for good reason: His chiseled features, sparkly blue eyes, and warm smile only got better with age.

Lowe had his sights on NBC. He shared an agent with Tina Fey and was a fan of her NBC sitcom, *30 Rock*. They had done a movie together, the Ricky Gervais dramedy *The Invention of Lying*. Lowe asked his agent if he could, perhaps, get a role on *30 Rock*. "Maybe you come in as a foil for Alec, or, who knows?" Lowe recalls his agent saying, in reference to Alec Baldwin playing the blowhard network executive character Jack Donaghy.

The network's response: Would he consider joining *Parks and Rec* instead?

Lowe knew of the show and that it involved a few *Saturday Night Live* alumni; this was a point in its favor, as he'd enjoyed hosting the sketch show three times in the past. But he hadn't seen *Parks and Rec*. "All I'd seen were pictures of Amy Poehler standing in a dirt hole," he says. "And I was like, 'It's about Amy Poehler in a hole that's trying to get filled?'" He asked his two sons, then teenagers, whether he should do it. They said yes. "It's a great show," they told him, "and people really like it."

He was more supernaturally handsome than Schur had been envisioning in Leslie's love interest, and that role was designed *for* Adam Scott. The network urged Schur to meet with Lowe anyway, just to see how it went. Schur agreed to a meeting with the actor, and Lowe, listening to his sons' advice, agreed to it as well.

As the two talked in Schur's office, toward the end of the second season's production, Poehler stopped by and said hi. Lowe felt instantly at ease with her sunny and funny presence.

During the meeting, Lowe—who seems affably delighted by his lifetime in Hollywood—told a story about his former *Outsiders* costar Tom Cruise, emphasizing Cruise's intensity. He imitated Cruise ordering a glass of water at a restaurant: "I would like *water*. I'd like it in a *glass*. I would like a *lemon*."

A character formed in Schur's head. "It was one of the only times this has happened to me, but I just immediately saw it," he says. "I saw the whole thing." Chris Traeger would be a fitness enthusiast who's in impeccable shape and has an inexhaustible supply of intense, positive energy. He would be a state auditor who visits struggling cities to enact budget cuts and would be paired with his opposite: a practical and no-nonsense accountant who does the real work. That guy, Ben Wyatt, would be played by Scott. The two would make the perfect good cop/bad cop team of state auditors: Chris would tell everyone what a fantastic job they're doing, and then Ben would slash budgets and deliver the dark truth. Lowe recalls reading the first iterations of Chris, described as "so likable that he could fire you to your face, and you leave the office and don't even know what's happening."

After the meeting, Schur told the NBC executives, "Look, I think there's a way to do this, but it requires both of them. It can't be one or the other."

To Schur's surprise, they agreed to hire the pair. A version of Lowe's Cruise impersonation would even make its way into a *Parks and Rec* script in which Chris Traeger orders a beer: "I would like a *local beer*. I'd like it in a *bottle*. I'd like the bottle to be *cold*."

And so a pop culture icon came to join the cast of *Parks and Rec*, and everyone on set was aflutter. No one could resist the allure of this.

Scott recalled watching *The Outsiders* and *Youngblood*. "So I was like, really? I'm going to be starting the show with Rob Lowe?"

Even Poehler gawped. "I can't believe I am Rob Lowe's coworker," she wrote, "let alone his friend."

Lowe gamely reminisced about his previous work. Scott fired off *West Wing* questions and loved hearing Lowe's stories about working with Emilio Estevez and Cruise. Poehler "hounded him," she wrote, about his Gen X touchstone films. "The scene when Sodapop comes out of the shower in *The Outsiders* was a very important moment in my adolescence," she wrote.

Costumer Kirston Mann approached these new characters differently from the others. "Ben and Chris are from the big city, from Indianapolis," she says. "And Ben, because he's an accountant, he got to be a little bit more low-key, like he might be wearing a plaid shirt with a tie, but it's long sleeves instead of short-sleeve, which would be more Pawnee."

Lowe, of course, required extra attention. "We kind of had a mayoral look for him," Mann says. "Rob always wants to dress like a Kennedy. We got to play with that. He just got to be perfection." She adds, "You cannot make Rob Lowe look bad. You *cannot*."

Lowe and Scott made their official debut in "The Master Plan," the twenty-third episode of the second season. In an indication of what their first appearances meant to the show, Dean Holland was supposed to direct the second-season finale, a great honor, but Schur asked him to instead take on the penultimate episode of the season. "Listen, we have Rob Lowe and Adam Scott coming in, and I want them to see your face first," Schur told Holland. "This is who the show is, and I want them to be directed by you first."

This was, Holland says, "the best compliment I had ever received in my entire life."

Holland says he "clicked with Adam and Rob immediately." Years into the future, he would still be golfing with Lowe. "And it was a game changer, the two of them coming in. It did add a ton of energy to the show."

Lowe and Scott met for the first time just minutes before doing their first scene together. But from the moment Schur saw them share the screen, he says, "It was very clear that it was going to work. It immediately felt like the right concept and the right two actors to do the job."

In this episode, Ben and Leslie spar with each other—a classic screwball comedy pairing, hating each other now only to love each other later. In their first moment of real connection, Ben takes Leslie to get a beer and clear the air. He tells her that it's evident to him that she wants to run for office one day. She hasn't said this on the show, this show that only recently began to see her as capable of such a thing. There's a special power in this, in someone seeing something in you that you want to believe but may not have admitted to yourself yet. I remember moving to New York City and suddenly being surrounded by people who *assumed* I would write books someday, who took me and my aspirations seriously. It transforms you. It means being seen and respected and believed in, as if your future success is a preordained fact.

In this case, it marks the beginning of love. "He's able to see something in her that she wasn't quite ready to see in herself yet," Scott says. "And she's also able to look inside of him and see who he is." That is, the guy whose teen mayorship is summarized by the headline "Ice Town Costs Ice Clown His Town Crown." And the guy who should be allowed to move on from that youthful disaster.

This was a time when Schur conceded to his director, Holland. "At the very top of the scene you see a beer being poured and we move off of it to Amy and Adam sitting at the bar taking a sip. Mike wanted to cut the beer being poured and go right to their dialogue, and I felt it was too abrupt, and the beer helped us ease into the scene," Holland recalls. "After many back-and-forths, he let me win. But every time we ever watched it, he would turn to me and say, 'I did that for you!'"

To Poehler, the new cast additions delivered. Scott impressed her with his ability to act with her in scenes as she grew increasingly pregnant with her second child and, as a result, exhausted. "When they came," she says of Lowe and Scott, "it really elevated everything in such an amazing way."

The duo's second episode was the second-season finale, "Freddy Spaghetti." This also marked the final appearance of Mark Brendanawicz. Writer Dan Goor sent Mark off with one of his favorite lines to make it into a script: "Recently I had been thinking about maybe leaving this job, but I felt like I needed a sign. And then Ann broke up with me the week I was going to propose, the government got shut down, and yesterday one of those pigeons took a shit on me. And I was indoors. So . . ."

Lowe and Scott, meanwhile, turned in another stellar performance. The storyline has Leslie working around the government-shutdown rules to uphold plans for a concert in a park by children's performer Freddy Spaghetti, played by Brian McCann (known for his sketch work on *Late Night with Conan O'Brien* as Pimpbot 5000 and FedEx Pope, among others). In the end, Leslie succeeds in putting on the concert, with a private financial assist from Ben, establishing him as a secret good guy and probable suitor. And when Ben and Chris show up at the performance, instead of shutting it down, Chris stands at the back of the crowd of extras in the concert audience, clapping maniacally as Leslie fills time with "If You're Happy and You Know It."

Lowe improvised the enthusiastic reaction, which officially changed him from possible villain to sympathetic goofball. "The point of the joke was she was trying to win over the audience, and they weren't having it," Lowe says. "Chris Traeger was *having it*. He loved it, and so my little clap rang out in the silence, and Amy looked at me like, *Oh, okay*. That was our first improv-connection moment."

As *Parks and Rec* finished its second season in May 2010, it was, like Leslie winning over Chris, beginning to win over critics and to be regarded as on par with contemporaries *The Office*, *30 Rock*, and *Community*—though all three of those got higher ratings. However, *Parks and Rec* did achieve what the industry called "stability in [its] time period," as *The Hollywood Reporter* (*THR*) said—in other words, it was a devil NBC knew. Something new in that spot was just as likely to do worse as to do better than *Parks and Rec*. The series was, *THR* said, a "steady," if "modest," performer. As network television was losing ground to cable, this wasn't nothing.

The show ended that second season as the 108th most popular show on prime-time broadcast TV, with an average of 4.6 million viewers per week, lower numbers than its first season. But it turned its public perception around in a big way: season 2 has a 96 percent positive rating on the review-aggregating site Rotten Tomatoes, compared with a 68 percent for season 1. It did well with wealthy viewers, a key to staying in network executives' good graces, since it meant they could sell advertising to higher-end companies. Among network comedies, it did better with this audience than any other series except the new sensation of the season, *Modern Family*—which annoyed Daniels a bit, as he'd already started to meet with *Office* writer Jen Celotta about doing their own mockumentary family comedy. Now, that was dead.

Dissent magazine later explained *Parks and Rec*'s turnaround this way: "Facing imminent cancellation, the writers came up with a plan to save the show: they would turn Leslie into a superhero. A series that began as a parody of the earnest take on government exemplified by *The West Wing* turned into its Obama-era equivalent. The producers hinted at the transition by adding a new name to the cast: Rob Lowe, last seen on NBC playing the fictional counterpart of George Stephanopoulos in Aaron Sorkin's glossy reinvention of the Clinton White House."

While that wasn't the motivation behind Lowe's hiring, Lowe thought the parallels were hilarious. He loved it when Schur told him that their original pitch to the network had been "*The West Wing* but with much lower stakes." Lowe says, "It's so fucking funny. And it made me realize how much I love low-stakes comedy. There's nothing funnier than incredibly low stakes that people take seriously." Lowe's characters on both are at least a little bit similar, with Chris as the smaller-time, dorkier version of the slick Sam Seaborn. Lowe puts it this way: "Chris would have been a big Sam Seaborn fan."

The show's small-but-desirable audience and its creative momentum were working in its favor but hadn't secured it a spot in the following fall's NBC lineup. On the other hand, Poehler was now several months pregnant, which could work against its chances.

She had found out in the middle of season 2. She felt like she was always pregnant these days. She had been pregnant on *Saturday*

Night Live, gave birth, and soon after went into production on the first season of *Parks and Rec*. Now she was hiding her pregnancy again at the end of season 2, and worried about how her growing midsection would affect the show's future—again. "When you're on TV and you've been pregnant on two different shows," she says, "you really feel like you've been pregnant for ten years."

She had been terrified to tell the producers at first, given how much her first pregnancy had messed with the show's debut. She was due in late summer, right when production would need to pick back up for a third season. Once they were informed, they considered their options. All they knew for sure was that Leslie couldn't be pregnant.

Finally, as the second season was nearing its high-note ending, the team came up with a plan to not just disguise Poehler's pregnancy or to ask for a production delay and hope NBC understood. They would instead use it to their advantage, to get NBC to pick up the show. They told the network they had to shoot more episodes right away, before Poehler was showing too much. The plan: They would bank six, then run them in September with the start of the new fall season, while Poehler gave birth and took maternity leave. She'd return to work just in time to keep the season going.

"We kind of forced them into a season three," Holland says.

It worked. They got an early pickup for the third season, announced in February 2010. The network explained that it was to "lock in actors' schedules," which was code for Poehler's condition. *Parks and Rec* had made it to a third season.

That meant taking just a two-week break after finishing the second-season finale, then rolling right into season 3 production, rather than taking most of the spring and summer off as they normally would. "So the writing staff and the production team ended up essentially making a thirty-episode season two," Schur says. "It was brutal. But it was also kind of thrilling, because it was like, 'We're making more of these! As long as we're making them, we're happy, right?'"

Mann's job would be to help hide Poehler's pregnancy as well as possible with her wardrobe. Mann recalls Poehler joking between scenes, walking out, hugely pregnant and exaggerating it, and saying, "This is good, right?" Mann was always charmed by Poehler's lack of vanity.

Going straight into production on the next season while everyone was still exhausted from the last one proved challenging for the writers, the first group that had to get cracking before anyone else could do their jobs. Schur created a mini arc with a serialized storyline that would stretch over many episodes to help propel them through; instead of many tiny stories, they'd have one big story broken into chunks: the story of the Harvest Festival. Leslie would work to revive an old Pawnee tradition to make enough money to save the parks and recreation department from budget cuts. If it didn't work, the department would shut down.

"It's an existential moment for the parks department," Schur says. "It's go big or go home." As *Dissent* magazine later pointed out, Pawnee's hemorrhaging budget was "a plot point that neatly brought together the real-life austerity crunch of 2010 and the show's own precarious standing."

Between late April and early June 2010, the writers had to outline, write, and polish six episodes before they went on hiatus. During that time, they worked to save the parks department, and *Parks and Rec.* Schur stood on a balancing board in the windowless writers' room, brainstorming with the six writers as they sat at a long wooden table, powering through episode after episode. Their day started at 9:30 a.m. As the day continued, he might drape himself across the nearby couch instead. Half-eaten food mingled with purple and white note cards on the table. White was for Leslie storylines, purple for supporting characters. The note cards, with story beats, would eventually need to go up on the corkboards, and, when they reached critical mass, would become a script outline.

In between ideas, the writers would play with Nerf guns, ponder the nutritional content of a microwaved sweet potato, or share stories about the single life. Talking nonsense was part of the process.

Still, this process was much easier when they had an ultimate goal in mind: getting Leslie to a successful Harvest Festival. Having that overarching storyline "makes it compelling, but it also fits the show, because the show is about a woman with ambition," Schur says. "It makes sense to have gigantic projects that she's working on at any given time. And that, in turn, leads you to be able to tell individual stories within those projects that are, by themselves, funny and interesting and good."

On the plus side, Lowe and Scott had become regulars with the start of season 3, and their energetic arrival had set the season up to be the show's best yet. The third season starts with their state-mandated Pawnee government shutdown, and further mayhem ensues with a town-wide flu epidemic that looks miserable for the characters but proved one of Poehler's overall favorites of the series.

In "Flu Season," Leslie is determined to ignore her own symptoms so she can continue working on the Harvest Festival, including making a crucial pitch to gain local businesses' financial support. She drowns herself in cold medicine and shows up at the Pawnee Chamber of Commerce meeting anyway. Poehler, in an improv tour de force, plays Leslie's drugged-up-ness to the hilt even as she's seconds away from taking the podium. "I looked at the meter and it had Egyptian hieroglyphics on it. Do you know the exchange rate?" she slurs, referring to the cab she took to the event. In another moment, she says, "The floor and the wall just switched. Walk very carefully." A show taking the easy, obvious way out would have ended the episode with Leslie bombing. In fact, season 1 Leslie likely would have made a total fool of herself.

But season 3 Leslie musters every bit of her energy, snaps into place, and delivers a beautiful pitch. Businesses are buying in. She has saved the day.

As soon as she's done it, she collapses back into medicated dementia, but a more important victory results: Scott, in his talking head as Ben, switches on an admiring twinkle in his eyes as he describes Leslie's speech. "That was amazing. That was a flu-ridden Michael Jordan at the '97 NBA Finals. That was Kirk Gibson hobbling up to the plate and hitting a homer off of Dennis Eckersley. That was . . . that was Leslie Knope."

The ancillary plots in the episode deliver some of the purest comedy ever seen on *Parks and Rec*, particularly a breakthrough moment for Lowe's Chris Traeger. The health fanatic is devastated by his body's betrayal of him when he, too, is struck with the flu. He lies splayed on the hospital floor saying, "This floor is my friend." He tells Ann, "I vomited somewhere in this room. I don't remember where, though. Wait. You might want to check that drawer." And in what would become one of his most famous lines, he looks at himself seriously in the mirror and commands: "Stop! Pooping!"

The "pooping" line materialized as an ad lib, cheered on by the writers and producers on the sidelines. "I remember people at the monitor laughing, and I was laughing," Lowe says. It was at that moment that he knew he'd be sticking with the show for some time. The Lowe halo of perfection came tumbling down, and the character was all the better for it. "One of the things that was nice is how we found additional colors," Lowe says, "and I'd say the main color that we found was the silliness of Chris."

"Flu Season" was also the first time Lowe's and Scott's characters were integrated into the action with the original main characters, not just acting as the enemy.

Scott had his own standout comedy scene in the subsequent episode "Media Blitz," when Ben has a breakdown on local TV while trying to do press for the Harvest Festival. Questions about his teen-mayor past come up, and he snaps under the pressure, blurting out, apparently, whatever is in his head to a startled Perd. His incoherent and off-subject rant includes: "Look, who hasn't had gay thoughts? . . . You know, sometimes I think I might need glasses. . . . Is there a bird in here? I swear, I keep seeing a bird in the studio." As Tom Haverford later explains, "And then he talked about feeling up Cindy Eckert for the first time for about five minutes, and then the show ended."

Ben finally pulls it together to defend himself later on Joan Callamezzo's show with Leslie by his side, saying, "Who doesn't do dumb stuff when they're eighteen?" She looks stricken, swallows hard, and chokes, "I stole my gym teacher's husband," then looks plaintively at the camera for an uncomfortable beat.

The scene required several takes before the three of them got through it without cracking up. "We're all just sweating, trying not to laugh, and in between we'd just bust out, and then we'd try it again," recalls Mo Collins, who played Joan. "It's the laughing-in-church effect." She appreciated that *Parks and Rec* was a set where laughing was allowed, wasn't frowned upon, even when it was a bit disruptive, because everyone understood they were there to make comedy. When she thinks about it now, she concludes, "It's heaven."

This run of episodes included "Indianapolis," in which Leslie and Ron go to the state capital to receive a commendation, and Ron throws a fit when he learns that his favorite steak house is closed. But the action heats up more back home in Pawnee, where we first meet local fragrance magnate Dennis Feinstein when Tom throws a party for him at his club, the Snakehole Lounge. Jason Mantzoukas, who had auditioned for those early versions of the Mark and Ron roles, plays Dennis with skeevy flair.

The actor had become a fan of the show as it aired, and he saw his role as the equivalent of *The Simpsons*' evil boss, Mr. Burns. "The opportunity to have him be a real villain for the town, I liked that," Mantzoukas says. "He's a megalomaniacal psychopath who just happens to traffic in scents, which is so funny to me."

His favorite fact about Dennis: He'd changed his name from the perfect fragrance-magnate name, Dante Fiero, to Dennis Feinstein, because that name seemed more exotic by Pawnee standards. "I thought that was incredible," he says.

Mantzoukas, yet another Upright Citizens Brigade alum among the many in the *Parks and Rec* universe, had actually had Poehler as a teacher at UCB. He got to see Poehler performing onstage regularly with Fey, Rachel Dratch, and Jon Glaser, and eventually got to perform with Poehler himself. Fey and Poehler also gave him one of his first jobs in Hollywood, a small part in their movie *Baby Mama*.

Mantzoukas loved that his debut on *Parks and Rec* was one of the silliest, improviest episodes yet, as all the characters in the club get drunk and otherwise mess around in ways we don't get to see at the office. "There was improvising, but then there was always a clutch of writers pitching jokes, and so it was fun," Mantzoukas says. "Everybody thinks that working on a comedy show must be just nonstop laughs the whole time. And you know what? Sometimes it is."

He admired the way that "the show feels like what the central ethos of improv is, which is a true focus on the ensemble." Poehler had taught him to not seek personal glory in comedy.

"My job in a scene with you is to make you [his fellow actor] look good," Mantzoukas explains. "Your job is to make me look good. And in doing so, in taking care of each other, we will make a scene together that is stronger than if one of us is just trying to get punch lines out."

This, incidentally, sounds a lot like something Leslie Knope might say about community.

As production stretched into the summer, the show reached another milestone: Daniels was stepping back and leaving Schur as the sole showrunner. He felt like they had fixed all the show's problems together and was happy to leave it in such a strong place. He also simply couldn't take any more of the pace he'd been maintaining. He had been bouncing between co-showrunning *The Office* and doing the same at *Parks and Rec* for two seasons now. "I had to lock scripts for fifty table readings, and I had to lock cuts for fifty episodes, in one year," he says. The two productions were about a half-hour drive apart, and he would have his assistant take the wheel while he sat in the back seat with a portable DVD player, reviewing edits in transit as he scribbled notes on a pad. Finally, he anointed Schur as the sole showrunner of *Parks* and Paul Lieberstein as the showrunner of *The Office*. "And I collapsed," Daniels concludes.

In a way, though, he was happy. Another of his TV production aphorisms was the "hit by a bus" standard: He wanted to get every show he created to the point where if he were hit by a bus, the show could carry on without him.

The third season would be *Parks and Rec*'s time to soar, if they could first face down yet another bout of possible cancellation.

CHAPTER 7

"You Take a Running Leap and You Learn to Fly"

Seasons 3 and 4

After all that—the second-season changes, the addition of Rob Lowe and Adam Scott, the creative momentum, the gambit to shoot the first six episodes of season 3 early—the show once again hovered in the crosshairs of cancellation.

The people behind *Parks and Rec* could not believe it.

The writers gathered at a hotel in Laguna Beach for a weekend retreat in the summer of 2010, when lead actress Amy Poehler was still on her maternity leave, to brainstorm ideas for the rest of the third season, the mood bleak. The production had just raced to make those early episodes, right after making twenty-four for season 2. And yet.

They had not long before gotten the news that the network wasn't going to put them on the air until the middle of the next broadcast TV season, in January 2011, which would mean a shortened season. A new show would be replacing *Parks and Rec* on the fall schedule, in the plum post-*Office* time slot. NBC claimed publicly that the network needed the chance to launch new hits. But internally, executives worried that *Parks and Rec* would never make it to syndication—a milestone at which a series is sold into reruns, and a major opportunity for the network, which owned the series, to net some long-term cash flow.

So not only had the *Parks and Rec* team rushed those six episodes for no reason, but the outlook for the show's longevity suddenly turned grim, again.

The writers decided to shift their approach: This could very well be their last season. They would leave it all on the floor. Every good idea they'd ever had, every new good idea they had on this retreat, it was all going into the show this season. They weren't saving anything for later. They'd worry about season 4 if they got there.

Poehler called this a "treacherous time." "The thought of them not getting on the air was so horrible we decided just not to think about that," she said of the finished episodes. "We just kind of, in the Midwestern way, went back to work."

Aubrey Plaza says now, looking back, "It always felt like we were the underdogs."

As a result, they were about to come up with one of their most memorable episodes—and one of their greatest guest stars, a small horse.

Li'l Sebastian arrived in the seventh episode of the season, the first one back after Poehler's pregnancy. The team already knew this installment would feature the Harvest Festival, the culmination of all of Leslie and company's efforts in the first six episodes that they'd already shot. The festival, which would either save or demolish the parks department, had guided the writing staff through those first six episodes. Now they had arrived, and their reality mirrored the fiction more than intended. It felt as if they were writing for the show's life.

"Harvest Festival" was Dean Holland's favorite to direct, and among Dan Goor's favorites to write. A major reason: the introduction of Li'l Sebastian, a mini horse who was a local folk hero in Pawnee. Mike Schur created Li'l Sebastian to satirize a common occurrence in small communities, unique local "celebrities" whom everyone in town knows and loves, even if their magic is lost on outsiders.

"Li'l Sebastian changed the show," Holland says. Holland knew the Li'l Sebastian phenomenon was already working when they shot the cold open, as Li'l Sebastian makes his first entrance into the parks department and the normally impassive Ron Swanson squeals with excitement. The rest of the staff goes equally crazy, except for Ben.

"We always had Ben as a voice of reason," Goor says. "I love the idea that Ben just didn't get it."

Though they had invented the Harvest Festival as a survival tactic that would make writing the first six episodes of that season easier, Schur says, "the incredible bonus of it was that it was really fun to do. And it gave us this template going forward; she should always have some kind of project that she's working on that allows us to tell mini arcs within the season. We started thinking of seasons not as just twenty-two or twenty-four half hours of comedy but as chunks of projects that she could be rolling out." While this kind of serialized storytelling is common now, network sitcoms had traditionally presented and solved problems within each self-contained half hour. Viewers could drop in on any given episode and understand what was going on, leaving satisfied. But as TV became more artistic and complex in the 2000s and beyond, keeping viewers coming back with suspenseful storytelling became more important.

That feeling of crescendo made "Harvest Festival" rousing. Greg Daniels called this "harvesting your seed corn" (though he didn't name this after the "Harvest Festival" per se). "The idea was you plant and plant and plant, and you tend to the crop, and you water it and fertilize it and you let it grow as high and as ripely as it can," Schur says. "And then in one fell swoop you harvest the whole crop. Those episodes where you're harvesting the crop are great, because you've been walking very slowly down this path for a long time with all the characters, and you get to then see the fruits of their labor pay off."

Though "Harvest Festival" has many sweet moments, they're tempered by a large helping of dirty humor. Holland explains, "There was a point when we're shooting the horse, and the horse was . . . *relaxed*. That was not planned. So then we were like, 'Oh, this is really funny. Every time we shoot the horse, we're going to show the horse relaxed, and we have to pixelate . . . his area." This led to some technical problems, though: "Then we were pixelating it when it wasn't there," Holland says. "And we'd go, 'It doesn't look right.'" The postproduction supervisor didn't understand, so Holland and Schur explained: "Something needs to be underneath it."

Next thing he knew, the post supervisor was googling for images of large horse penises. "Hey, I'm not going to get in trouble, right?" he asked Holland.

The director assured him that the production would vigorously defend him against any human resources complaints. "We're backing it up," he said. "It's right there on camera." And, indeed, in the end, he says, "Mike was right. It made a difference."

Attention to detail at all times makes a good sitcom great.

Encouraged by Schur's edict to leave it all on the floor, the writers sped ahead recklessly with stories. They had been planning a long, slow, fumbling romance between Andy and April. But at the fateful season 3 writers' retreat, Schur said, "They should get married. Like, it'll be funny. It'll be unexpected. No one will see it coming."

What would happen next?

"Who knows, but it'll be surprising," Schur remembers thinking. "The goal was to be as surprising as we could possibly be."

April and Andy had proven their chemistry in the season 2 episode "Hunting Trip," when the rest of the characters go off into the woods for the day, leaving the two of them back at city hall, where they play games like Marco Polo and flirt. April considered quitting her city job but instead got hired as Ron's assistant when she realized that sticking around would allow her to stay close to Andy. She finally broke up with her boyfriend (who has a boyfriend), and their flirting intensified just as Andy realized April was still under twenty-one, which made him uncomfortable, and then Ann kissed Andy, infuriating April. They finally got together once she'd turned twenty-one, with a few more blips along the way (like April's Venezuelan boyfriend, Eduardo, and Andy greeting April's first declaration of love with the one-word response "Awesomesauce"). Now they were finally together. And suddenly, it seemed like it might be for good, against all sitcom rules.

So in the ninth episode of the third season, Andy and April throw a "fancy party" that turns out to be a surprise wedding, April in a plain white cotton dress and Andy in the football jersey she bought him before they started dating. Katie Dippold was assigned to write the script, though she had opposed the coupling at the beginning. She had originally preferred focusing on Andy's attempts to get Ann back.

"So how dare I be able to have my name on their wedding episode?" Dippold jokes.

But she had come around and was honored to unite them in matrimony. "I think they brought out a really funny side of each other's characters," she says. "I like someone as dark as April ending up with someone as sweet as Andy."

Some fans have noted, with startling accuracy, that April is like a cat, while Andy is like a dog.

Dippold, who was in her twenties at the time, came to love writing for the young couple, who were in her age range. "I always had my ATM card sticking out of my back pocket," she says, "so maybe I related to them." Two episodes later, for instance, we learn that the two share one fork. She liked the idea that they'd throw themselves an impromptu, casual wedding. "It was fun, because it was like, what kind of weird shit would they have at this wedding?" One joke that was cut, for example: When Leslie arrives at the wedding, she asks where April is, and Andy answers that she's upstairs watching *The Skeleton Key*. Dippold thought, "That's what she would do. She wouldn't be at her wedding, entertaining people. She just wants to finish this movie she was watching while getting ready."

Aubrey Plaza had been pushing for the Andy–April relationship since early in the show, so she was excited to see it turning in such a committed direction. "There's something actually mature about their relationship and their dynamic, and I felt like it was a cool thing that I had never seen before," she says. "That relationship was a great way to watch her grow. There was this underlying feeling of a healthy, not toxic, romantic relationship that is nice to watch."

In the episode, Leslie worries that the couple are moving too fast and are too young to make it work. During a moving scene, she confesses to Ron how concerned she is, and he points out that he's in his forties and has been married twice, and both ended in disaster. "Who's to say what works?" he says, offering the show's thesis on long-term romance. "You find somebody you like, and you roll the dice. That's all anybody can do."

Schur adds, "That was Ron giving voice to what we were feeling in the writers' room, which was: Who knows if this is the right move, in terms of the show? We're just going to say, we think this is a good idea, and it's interesting, and we're gonna let it fly and see what happens."

Plaza, for one, felt emotional throughout the episode, between the

Andy–April connection and Leslie's outpouring of motherly worry toward April. "It felt weirdly real," she says. "There were tears. Every time Amy would come up to me, I'd be like, no, stop, go away, because she'd be crying. It was so, so sweet." While talking about this, even now, Plaza stumbles around in her reverie of emotion.

The wedding—and more important, the impending marriage—opened up new possibilities for Plaza in playing April. "I wanted to make sure that I was always playing her to the top of my intelligence," she says. "She's very, very smart, and she knew exactly what she was doing at all times." Plaza wanted to find ways to show that April was growing up, just as Plaza was in real life, and to take her beyond what she'd become known for, which was her deadpan, cynical presentation. "For me, the challenging thing was not to repeat my own thing," she says. "When you're doing that many episodes, the challenge is not to be lazy about it. It's an easy game to play with my character. It's like, 'I hate everything, blah blah blah.'"

Startlingly, the wedding almost didn't work as an episode. When Holland first edited it together, he says, he and Schur watched, "and we were like, how the hell do we make this a show? This is not good." Leslie's story wasn't tracking right. "She was just being a busybody, telling April she shouldn't do this, she was too young, and so on," Schur explains, "and it seemed like meddling beyond the 'kind and familial' meddling Leslie usually engaged in."

Holland sat with it in the edit room for a few weeks by himself, cutting and recutting. Then he and Schur came up with plans for more talking heads and a few reshoots. The crew had already pulled down the set and had to reerect it. Most critically, they filmed more Leslie talking heads in which she references her own bad relationships, making it clear why she was so worried about April. This also played into Leslie's decision, after talking to Ron, to ask Ben to stay in Pawnee. "And it turned out to be this amazing episode," Holland says.

In the end, "Andy and April's Fancy Party" gives us not only a surprise wedding and a look at Leslie's growing maternal instinct toward April, but also yet another glimpse of Chris Traeger's unabashed dorkiness, this time when he dances at the wedding party. In the script, it was a blip, but the producers asked Lowe to choose what song he would dance to as Chris. He chose House of Pain's 1992 hit "Jump Around" . . . and then he *did*.

"The cutaways of everybody looking at me are the real thing," Lowe says. "There's a particularly good one of April looking at Chris like, 'What the fuck is happening here?'" To Lowe, these goofier moments fit into Chris's overall character, from his penchant for seeing the good in everyone to his meticulous care of his own physique.

"Every time I would try to do something other than the most exuberant, committed version, it just wasn't him," Lowe says. "So whether it was dancing or anything else, the committed, super-enthusiastic Chris never got old."

In fact, he says, "particularly in comedy, the harder you commit, the funnier it is. And no cast committed harder to what they were doing than this cast."

Romance done differently turned out to be one of *Parks and Rec*'s true strengths. *The Office*'s Jim and Pam had entranced viewers with their slow-burn journey from coworkers to, as of the previous TV season, spouses. They had faced a number of increasingly unique obstacles, most notably Rashida Jones's character, Karen. Beautiful and cool, she read as a genuine threat because she wasn't evil.

"The playbook would have been, in an ordinary show, to give one of them a boyfriend or a girlfriend who is obviously kind of crappy, right?" Schur says. "Greg had given him a nice, attractive, interesting girlfriend. His idea for that was you want half the people watching the show to come to the conclusion that Karen is a better girlfriend for Jim than Pam is."

But once Karen and Jim broke up, the show did something even crazier: It allowed Jim and Pam to start dating each other and to *not* break up. They would not torture viewers for seasons to come the way Ross and Rachel did on *Friends*. "What Greg wanted to do was to say, we're going to keep these two apart as long as we plausibly can," Schur says. "And then when they get together, they're not breaking up. They're just soulmates. Why would they ever split apart?"

Jim and Pam had set the bar high for sitcom couples, and *Parks and Rec* had struck out with its first attempt at giving Leslie love with Mark Brendanawicz. So the team had taken their time, trying out Louis C.K.'s Dave and Justin Theroux's Justin, just to see what Leslie was like in a dating relationship. Now, with the introduction of Ben, things seemed to be working. At least so far.

With Andy and April married, the writers turned their romance-making superpowers toward Ben and Leslie, most notably in the episode "Road Trip," which aired on May 12, 2011. In it, a smitten Leslie determines not to allow herself to be alone with Ben, given that Chris, who has become the city manager, has forbidden employee relationships. Soon after, however, Chris assigns them to drive to Indianapolis together to pitch Pawnee as the site for the next Indiana Little League baseball tournament. After Ben's heartfelt speech about the allure of Pawnee—the subtext of which is clearly about Leslie—they kiss for the first time. ("Adam always has fresh breath for kissing scenes," Poehler wrote in her memoir.) The sweetness is tempered by plenty of *Parks and Rec*–style hijinks, like Chris tagging along for the drive and playing air banjo in the back seat, or a memorable secondary story at home in Pawnee in which Ron explains to a visiting schoolgirl how taxing people is like stealing her lunch.

But it's among the series' most swoonworthy outings. "The writing, for sure, is why it's so special, and where it all starts," Scott says. "But also Amy and I just loved doing that stuff."

He continues: "We connected. We never rehearsed. We just showed up and locked in and did it. It was a special, special time." His tone here is wistful, not unlike Plaza's when she speaks about Andy and April's wedding. Scott adds, noting how much he misses it, "I haven't watched any of that in so long, because I feel like it would be sad."

With Ben and Leslie, Schur determined to follow a similar model to Jim and Pam while charting their own unique path. The characters would know they were right for each other. "There are other obstacles we can throw in their way, like their careers," Schur says. "But it was always going to be the case that it felt like this was the right person for her."

Leslie's ambition, her defining trait and also the reason Ben loves her, would cause more problems than anything else.

Costume designer Kirston Mann began to work more red into Leslie's wardrobe in this period, to symbolize her falling in love. "When Leslie and Ben are together, we splashed red in there," she says. "It might have even been just between Amy and me, feeling like that would be a fun thing to do." Everyone working on this show seemed to be a romantic, in one way or another.

The list of this season's go-for-broke ideas contained plenty of silliness as well. The April 28, 2011, episode "Jerry's Painting" has department laughingstock Jerry making a (quite competent) classical Enlightenment-style painting of Leslie as a topless centaur (and Tom as a cherub). The joke, of course, is that, as art director Ian Phillips says, "we come to find out that he's an artist, and not just any artist, but he's a *good* artist. And everybody still picks on him for it." Centaurs had, believe it or not, made recent news, thanks to a gossip magazine report that New York Yankee Alex Rodriguez had two paintings of himself as a centaur. (He later denied this.) "It was like, how and why did Jerry think of his own coworkers like that?" Phillips says.

Inspired by the Pawnee City Hall murals depicting the town's most offensive historical moments in soft pastel colors, writer Norm Hiscock pitched the idea of Jerry making a painting that was upsetting in a different way. "The pitch was that Jerry did nude paintings, and people discovered that he had done all these very classy and highbrow paintings of everyone in the office, and he was really good at it," Hiscock says. As the writers outlined the story, they brainstormed and came up with the idea of Leslie as a centaur and Tom flying in the corner as a cherub.

The episode put Phillips's work in the foreground. He and Schur had many meetings to discuss the painting: How would it look? Was it modern or classical? Bright, muted, or naturalist? They began with some basic illustrations followed by several back-and-forth revisions. Where would Leslie be? Where would Tom be? Once they had settled it all, Phillips hired a painter to make a few copies of the final version.

The one thing that remained constant throughout the conversations was that Leslie would be topless. That made it funny. That, however, also meant many awkward discussions between Phillips and Schur about how to portray the centaur's body. They had no intention of asking Poehler to pose for it, but they wanted her to feel good about it.

Hiscock remembers going to see the finished painting for the first time. "In our *minds*, it was funny," he says. "But then you see, actually, a picture of Leslie topless. And then you go, *Oh, that's now actually painted.*"

Poehler, who of course knew it was coming, told him it still felt weird to see it finished.

Hiscock replied, "I know, it freaked us out, too."

Similarly, Leslie's coworkers struggle to notice Jerry's skill, given her centaur's state of undress. "If you look at most classical paintings, they're all like that," Phillips says. "A lot of the women are either in a very sheer outfit, or they're breastfeeding, and it's what you would see if you went to a museum. The joke is not that Jerry is this amazing artist but that he painted Leslie topless. Not that she's a strong centaur woman but that she's topless."

In the following episode, we learn about the ritzy neighboring town of Eagleton, the target of much Pawneean resentment. Leslie's friend-turned-nemesis, Eagleton parks director Lindsay Carlisle Shay (played by the incomparable Parker Posey), has erected a fence in the towns' shared park to keep Pawnee residents from coming over to the Eagleton side.

"Springfield has its Shelbyville, Cheers had its Olde Towne Tavern, Seinfeld had his Newman," critic Rick Porter wrote on Zap2it. "And in the world of 'Parks and Recreation,' Pawnee has Eagleton." The episode introducing Eagleton, which makes its first appearance here, Porter wrote, "worked nearly as well as some of those classic 'Cheers' episodes." The Eagleton–Pawnee rivalry would become a driving force in many storylines to come, too.

In another silly, memorable episode, we get to know Janet Snakehole. Plaza's mid-Atlantic-accented alter ego originated with Plaza and Poehler goofing around together. April first takes on the name earlier in the season, when she and Andy try to get as much free stuff as possible while at the Snakehole Lounge; she uses the name to pretend she's related to the owner of the establishment.

But Janet wouldn't take on her defining qualities until the thirteenth episode of the season, "The Fight," when many of the characters get extremely drunk on Tom's powerful alcohol, Snake Juice, at the Snakehole Lounge, where he's an investor. Written by Poehler, the script's main storyline focuses on a fight between Ann and Leslie over Ann's reluctance to work with Leslie at city hall, where Leslie urges her to apply for a job as the PR director for the health department. In the secondary plot, April riffs as the old Hollywood dame she calls Janet Snakehole.

"Since I was a kid, I've had this big obsession with Judy Garland," Plaza says. "Amy knows that about me. The two of us were like, it would be really funny to have me have this other persona where I'm this kind of femme fatale, film noir character."

Janet, a widowed heiress, would appear in a role-playing flirtation with Andy's alter ego, FBI agent Burt Macklin, known for "stealing the president's rubies."

The episode overall, in which all the characters get drunker as it progresses, allows for an improv extravaganza, culminating in a montage of slurring talking heads: Ben saying "Baba Booey," Andy singing in his most nineties rock/Mouse Rat voice, Ron dancing in April's Janet Snakehole pillbox hat. Tom's list of business ideas comes a close second, rivaling *Saturday Night Live* character Stefon's club picks: "a baby tuxedo clothing line," "a department store with a guest list," "white fur earmuffs for men," "a new brand of bottled water called H-2-Ho," "contact lenses that display text messages," "a phone that smells good," "a nightclub called Eclipse that's only open for one hour two times a year."

Chris Traeger, meanwhile, is on a cleanse and bragging about it at every turn—and around this time is when he established his catchphrase, the word "literally," pronounced "lit-rah-lee," and emphasized with his Tom Cruise impression cadence. In this episode alone, he says it twice: "Every time I cleanse, I can *literally* feel the toxins leaving my body!" And on Snake Juice: "I believe an ounce of that would *literally* kill me."

"I really loved 'The Fight,' because we were all together in that nightclub for so long," Poehler says. "And Rashida and I got to fight, which was so fun. Leslie didn't get to fight a lot."

Ann eventually pulls it together and lands the job at city hall, a way of finally explaining why someone who works as a nurse spends so much time there—beyond the fact that her dating life has often been centered there. Jones told *Salon* at the time that she understood why her character had to date so many guys, plot-wise: "The people who are together are together, and they didn't want to link me up with somebody and have me done, because that's not fun from a story perspective. So I'm the town slut. It's totally fine. I'm fine with it." With so much going on in the third season, viewers could miss that Ann was breaking out of her straight-woman role in the show's comedy, thanks to a mini-breakdown after dating Chris.

"My favorite stuff is when Ann's super confused and a little bit crazy, and hopefully, Ann is primed to have a major moment," Jones said to *Salon*. "We've talked about it, and I'm sure we're primed."

Everyone's maximum efforts on the season paid off: *Outsourced*, the workplace comedy that had replaced *Parks and Rec* on the fall schedule, faltered, and NBC pulled it off the air. *Parks and Rec* was waiting, with its best run of episodes yet, to swoop back in to the Thursday-night time slot, this time in the spot after *The Office* (where *Outsourced* had been) instead of before.

As *Parks and Rec* prepared to return to the schedule on January 20, 2011, the cast shot a promo targeted for online. They were playing themselves, celebrating their triumphant reemergence.

Lowe, portraying himself as a diva, explodes when he learns that he hasn't appeared on TV in months. "How fucking long have I not been on television?" he demands. He pitches a fit and throws coffee in Aziz Ansari's face.

"It's a very, very, very funny clip, and Mike wrote it," Lowe recalls. "I always liked that he wrote that I'm Robert Bosephius Lowe. I love Mike's fetish for writing the weirdest names he could come up with."

The long-awaited third season, which would be nominated for an Emmy and earn a 100 percent rating on Rotten Tomatoes, premiered to great acclaim, with a generous side of contempt for the network's decision to keep it off the air for so long. *The Hollywood Reporter* called the show, upon its season premiere, "one of NBC's finest and funniest sitcoms, making a midseason return because NBC is NBC, and there's no room for logic." *THR* further praised the show's impressive turnaround: "During its debut season, *Parks* took five of its six episodes to get beyond seeming like a less-funny version of *The Office*. By the sixth episode, the characters were more defined, their quirks and rhythms understood, but the show didn't exactly arrive until season 2, with 24 superb episodes, that made it the best comeback story on television and a top-tier comedy." The publication noted its "nuanced characters, superb writing, and a willingness to be different in its premise from other formulas."

The review continued, "True, NBC deserves credit for sticking with a show that had dismal ratings and seemed to fail its freshman tryout, but the network proceeded to choke horribly in giving egregiously unfunny *Outsourced* the fall slot, right when *Parks* was on a creative roll. . . . But put your bitterness aside—seriously, one day NBC will be run like a real network—and bask in the fact that our Pawnee pals have returned, and there are plenty of excellent episodes in store."

What distinguished the show's third season, in particular, was the characters' growth and change, a direct result of the writers' throw-everything-in reaction to nearly being canceled. The second season had, as *THR* said, "quirky gusto." But the third season proved compulsively watchable, propulsive even. Would Leslie and her team pull off the Harvest Festival and save the parks department? Would the smoldering tension between Ben and Leslie ignite soon? *Parks and Rec* had found the right tone and pacing at last.

It was living up to its vaunted spot in NBC's excellent Thursday comedy lineup. *New York Times* columnist David Carr wrote, "Even NBC, which was sold for parts as near as we could tell, put together a Thursday night that is actually a destination at our house: 'Community,' 'Parks and Recreation,' 'The Office' and '30 Rock.' That reminded us that a suite of shows, carefully threaded, can keep you planted all night, or at least until Leno comes on."

The sixteen-episode run would finish in May 2011 at 116th place among prime-time broadcast shows, with an average of 5.1 million viewers per week—better than the previous season's 4.6 million, if far short of *The Office*'s 7.7 million.

Dissent magazine later noted that perhaps the series had an extra allure for certain viewers at the time, as Republicans were taking over the US House of Representatives and several state governments. *Apprentice* star Donald Trump was also busy spreading birther conspiracy theories about President Barack Obama. "The major legislative accomplishments of the Obama administration were all in the rear-view mirror," *Dissent* said, "but frustrated liberals could watch Leslie put together an epic town harvest festival."

As promised, the writers didn't take their foot off the gas until the end of the season. "There were weddings, and people dying," Poehler says. "I mean, animals dying. I'm thinking of Li'l Sebastian."

The season signed off with perhaps its greatest episode, "Li'l Sebastian," which was, like "Harvest Festival," written by Goor. This brought together the magic of the mini horse, the peculiarity of the entire town of Pawnee, the teamwork of "Harvest Festival," the music of Mouse Rat, and the sweetness of Ben and Leslie's burgeoning love, all well-earned by the opening blow of Li'l Sebastian's death, and the more devastating ending blow—Leslie being forced to choose between following her dream of running for office and being with Ben.

The cold open reveals the death of Li'l Sebastian. As Goor originally wrote it, he says, "We were going to start with the flags at half-mast, establishing shots, people walking around with black armbands, black crepe paper all over." But as they shot, Goor and director Dean Holland realized it was depressing. "The joke was supposed to be that they're treating the death of this little horse as if Kennedy had died, or FDR," he says. "Those famous pictures, *Time Life* pictures, of people along the funeral path weeping, but it just read as sad."

So right there during shooting, Goor and the producers came up with an alternative.

In the revised version, Leslie says to the staff in the office, "Hey, do you guys remember Li'l Sebastian?"

Everyone cheers and talks about how great and meaningful he is.

Then she says, "Well . . . he died last night."

Ron presents a framed picture of the horse with a black ribbon across it.

"It's like a record scratch," Goor says. "And it really worked. That was fun—I always liked when we would come up with stuff on set, and the actors are so unbelievable that they can do anything."

As the parks and rec department rushes to plan Li'l Sebastian's town-wide memorial, it becomes apparent that Mouse Rat will need a grand song to rise to the occasion—something that is, as they say, "five thousand times better" than Elton John's "Candle in the Wind," which the star modified for the death of Princess Diana in 1997. Goor wrote the first verse and chorus of the song that Mouse Rat would perform, "5,000 Candles in the Wind."

Up in horsey heaven, here's the thing
You trade your legs for angel's wings
And once we've all said goodbye
You take a running leap and you learn to fly

Bye bye, Li'l Sebastian
Miss you in the saddest fashion
Bye bye, Li'l Sebastian
You're 5,000 candles in the wind

Parks and Rec had beat the odds to get to this third season. And now it had its own anthem. Composer Mark Rivers, heretofore best known for the rousing Mouse Rat song "The Pit," stepped it up a notch for the occasion. "Mouse Rat *was* Mark Rivers," Holland says. "Andy Dwyer is Mark Rivers."

And, to be clear, Mark Rivers *actually* continued to play the on-screen drummer for Mouse Rat, though it was hard to confirm that at times. Rivers can't prove that the producers were trying to never show him, but, he says, "There are some episodes where I'm so perfectly blocked by the camera angle. You see the drums. You see the cymbals being hit. I'm back there. I know that's me."

Rivers calls "5,000 Candles in the Wind" "Andy's most inspired songwriting moment. He really pulled out all the stops for that one, inspired, I guess, by the death of Li'l Sebastian. There are some more clever chords in there. There's a minor chord or two." In fact, there's a B minor and an F-sharp minor, not to mention two suspended chords.

To write it, he began with Goor's lyrics and the tempo of "Candle in the Wind." He knew it had to start with Andy on the acoustic guitar and build to a big power ballad, with the band joining in for the chorus. Rivers had learned some rules for writing comedic songs for television shows: No long instrumental introductions. Get to the lyrics quickly. Craft them as catchy, good songs; don't let the musical part give away that they're jokes. Though, he says, "again, there are limitations on Mouse Rat songs. They can't be too good or too clever."

The on-screen band did learn the songs to play along accurately, though the show as it aired would use recorded instrumentals from Rivers, with perhaps a bit of the on-screen band's playing mixed in for a more "real" sound. "It didn't sound like prerecorded songs," Rivers says. "They did a good job of mixing."

Holland was overjoyed to be directing what was essentially a Mouse Rat concert, with five hundred extras and a big stage. As soon as he read the script, he thought, "All right, Andy's alone on the stage with a guitar, spotlight on him. And then we pull back and reveal the band behind him." He adds now, "Oh god, that was a good episode. And how often do you write a really good song that is funny as heck? It's a 100 percent legit song. If you wrote a shitty song, it wouldn't be as funny."

"It *is* a good song," Goor jokes. "And the residuals ain't too bad, either."

At the end of the episode, Leslie's dreams—and her nightmare—come true. Some local political operatives approach her, encouraging her to run for office. "When you run, even in a local election, your life becomes an open book," they tell her. "So if you so much as stiff a waiter on his tip or use a government stamp for personal mail, it will come out."

She insists she has no scandals they need to worry about. Except, of course, that she does: She's in love with her coworker, her superior, Ben Wyatt. And they can't be together if she pursues her ambitions.

Nevertheless, Leslie Knope was running for office, and *Parks and Rec* was about to become an even clearer allegory for Obama-era politics.

CHAPTER 8

"Prime-Time Television's Most Committed Political Enthusiast"

Seasons 4 and 5

In the fifth-season premiere, Leslie has been turned away from an in-person meeting at the Department of the Interior in Washington, DC, where she was hoping to present Pawnee's application for a federal riverbed preservation grant. And two DC mean girls have just passive-aggressively insulted her at a cocktail party: "Local government is *so* important. My grandmother's on the city council in her town. Gives her a reason to leave the house."

Leslie escapes to a nearby balcony and delivers a talking head to the camera: "Ben and I both did some amazing things today. He scored a victory for the congressional campaign he's working on, and I was mistaken for Beverly D'Angelo by a Japanese tourist. So, pretty big day for both of us."

The shot looks particularly gorgeous by *Parks and Rec* standards. The cocktail party scene is taking place in the Hay-Adams Hotel, which overlooks the White House, with the Washington Monument towering behind it. The Hay-Adams, famed and grand, has inlaid ceilings, gilded chandeliers, and walls lined with lots of old oil paintings of important-seeming men. Its tagline is "Where nothing is overlooked but the White House." Its restaurant is called the Lafayette, and its bar is called Off the Record. The *Parks and Rec* cocktail party, filmed on location, takes place in the Top of the Hay, where the wraparound balcony and French doors allow for plenty of opportunities to enjoy the famous view from the ninth floor.

While the crew was shooting the sequence, producer Morgan Sackett got a call: The Secret Service was sorry to inform him that cameras weren't allowed there. But Sackett had just been in Vice President Joe Biden's office working out details for another scene, so he called his contact there and asked for some help. Soon, the vice president's office had called the Secret Service to say that the *Parks and Rec* crew could keep their camera in place.

Sackett says it was "the biggest power move I've ever made . . . the biggest thing I've ever been able to pull off in my life."

It was a pretty major moment for the show as well. After years of the series hinting at Leslie's crush on Vice President Biden, the production had decided to go to Washington. Sackett had attended college with someone who worked for Biden, and then Obama, but what really helped was that many of the young people staffing congressional offices of both political parties loved *Parks and Rec* and helped the show to infiltrate the highest levels of government.

Leslie Knope may not have felt it, but she, as a character, and her show, *Parks and Rec,* had made it. She had become a hero to politicians and their staffers from the local to the national level. And her boss, Ron Swanson, had become a symbol in the world at large as well, as we will see, a champion to conservatives and manly men, though perhaps not in the way his creators preferred. The show was influencing real-life politics as much as it was reflecting the times.

* * *

Poehler, in her gray suit and red Keds for the party scene, delivered her lines in what Leslie describes as a "swamp town"—which she means not in a "drain the swamp" way but in a July-at-maximum-humidity way. Which was true—high temperatures were hovering in the nineties when they filmed the scene. New writer Megan Amram was sweating for a different reason, worried because she'd pitched the Beverly D'Angelo joke. When Amram first suggested it, she wondered what Poehler would think, but the actress said, "That's good. Everyone does think I'm Beverly D'Angelo." Amram got her first joke onto the show.

After that scene, Poehler and the rest of the cast and crew had to wait a bit for senators Barbara Boxer, John McCain, and Olympia Snowe, who would appear in scenes later in the episode but were tied up in a vote at the moment. This whole operation was a big deal, and everyone knew it; *New York Times* reporter Bill Carter was on hand to document it, describing Leslie in the piece as "prime-time television's most committed political enthusiast." Poehler joked to Carter that she hoped McCain remembered "the time we shot a scene in the shower together" on *Saturday Night Live* when the politician hosted in 2002. "It's all a beautiful, hazy blur, what happened in there."

When it was apparent that her feet would be visible in a coming scene, Poehler traded her Keds in for black heels that had already torn her feet up earlier in the day. This was among the day's disappointments, along with the fact that the Emmy nominations had been announced, and *Parks and Rec* hadn't made the Best Comedy list as it had the year before.

But Poehler's day brightened when McCain arrived for his scene and greeted her with, "Do you remember when we shared a shower together?" The two laughed as they prepared to shoot their scene, this one taking place in another confined space, a coat closet.

One politico, however, balked at *Parks and Rec*'s ideas for him.

Kentucky senator Rand Paul, a Republican famous for his libertarian views, had tentatively agreed to a scene in which he would have lunch with Ron to talk about their shared interests—like woodworking.

"His staff was so excited," Sackett says, "because his likability factor wasn't so good. And they were like, 'This is going to make him feel so much more human.'"

But when the senator read the script pages, Sackett says, he thought the show was making fun of him, perhaps because he didn't understand that Ron was a beloved libertarian. He backed out. "I think he just didn't get it," Sackett says.

Parks and Rec had dabbled in political satire in its first few seasons, with its gay penguin wedding and its philandering local officials. But it got more overtly political when Leslie decided to run for Pawnee City Council in the fourth season. The story arc included many plot twists, each one designed to deliver *Parks and Rec*–style emotions along with political commentary, leading up to the show's final pilgrimage to Washington, DC, and its dive into national politics.

From the beginning, Leslie's political career brims with challenges. Her first stumble comes when her relationship with Ben is exposed and the two are subjected to a professional trial, as dramatic as any congressional hearing, for having violated Chris's edict against relationships between city employees and their supervisors. In the end, Ben requests a private meeting in which he resigns as assistant city manager to save Leslie's job. She'll be suspended, but not fired. Confused as to why she isn't being fired, Leslie meets with the court stenographer, Ethel Beavers (Helen Slayton-Hughes), who reads her the transcript of his meeting, in which Ben says it's worth losing his job because he loves Leslie. In response, Leslie asks Ethel to reopen the transcript so that she can declare her reciprocal love for Ben on the record. In history's nerdiest romantic gesture, she brings Ethel to her house that night to read the official testimony to Ben.

Her campaign, however, is still in doubt. The next episode, "Citizen Knope," has Leslie filling her suspension downtime by forming a political action committee, Parks Committee of Pawnee (PCP), and wondering whether her campaign can continue after her professional advisers quit. Leslie sends over the perfect Christmas gifts for every parks staff member, delivered in absentia, including a painting of April killing the Black Eyed Peas and a personalized leopard-print robe for Donna. The episode marked new writer Dave King's first official credit on the show, and he was blown away by the excellence on display all around, from the painting to the marshmallow Ron in the gingerbread city hall that the staffers make for Leslie in return. "That was definitely one of my first experiences of, here's a silly joke on paper, and then someone takes all this time and makes the joke so much better, because they're so good at *their* job," King says of the props department. "And that was very common at *Parks*."

That went for the actors as well. Jim O'Heir had to react to Leslie's grand gift for Jerry, beige socks. "Aw, jeez," he says with genuine emotion. Then, in the talking-head shot, overcome with gratitude: "Socks. She gets me."

King watched in awe as O'Heir delivered different versions of the talking head, some of which included the word "beige," though that didn't make the final cut. "I was like, 'This guy's hysterical,'" King recalls. "He did six different versions of it. And just hearing him say the word 'beige,' I was like, 'Oh, every person on the cast here is a home run hitter.' It's not that I didn't think he was funny watching the show, but you just get something different when you're on set. You see multiple takes, and I was like, 'This guy rules.'"

Leslie has always excelled at giving gifts, and here it all comes full circle. The parks staff works together to cheer Leslie up with a gingerbread-house version of city hall for Christmas, and when she returns to the office, they surprise her with an even better gift, volunteering to staff her campaign. "Gift giving was one of her love languages," King says, "and she preferred to *give* gifts. This was a great slow-burn payoff of everyone giving her a gift that only they could give her."

On a show known for sweet moments, this stands out among them. And it works. "It's the performances," King says. "When the performances feel real and not overly treacly or emotive, you can get away with more sweetness. All the actors are genuinely emotional, grounded people who are capable of nailing those performances in a way that feels real. So a guy like Nick Offerman is both hysterical as a character and is also incredibly empathetic and kind, and he understands where those emotions come from. And I don't know who better than Amy Poehler or Adam Scott or Aubrey Plaza or any of those people to make you feel okay about caring a little bit."

Scott says he played his character the same whether the material was funny, dramatic, or sweet. "If it's comedy, then playing it completely straight will be funny, because the stakes and everything are set up by the story, not by the actor," he says. "The actor needs to attack it truthfully and the comedy will emerge. *Parks and Rec* was a pretty grounded show—particularly the stuff with Leslie and Ben. We always tried to keep that really honest and real. The flexibility of the tone on that show was really fun. It was a couple of degrees cranked from the complete naturalism of some mockumentary comedies."

But, King says, the writers tried to resist the urge to undercut emotional moments. "For the actual moment of heart, don't get in the way of it," he explains. "Don't try to cut it with a silly, dumb pun or joke. After or before, that's okay. But let people feel the moment and don't worry about it being too emotional. You *should* feel emotional."

The gang's first major outing as her campaign staff, "The Comeback Kid," leans hard in the other direction of pure slapstick. No one knows what they're doing in their new roles, and her first rally ends up accidentally booked in the middle of an ice rink. In the series' funniest bit of physical comedy, the entire team, having sworn to stay in this together, tries to make their way to the platform in the center of the ice to Leslie's upbeat walk-on music, Gloria Estefan's "Get on Your Feet." Ironically, no one can remain upright as they try to take the tiniest, most careful steps, yet all of them—Leslie, Tom, Ann, Andy, April, Andy and April's three-legged dog, Champion, and Ron—remain committed until the end.

Plaza names it as one of her favorite scenes in the entire show. "We were dying laughing," she says. "Because it was just all of us out there, and it wasn't fake. We actually were on the ice, and we were falling."

Meanwhile, Ben, who should have been her campaign manager, remains unemployed and depressed at home because he and Leslie worried that associating him with her run would remind people of their dating "scandal." To occupy himself, he makes a stop-motion Claymation video called *Requiem for a Tuesday*. After working quite industriously throughout the episode, he presents it to Chris to prove he's not depressed—and it consists of about four seconds of action to the beginning of R.E.M.'s "Stand." (The video only plays the first couple of words, then cuts off.) The clay man only manages to get out of bed before it stops cold. The props department, of course, had to make Ben's Claymation set, which Scott still has on a shelf in a closet, while Ben holding up his Claymation figure to show what he's "accomplished" has become a popular meme since.

The sequence also introduces what would become Ben's signature depressed look: wearing a T-shirt from the indie rock band Letters to Cleo, his hair askew. Schur had long followed the band and seized the chance to pay homage, though it took on greater significance than he could have anticipated given the show's increasingly enthusiastic social media fandom.

Lead singer Kay Hanley had met Schur at a fundraising event in 2004, the two of them introduced by Mike O'Malley, the other final candidate for Ron Swanson. All of them were from Boston and were attending an annual charity event called Hot Stove Cool Music. When Hanley met Schur, she didn't think much of it. He was "just a very unassuming guy who was hanging out with us all night," she says. They started following each other on Twitter. "And that was that."

When the shirt showed up on *Parks and Rec*, the unexpected wave of social media attention surprised Hanley. Her band, which had broken up in 2000, was suddenly trending on Twitter in 2012. "People weren't lining up around the corner to see our band [before that]," she says. "People weren't writing big think pieces about Letters to Cleo. So it was really unusual."

Even more extraordinary: The wardrobe department had made the shirt especially for the show. It featured the cover of the band's best-known album, 1993's *Aurora Gory Alice*. But the band started selling it after it appeared on *Parks and Rec*, and they continue to sell it to this day.

Politics took a more central role on the show when Paul Rudd showed up as Leslie's dim-witted opponent, Bobby Newport, heir to the Sweetums candy empire that rules the town. Their showdown expressed politics as many of us wished they could be in the Obama era, allowing a capable and experienced woman to triumph over an unfit and spoiled scion whose dad is trying to buy the election for him.

Rudd wanted to work with Schur, whom he describes as "this really bright guy, hysterical and kind. I'm always kind of awed by Mike Schur." Rudd had been watching the show and loved it, plus he was friendly with most of the cast, so joining was a foregone conclusion. "They built that show around the nicest, funniest people," he says. "I was a fan of everybody, so it was a very fun experience to get to join in for a few episodes."

Bobby Newport represents the antithesis of Leslie Knope: He has the power to thwart her greatest dream, being elected to the city council, when he clearly doesn't care about it himself. "He's completely unqualified," Rudd says. "And he doesn't understand why that would ever get in the way, which, by the way, might be prescient."

On the other hand, Bobby does not come across as evil or conniving. He says exactly what he feels. He doesn't pull dirty tricks. He doesn't lie. In fact, he seems incapable of it. "There's an optimism to him," Rudd says. "He likes people, and he wants to be liked. He has no awareness of nuance, or the way normal people behave."

Rudd plays Bobby's kind of dumb perfectly, with wide, blank eyes. "He has no irony, because he doesn't understand it," Rudd says of Bobby. "There's just something undercooked. There's an innocence." Bobby's stand on abortion sticks with Rudd as indicative of the character's entire spirit: "I guess my thoughts on abortion are, you know, let's just all have a good time," Newport says when asked about the issue.

With Bobby Newport's arrival came another memorable guest star, Kathryn Hahn, as his overpriced, overpowered campaign consultant Jen Barkley, who usually works at the national level. "He would be the worst person for the job, but she doesn't care," Hahn says of her character. "She's getting a lot of money from his dad. She knows he's an idiot, knows there's no way that man should be anywhere near a public office."

To play the character, Hahn thought about Mary Matalin, the Republican campaign operative who appeared in the 1993 documentary *The War Room* helping to run the George H. W. Bush reelection operation against her husband, James Carville, who led Bill Clinton's successful challenge. What struck Hahn most about Jen Barkley is that, she says, "she's very clear. She says what she means. There's no massaging around the edges to try to soften anything. Time is money. She has no time to waste on people's feelings or egos. She just needs to win." She works in the inverse to the main characters on *Parks and Rec*, who freely mix work and feelings, professional and personal.

Hahn and Rudd had appeared in a few movies together, including *Anchorman*, *Our Idiot Brother*, and *Wanderlust*, and connected over their similar senses of humor. "Very few people make me laugh," Hahn says. "We just hit each other's funny bone. Coming on with him was an added power move, because if I had just walked in by myself, Kathryn Hahn playing Jen Barkley, into this well-oiled machine of an ensemble, it would have taken a little more time than strutting on with my friend Paul."

Hahn couldn't believe how much frivolity she found there on set. One day, she went to the hair and makeup trailer after lunch to get touched up for the afternoon and discovered a ritual that Poehler led: post-lunch dance parties.

"That was like a mandate by Amy," Hahn says.

Just three to five minutes, just a song's worth to boost everyone's spirits for the afternoon.

"It was dumb how fun it was," Hahn says.

Hahn also enjoyed the more professional parts of the job, as when Poehler wrote and directed the episode "The Debate." "She doulas and produces," Hahn says of Poehler's approach to directing. "She'll help you create. She was the perfect director for that show in that moment, because she knew the inside of it so well, and all she wants is for her actors to succeed. There's no ego involved. There's just intention and then freedom. So much freedom."

Both Hahn and Rudd were also close with Adam Scott. Rudd and Scott had gone to the same acting school, the American Academy of Dramatic Arts, and had been friends ever since. "He and I have been best friends since he was a teenager and I was twenty," Rudd says. "In fact, he's probably my oldest, closest pal." This made it all the easier for them to meld with the cast, which was obviously hell-bent on fun.

During one episode, they noticed that they were all wearing business suits—Rudd, Scott, Hahn, Poehler, and Rashida Jones—which they thought was hilarious, and they took a photo in front of the building where they were shooting, which featured Neoclassical details. They arranged themselves in two rows—Scott and Rudd in the back, with Poehler, Hahn, and Jones in the front—like a cast photo. They all stood sideways and shot serious looks at the camera. Scott and Jones have their arms crossed, while Rudd leans back on a nearby ledge with confidence.

When they saw the photo, they thought it looked like a promo for a lawyer show, a *Law & Order* kind of thing—"not prestige," Rudd says, "but an old-school, twenty-three-episodes-a-season law procedural show."

They took to calling it *Philly Justice*. But with this group, that one observation couldn't be the end of it. "If you ever hang out with that crowd, everything's a bit," Rudd says. "And so *Philly Justice* turned into this extreme bit that we were doing."

In their imaginations, Dylan McDermott, who had played a lawyer on *The Practice*, served as the lead on their fictional show. Scott went so far as to start an email chain with the fake address dylanmcdermott75@gmail.com so that "Dylan" could tell everyone how excited he was to join the show. Scott would then log out of his dylanmcdermott75 account and log back in as himself to reply that he, too, was excited to work with Dylan McDermott. They got *Philly Justice* T-shirts made.

"There was *merch*," Hahn says.

Then it went, if you can believe it, further: Sackett arranged for them to shoot actual scenes of a *Philly Justice* pilot on the set. "Like we used the courtroom set," Hahn says. They even got McDermott to join them, though, Hahn says, "I don't think he quite knew what was happening, because it was a lot of inside jokes."

Yes, professional actor Dylan McDermott came and shot parts of a fake pilot with the cast of *Parks and Rec* for no good reason besides their own amusement.

The bit went public at a 2012 Paley Center panel discussion with the cast, where Poehler explained, with deadpan seriousness, that *Philly Justice* was a "pilot we did in 2003, and what was weird about it was that Rudd didn't connect with the producers and he was replaced after the pilot with Dylan McDermott."

Schur added, "And then Dylan McDermott was replaced with Dermot Mulroney."

Scott's character's name was Nick Bellows and "he's still reeling from 9/11, and his character went to Iraq. . . . And he's a real loose cannon," Poehler explained. Jones, she said, played "Joanna Suarez, we call her Joey. She's fiery. She likes to stop gang violence. Halfway through the series, she's testing a little angry, so the producers pull her back, they put on some crazy glasses, and she's a little sweeter."

They would all tease Rudd on set about the fact that he'd been fictionally replaced in their fictional creation. He would retort that he was instead doing a stage production of *You Can't Take It with You*.

"You know what, we need to go pitch it to CBS," Scott says now. "Start that show."

Hahn agrees: "I still think it should happen."

They have a presentation ready to go. They cut together a trailer, which Sackett still has and allowed me to see. (It recently surfaced online.) It claims to be a trailer for the show's release "for the first time ever on DVD . . . the legendary courtroom drama that no one has ever seen."

Offerman plays a bespectacled judge.

Scott's lawyer character inexplicably has his motorcycle helmet with him as he appears in court. He exchanges tense words with McDermott: "What the hell are you doing here?" "What the hell are *you* doing here?" "I work here now." "*I* work here now."

Poehler's character quips, "Keep your history in your pants, boys."

In another scene, McDermott, presumably finishing a rousing closing statement, declares, "Let there be justice in Philadelphia once again!" It is one minute and fifty-four seconds of extraordinary commitment to a bit.

Back in the world of Pawnee, Leslie was running the campaign of her life against Bobby Newport in the actual show the cast was making. In the end, she emerged triumphant, but only after a recount (and after learning that Bobby himself voted for her). It counts as a dizzying achievement for the character, given where Leslie started the show. She has fulfilled a dream that seemed impossible then, putting her on par with her imperious, politically minded mother, Marlene Griggs-Knope (Pamela Reed).

This seems like liberal wish-fulfillment, perhaps even of the *West Wing* variety: The very qualified and conscientious female candidate beats an exaggerated George W. Bush–like figure, a wealthy, coddled, dim scion pushed into politics by his father. It's even more satisfying to witness Bobby's palpable relief at having dodged a position of real responsibility.

That run of campaign episodes would stand out among the actors' favorites. "Being out around Los Angeles on a campaign bus with Hahn and Rashida and Amy and Pratt and Aubrey—and Rudd was around for a few episodes—it was so fun," Scott says. "It was springtime in LA. We were all laughing all day. It was the best. I badly miss those days. We were just running to work in the morning, you know?"

All this fun translated to the screen, at least critically. The fourth season of *Parks and Rec* has a 100 percent rating on Rotten Tomatoes. It retained its Thursday-night spot on NBC for the 2011–2012 season, coming in at No. 134 in the ratings, with 4.4 million viewers per episode, a slight downtick from the previous season's 5.1 million viewers. It seemed unlikely at this point in the show's run that the ratings would improve, but creatively, it was on a high.

The producers decided to go big for the fifth season, which is how the trip to Washington, DC, came about. They began making calls to congressional staffers, one of their most enthusiastic audience niches, asking for politicians to be on the show.

"I think having fans in all those offices was the real linchpin," Sackett says.

Many of the guest stars the show netted signed on because their staff told them to.

"Believe me, Orrin Hatch had no idea what show he was going to be on," Sackett says.

Senator Olympia Snowe *did* know what show she was on by the time she was in front of the cameras, but she hadn't known much about it until her office got a call asking her to be in the party scene with Senator Barbara Boxer. Snowe, a moderate Republican from Maine, was about to retire after eighteen years because of increasing partisanship. Boxer was a longtime Democratic senator from California. Their cameo would serve as a small symbol of *Parks and Rec*'s bipartisan ideals and admiration for pioneering women in government leadership. (Boxer and Snowe are Nos. 4 and 26 on Leslie's list of amazing women.)

Snowe says her staff was "just exuberant" about the opportunity. She had heard of the show but had not watched it. However, she had always liked Poehler's work on *Saturday Night Live*. After the offer to appear on *Parks and Rec*, Snowe pulled up YouTube and watched a few episodes "to make sure I knew what it was all about," she says. She was sold. "I love the sense of humor and the passion and commitment to public service—which we all need, which politics requires." She decided to do it, though she'd had no previous acting experience, not even in playing herself.

Boxer had more practice, perhaps because she was from California; she had played herself in the film *Traffic*, the improv-heavy TV show *Curb Your Enthusiasm*, the sitcom *Murphy Brown*, and the dramedy *Gilmore Girls*.

In the senators' *Parks and Rec* scene, Leslie meets two of her political idols just after her ego's been bruised. She came into the trip full of her normal excitement. But she found herself turned down for the one meeting she'd hoped to get, making the case personally for a federal grant to clean up a river in Pawnee. Now she's surrounded by beautiful young women working at the highest levels of government alongside Ben as he staffs a congressional reelection campaign. Snowe found the situation affecting: "Once I understood the context of it and what that scene would be all about, I appreciated what she was going through. It puts us back where we were, starting out in the political world."

Once they got the script, Snowe and Boxer rehearsed together for at least an hour in Snowe's office conference room. Staffers served as stand-ins for Ben and Leslie. Snowe had two lines: "Pleasure to meet you," upon meeting Leslie, and "I'm sure that's not true," in response to Leslie saying Pawnee was "small and unimportant." But they wanted to practice as much as they could, Snowe says, because "it's all in the gestures. So Barbara and I rehearsed and rehearsed. We didn't want to be responsible for any interruptions in this episode." The fear of holding up production haunted her. She had consulted on the 1987 film *Suspect*, a DC crime drama starring Cher.

"Watching the directors having to redo a shot every time became painful," she says. "So we did everything we could to make sure it went smoothly, at least on our end."

It paid off: *The New York Times* reporter Bill Carter wrote, "Both senators delivered their lines flawlessly, allowing Ms. Poehler to land the jokes." (The article had a deadpan title: "Official from Pawnee, Ind., Buttonholes Senators.") For their scene together, the Republican wore blue and the Democrat wore purple, perhaps symbolizing bipartisanship.

Snowe reports that they had fun, too, more fun than they had anticipated, because the cast and crew were so welcoming and her staff got to be extras. "We could not have been more impressed with their level of professionalism and graciousness and generosity," Snowe says.

She was surprised to find, after the episode ran, that she was often recognized from it. Not long afterward, she was in line at a Starbucks in Washington when a tour bus full of students from Connecticut pulled up. When some of them came in, one boy tapped her on the shoulder and said, "You were on *Parks and Recreation*!" Telling this story brings out her New England accent: *Pocks and Recreation*. "It shows that you can combine humor and the pursuit of public service and doing good," Snowe says of the series.

The *Parks and Rec* team shot the hotel party sequence, then a scene with Vice President Biden, Leslie's longtime crush. For that, they headed over to the Old Executive Office Building, which is next to the White House. They prepared the room, opening the French doors to the office to maximize the natural light. Biden was in a meeting with Obama, they'd been told, and then he would be over to rehearse.

As the cast members in the scene, Poehler and Scott, waited along with the crew for the vice president, they went out through the French doors and onto the balcony. They could see Marine One running just outside the White House, the helicopter's blades churning. As they spotted Obama leaving the White House and heading for the helicopter, they all lifted their phones to catch the moment on video.

Everyone was mesmerized by their proximity to power when a vice presidential staffer rushed out to the balcony, panicked. "Come on, you guys gotta get in there. The vice president doesn't walk into a room that's empty!"

Holland and Sackett grabbed Poehler and pulled her into the room just in time. "Could you imagine?" Holland says now. "You're the vice president and you walk in and you're like, 'Where is everybody?'"

In the scene, Ben has arranged the meeting as an engagement present. "You must be Leslie Knope, welcome," Biden says.

"My name just came out of your mouth," she stammers incredulously.

After a very awkward exchange in which she flounders verbally and accepts the job of secretary of state, replacing Hillary Clinton, though it was never offered, Biden gets things back on track by congratulating Leslie on all her public service. She grabs his outstretched hands, and then his face.

"I just want to say thank you," she says, seemingly going in for a kiss before he manages to distance himself and say, "You're very welcome."

That wouldn't air until the seventh episode of the season, just after the 2012 presidential election. If it ran before, it would have triggered the equal-time broadcast law and NBC would have been required to give the same amount of air time to Biden and Obama's Republican opponents, Mitt Romney and his vice presidential pick, Paul Ryan. In fact, the production had chosen the congresspeople for the previous scene based partly on who wasn't up for reelection. "Universal suddenly wanted to send a governmental affairs person with us," Sackett says.

NBC's parent company, Comcast, "always has fifty things in front of regulatory bodies," he says. "And the last thing they want is to have some sitcom blowing up their goodwill."

In the end, they didn't need to worry, since it would simply air after the election—and after Ben and Leslie had gotten engaged, another beautiful blend of work and love and politics for the characters of *Parks and Rec*.

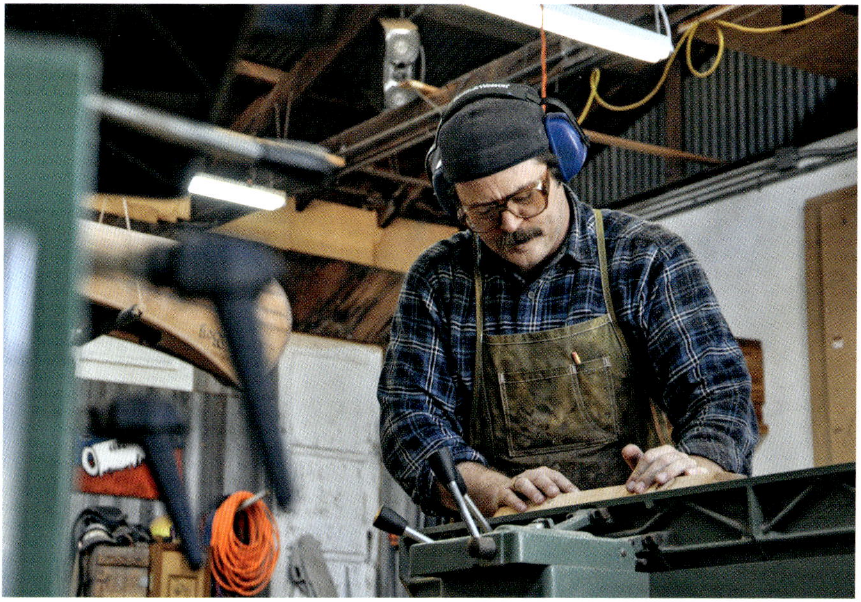

Above: Offerman working in his woodshop.
Below: A stage set for the show's fictional band, Mouse Rat.
Courtesy of Norm Hiscock

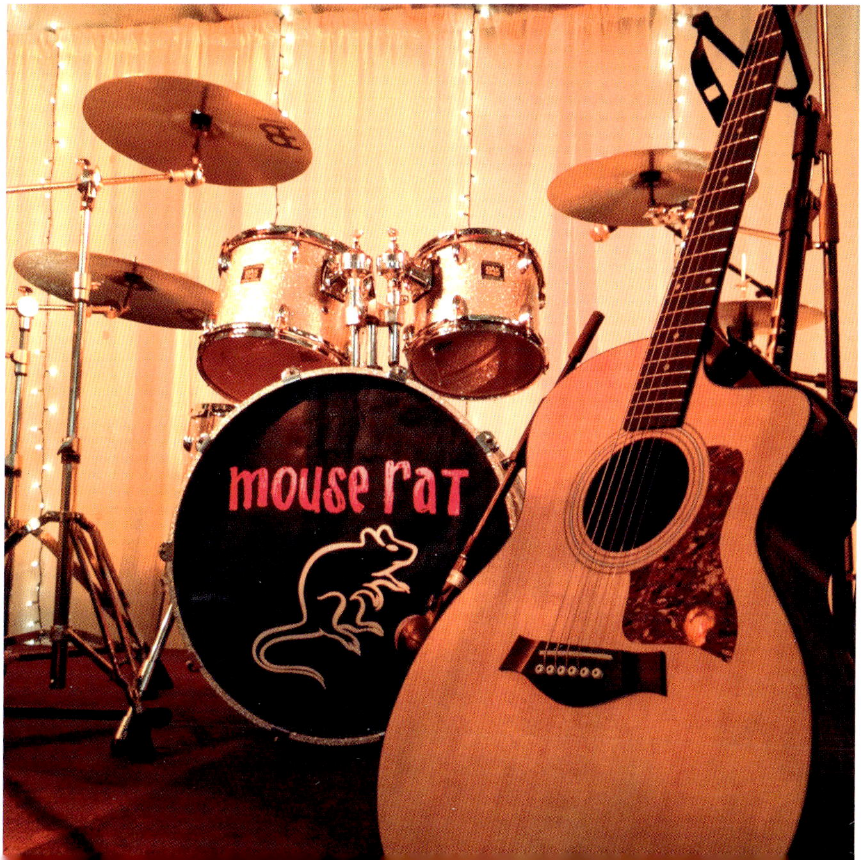

The writers and assistants on a writing retreat (left to right): Harris Wittels, David Phillips, Alan Yang, Katie Dippold, Aisha Muharrar, Greg Levine, Brian Rowe, and Charlie Carlisle.
Courtesy of Norm Hiscock

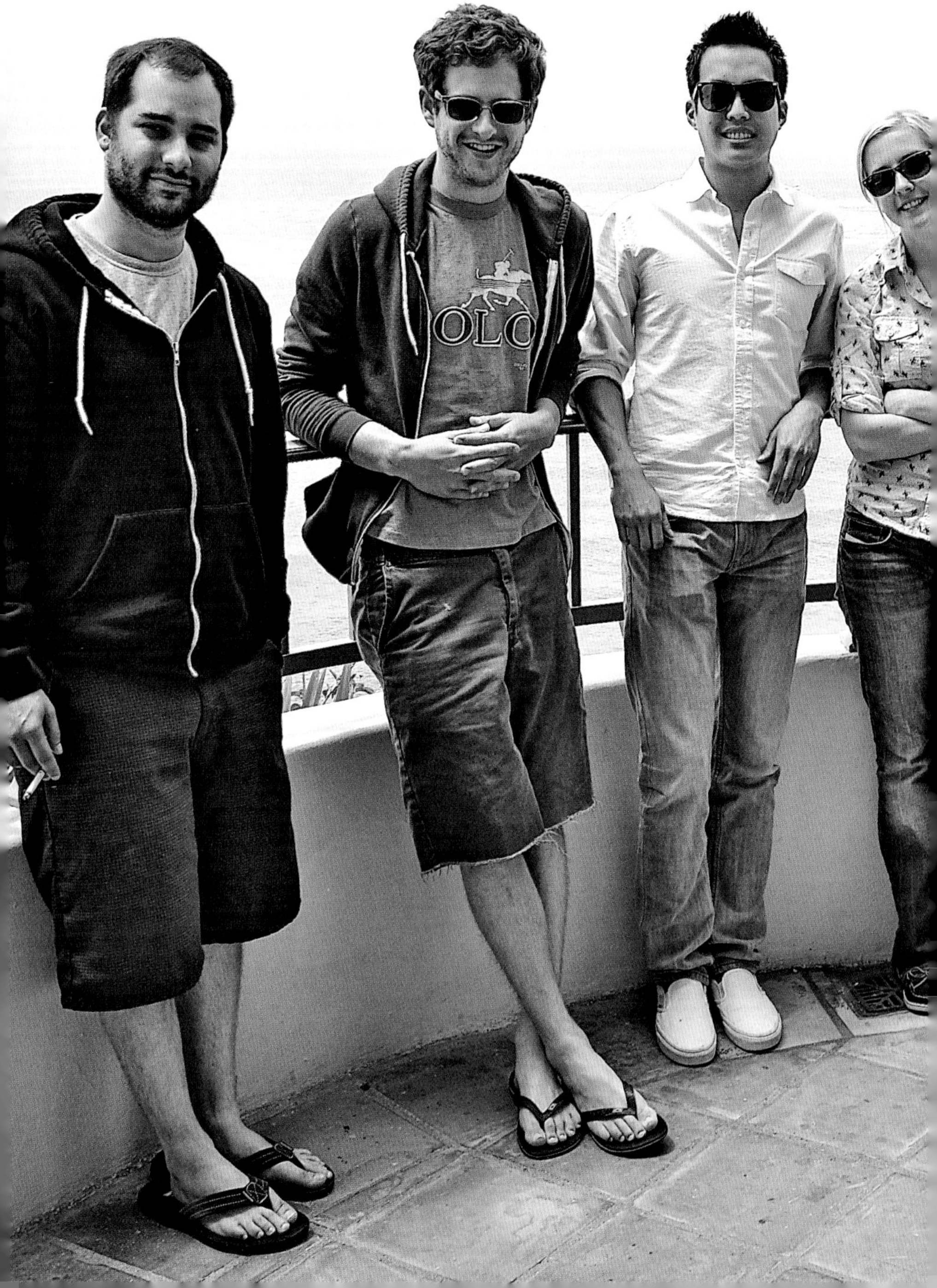

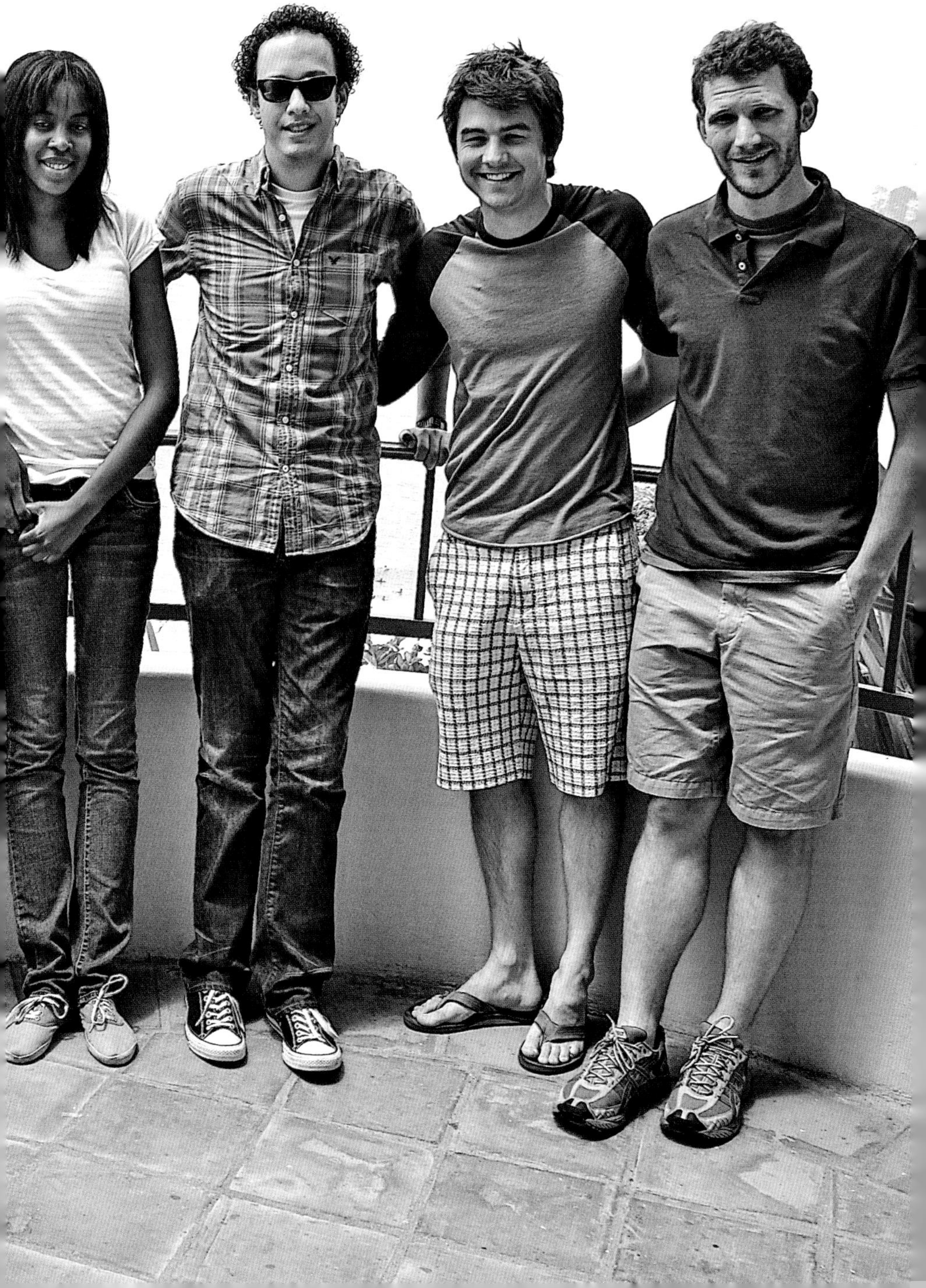

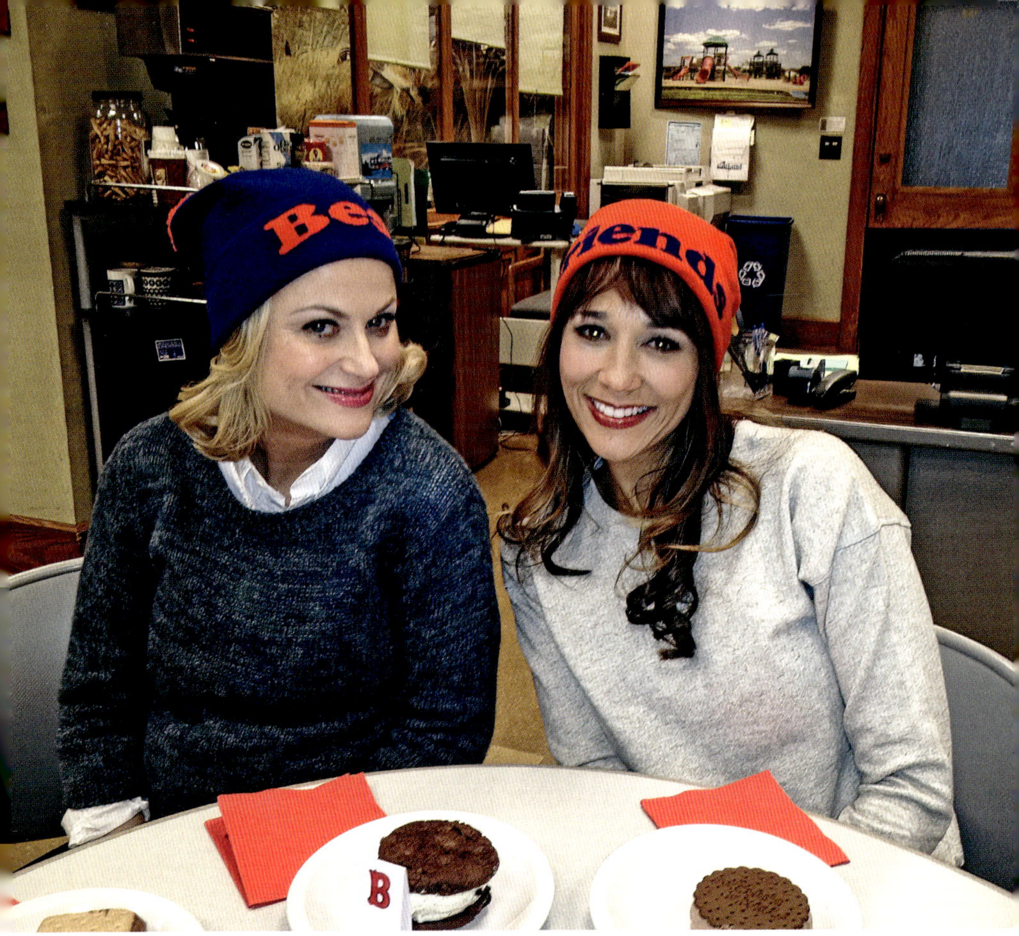

Amy Poehler and Rashida Jones celebrating their "best friendship" on set.

Courtesy of Kirston Mann

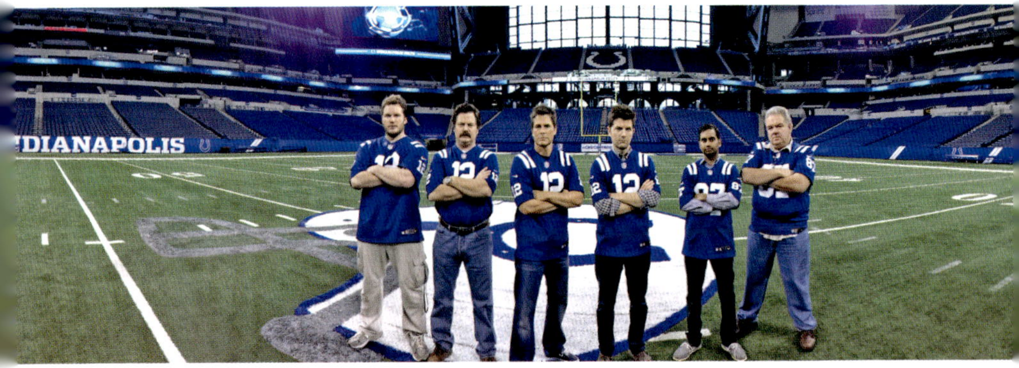

The male cast members on their visit to play with the Indianapolis Colts: Chris Pratt, Nick Offerman, Rob Lowe, Adam Scott, Aziz Ansari, and Jim O'Heir.

Courtesy of Michael Schur

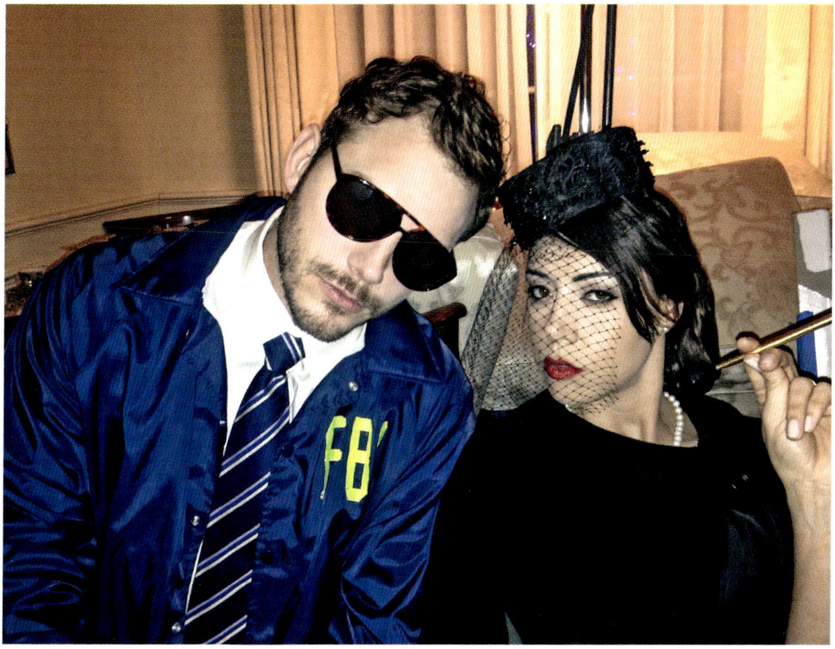

Chris Pratt and Aubrey Plaza as their characters' alter egos: Burt Macklin and Janet Snakehole.

Courtesy of Michael Schur

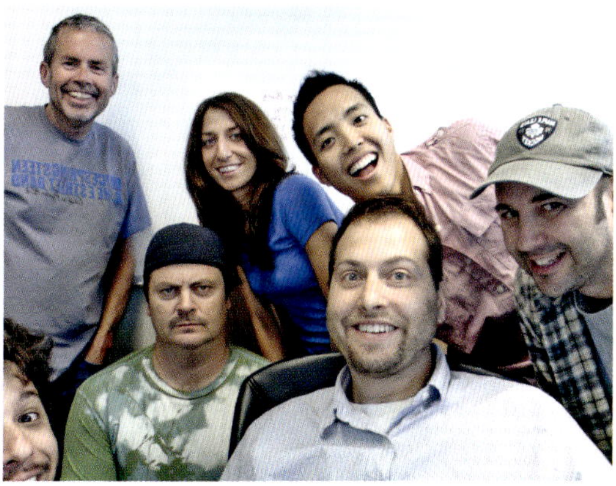

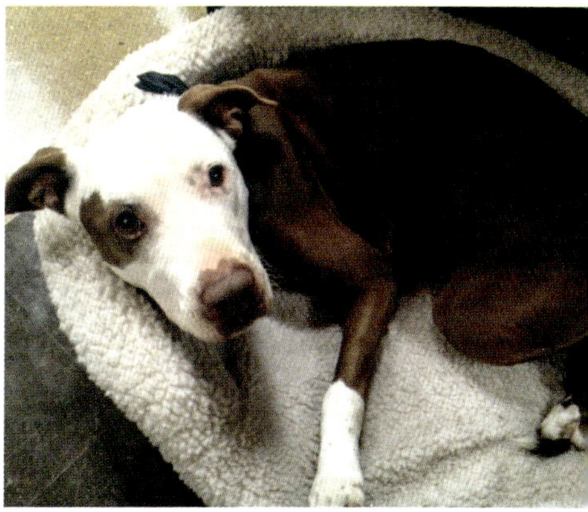

Left: Writers Dave King, Mike Scully, Chelsea Peretti, Alan Yang, Dan Goor, and Norm Hiscock (in foreground), with actor Nick Offerman.

Courtesy of Dan Goor

Right: Champion, Andy and April's dog.

Courtesy of Michael Schur

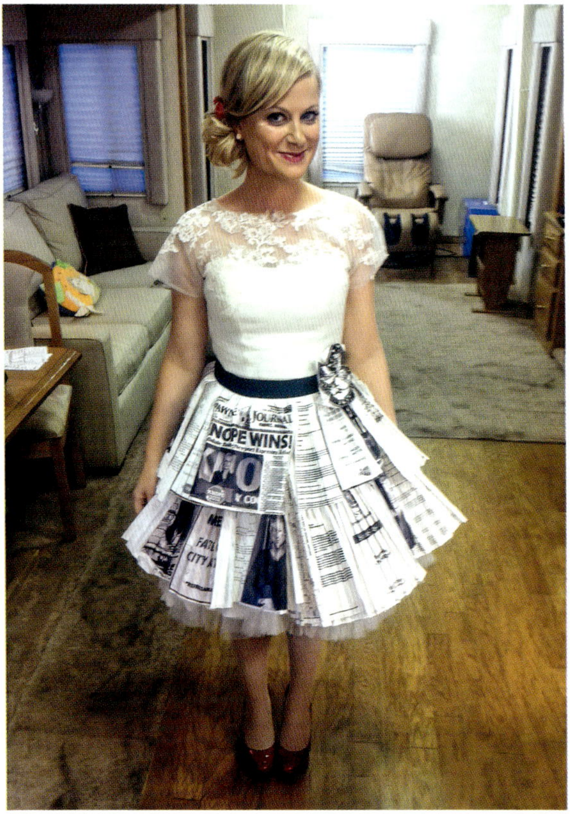

Poehler models Leslie Knope's wedding outfit.

Courtesy of Kirston Mann

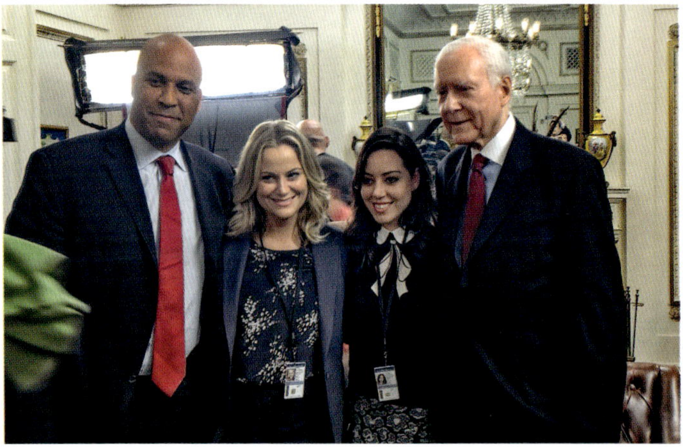

Senator Cory Booker, Amy Poehler, Aubrey Plaza, and Senator Orrin Hatch.

Courtesy of Michael Schur

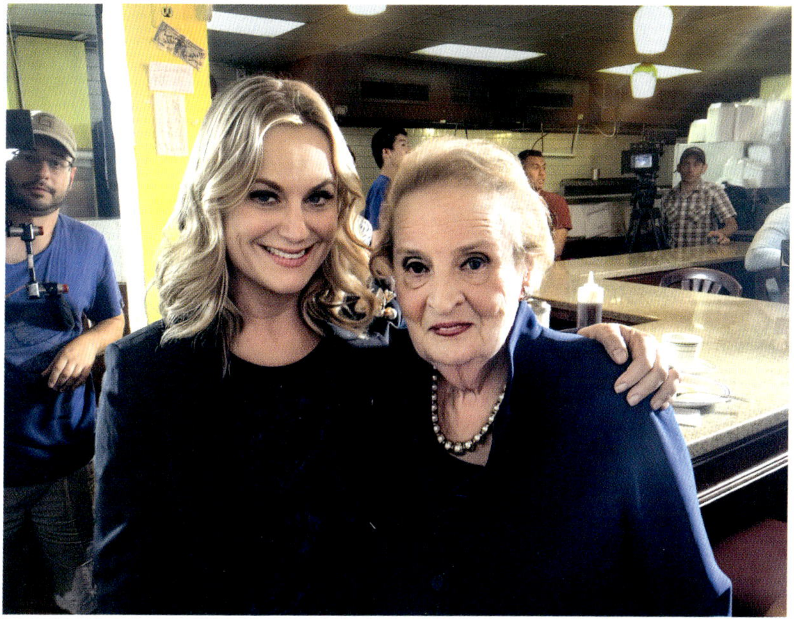

Amy Poehler and Secretary of State Madeleine Albright.

Courtesy of Michael Schur

The cast in the Pawnee City Council chamber.

Courtesy of Michael Schur

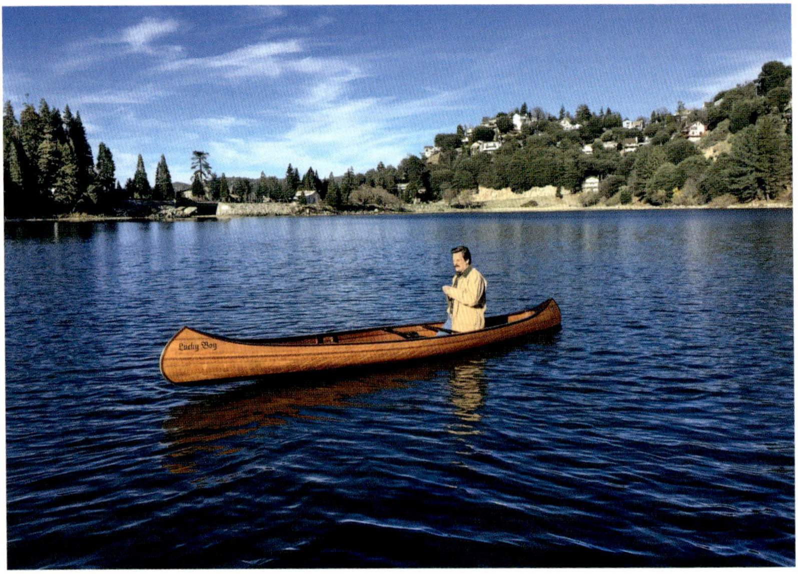

Offerman in a canoe.

Courtesy of Michael Schur

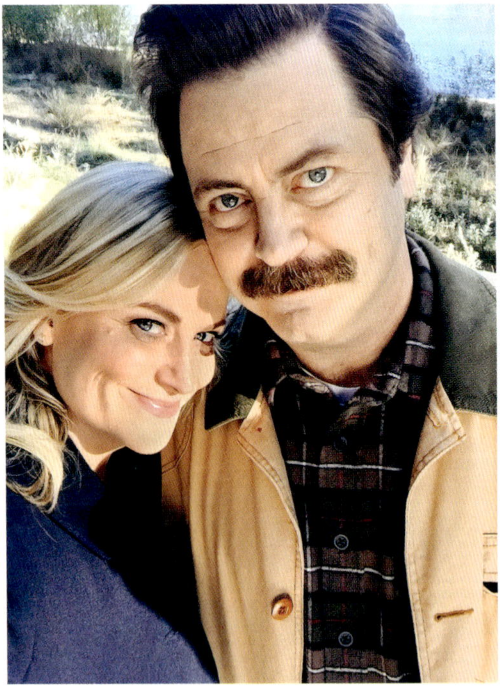

Poehler and Offerman.

Courtesy of Michael Schur

CHAPTER 9

"A Singularly Compelling Representation of the Liberal Spirit"

Political Philosophy in *Parks and Rec*

The memorable episode "Women in Garbage" has April and Leslie volunteering to work on a garbage truck to prove that women are as capable as men. In an interesting twist, they encounter an industrial-size refrigerator that they can't move, thus showing their limitations. But they eventually arrange for a local soup kitchen to take it, since it's working, and they load it onto a truck with a group of women. *Bitches get stuff done.*

The same episode introduces Paula Horke (Bonnie Bartlett), Pawnee's first female city council member, who was elected forty years prior and is now eighty-two. Some things are unchanged for women after four decades; the wall of council members' photos shows only men between Paula's time and Leslie's. "We still have quite a ways to go," Leslie says. In fact, she explains as she stands outside the conference room where she's meeting Paula, "Technically, I'm not allowed to reserve this conference room without my husband['s] or father's signature."

It was unusual for *Parks and Rec* to get involved directly in partisan politics. The show avoided any mention of political parties. Leslie is not explicitly a Democrat (until one hint at the very end of the series), and Ron is not a Republican. The producers made great efforts to include cameos by Democrats and Republicans. "We try to keep our own beliefs out of the stories, and we've done stories that are very traditionally conservative," Schur claimed to *Newsweek*.

But the show has a clear political message. And that message is left-leaning, if moderate. It argues for the power of government to help people, though it also believes that people of different political persuasions can work together on that project. Its national politician cameos underline that message. "Without a doubt, Leslie was a liberal Democrat," Poehler says. "But it was a different time." She was also *explicitly* feminist, an inherently liberal identification.

In the 2024 book *Liberalism as a Way of Life*, University of Sydney professor of politics and philosophy Alexandre Lefebvre cites Leslie Knope as his example of the perfect representation of nineteenth-century liberalism. He returns to Leslie and *Parks and Rec* to illustrate principles and arguments throughout the book, and insists, just to be clear, "I am serious about Leslie being a singularly compelling representation of the liberal spirit."

This came, at least in part, from Poehler's natural personality, Offerman says, just as his own character sprang from his God-given characteristics. "Amy's an ebullient unflappable sunshine machine, that is her face and her talent," he says. "And so the writers make her positive to a fault, to the point of driving herself into the ground or driving people crazy around her."

As the show goes on, Leslie's feminism, another characteristic she shares with Poehler, becomes more overt. Though the other female characters should get some of the credit here, too. April in particular charts her own path as a cynical but increasingly competent presence at city hall, and as the smart, dominant half of her marriage. She underlines her singularity among female TV characters when Ann asks her who her favorite *Sex and the City* character is, and she deadpans, "Alf." The men even get in on the act. In the fourth season, April's husband, Andy, takes a women's studies class at the community college, and Ron, of all people, takes a romantic interest in the teacher.

Critics and bloggers cheered the show as "a giant feminist treat," "the most feminist show on television," and "the most feminist sitcom on TV at the moment," with a message of "feminism for everyone." This was still unusual for the time, though it was becoming more common. The series coincided with a resurgence in the feminist movement termed "fourth-wave feminism," which focused on issues such as street and workplace harassment, violence against women, body shaming, online sexism, rape culture, intersectionality, and, critically for *Parks and Rec*, media representation. *Parks and Rec* was among the first major TV series at the time to lean into feminism. Leslie even dressed as Rosie the Riveter on the fourth-season DVD packaging.

Leslie's feminism became a subject of academic studies. A GenderWatch paper by Erika Engstrom, a gender and media scholar, noted the ways that *Parks and Rec* "simply treats feminism and feminist values as something normal. . . . Its low-key approach and Everytown, USA, setting combines with the treatment of its women characters in non-stereotypical ways to offer viewers a look at small-town life as lived by unique individuals."

Engstrom argued that *Parks and Rec*'s feminism was "a means by which people collectively and with intention effect changes in the current power structure . . . a positive version of the core tenets of feminism: gender equality and the progress of women." Engstrom sees

Pawnee's history of entrenched oppression as a major way that the show asserts its views. "The city of Pawnee itself serves as a text that provides an opposition to Leslie Knope/feminism," she writes. "One can read Pawnee as a symbol of the U.S. itself, and, by extension, patriarchal views that prevent feminist progress."

This is evident in the "Women in Garbage" episode, as well as another in which Leslie proposes repealing 110 antiquated Pawnee laws, including, as Engstrom points out, "those that confine menstruating women to their bathtubs, and allow land-owning men to crack an egg on the head of any woman who raises her voice to them." One citizen, played by Patton Oswalt, is opposed to this change, citing the importance of tradition and then filibustering by describing his detailed pitch for *Star Wars: Episode VII*, which includes the resurrection of villain Boba Fett. This mimics a common dynamic that was emerging online at the time: nerdy guys opposing women's advancement and using the concept of tradition to back up their arguments. (Director Jon Favreau later seemingly mimicked what Oswalt described in his pitch when making the 2021 *Star Wars* spin-off series *The Book of Boba Fett* for Disney+.)

It's crucial to *Parks and Rec*'s depiction of gender politics that Ben and Leslie are both ambitious. They negotiate their priorities as a couple, developing their own feminism and the show's. In the same season when Leslie has conquered the city council (at least for the moment) and Ben is moving up to national politics, the couple gets engaged. Leslie will *not* be changing her name, of course, and, furthermore, she has found a guy who understands that between the two of them, *she's* the more likely potential future US president. He gets her a meeting with Vice President Joe Biden as an engagement present.

Her wedding dress is made from newspaper clippings about her accomplishments. Costume designer Kirston Mann asked prop master Gay Perello for lots of fictional magazine and newspaper articles about Leslie Knope. Mann took inspiration from her son, who was into origami at the time, and folded the papers up so that they lay together to make a dress. "It was this big art project that was so full of love, so full of *the show*," Mann says.

Even Scott's straight-man performance, compared to Poehler's unpredictable improv, reads as feminist. Not since Desi and Lucy has there been a TV husband so content to let his TV wife's comedy shine. Yes, Ben had his eccentricities, like his fear of cops and his Claymation hobby. But, as Scott says, "It's fun to have someone there that's like, 'Sorry. Are you insane?' It's good to have that person that can react in a grounded way."

As a modern, demonstrably feminist man, Ben stood in contrast to the other important man in Leslie's life, her friend and mentor Ron Swanson, a hypermasculine libertarian. And Ron was grabbing at least as many headlines as Leslie for his political implications.

As someone who comes from just a few suburbs over from Nick Offerman's hometown of Minooka, I feel an intense and emotional pull toward his portrayal of Ron. He makes me feel safe. My father was a stoically masculine, Chicago-accented, mustachioed, meat-grilling, conservative guy who was literally named Ron. Think the Belushi brothers, Dennis Farina, the "Superfans" sketch on *Saturday Night Live*. Offerman says a lot of Ron Swanson "is actually just the color Mother Nature painted me." I wouldn't be surprised if others from the Midwest have the same reaction to Ron Swanson that I do, Republican, Democrat, or libertarian.

But Republicans certainly embraced him. In May 2010, Republican representative Joe Wilson of South Carolina wrote an op-ed piece for *Politico* praising the character: "America has a new champion of limited government and spending restraint. For six years straight, Ron

Swanson, director of the City of Pawnee's Parks and Recreation Department, brought his agency in under budget. He set citywide records by spending only 60 cents of his department's discretionary fund. Regrettably, Swanson is not running for Congress. Instead, he is leading the limited government fight as a fictional character on NBC's primetime show 'Parks and Recreation.'"

Elected in 2001, Wilson was regarded as a "folk hero," *Politico* said, by his like-minded colleagues and activists. In 2009, he had become famous for yelling out "You lie!" during President Barack Obama's televised speech to a joint session of Congress about his plans for overhauling health care, an act the Associated Press characterized as "an extraordinary breach of congressional decorum."

"The movement has been waiting for someone to have a defiant attitude, and what he did was very reflective of what everyone feels," said Eric Odom, executive director of the American Liberty Alliance, a libertarian-oriented group.

Ron's position as a libertarian on television, one who often made libertarian arguments in prime time, was making *him* a folk hero now. Conservatives cheered at seeing one of their own humanized instead of demonized on mainstream TV, perhaps more so because the show was clearly, if not explicitly, aimed at liberal audiences.

His cultural predicament was not unlike that of Archie Bunker of *All in the Family* in the 1970s, a conservative figure created as a bit of a joke, by people who held opposite political beliefs, who is hailed as a hero despite his creators' intentions. Ron held particular sway as a man's man, the kind that people will often say you just don't see enough of anymore. (From the *All in the Family* theme song, "Those Were the Days": "Girls were girls and men were men.") Ron says at one point, in his classic deadpan, that he's only cried twice in his life. He loves steak. He hates hugging and feelings. He loves guns, woodworking, and the outdoors. He has a deep voice and a mustache.

Of course, his masculine aspects are tempered by a number of sneakier factors, especially as the series progresses. He mentors and admires Leslie, a pro-government heroine who subscribes to feminism. When he receives the Dorothy Everton Smythe Female Empowerment Award, he uses the moment to point out to an enraged Leslie that she relies too much on outside validation, but he also tells the awards program that he believes that she deserves it, not him. He's a feminist, though he doesn't admit it. Ron is, in fact, the ultimate father figure for any liberal viewer who might be craving one. Perhaps that's the secret to his success: He can be whomever a viewer wants him to be.

Parks and Rec makes him a conservative whom liberals can accept in several ways. He's a libertarian, rather than a Christian conservative, and he's never racist or sexist. Left-wing liberals have a lot more sympathy for the libertarian point of view than for Moral Majority theocrats. By his mentorship and public expressions of respect toward Leslie and other women and girls, he telegraphs that he's not a sexist. He disagrees with liberal viewers in ways they find acceptable because the show makes clear that he respects women and mentors not only Leslie but also April and Tom.

Like Leslie, he was tapping into a part of the zeitgeist. "Ron Swanson is more than the MVP of the *Parks and Recreation* squad, more than just the funniest character on TV—he's the perfect depiction of aggrieved American manhood at the twilight of the empire," Rob Sheffield wrote in *Rolling Stone* in November 2011. "As embodied by the great Nick Offerman, who says more by clenching two-sevenths of his right eyebrow than most actors say with their whole bodies, Ron Swanson is the familiar sitcom archetype of the ornery boss, in the tradition of Ed Asner on *The Mary Tyler Moore Show* or Danny DeVito on *Taxi*. The big difference is that he's the boss of a petty government bureaucracy that embodies everything he hates."

As Sheffield noted, "Ron has existed for less than three years, but his fringe political views have turned into the Republican mainstream, if not the whole message of the primary debates, which are *Parks and Rec*'s main comedy competition this fall."

Several new sitcoms in the fall of 2011 featured similar types: white, middle-aged men trying to assert their masculinity in a changing world—Kevin Dillon in *How to Be a Gentleman* (which was canceled after two episodes) and Tim Allen in *Last Man Standing* (which coasted on the *Home Improvement* star's lasting broad appeal), among them. But none of them were as finely realized as Ron Swanson.

Offerman played him so well that he won the Television Critics Association's Award for Individual Achievement in Comedy. If fans knew anything about the show, it was that Ron loved woodworking, meat, breakfast foods, and stopping the government from infiltrating his life, if not the lives of those around him as well.

"I feel like our society longs for someone to have the simplicity of vision that Ron has," Offerman told *Newsweek* at the time. "In this day and age, we're bombarded with so much information and choice that to see this heroic edifice of a man who lives by a set of simple rules is really inspiring to me. People wish they could just say, 'Yes, I want to eat red meat and only use tools and firearms. That sounds like a happy, simple life.'"

Political polarization among Americans was already increasing before and during the series' run. Polarization became a talking point in the early 1990s, when Republican presidential primary candidate Pat Buchanan delivered a speech at the 1992 Republican National Convention where his opponent, incumbent George H. W. Bush, accepted the nomination. The landmark speech declared a "culture war" for America's future. Though Democrat Bill Clinton beat Bush, Republicans swept the midterm elections two years later, taking control of Congress for the first time in forty years. By the 2000 presidential election, polarization was accelerating, and presidential elections from then on would become increasingly contentious and close. In 2004, historian Simon Schama said that America had not been so polarized since the Civil War, quipping that the country should be called the Divided States of America.

Between the years 1994 and 2014, the number of Americans who identified as "consistently conservative" or "consistently liberal" doubled from 10 percent to 21 percent, according to a 2014 Pew Research Center survey, and during that same time, the average Republican shifted further right, while the average Democrat shifted further left.

Schur's philosophy, which runs throughout *Parks and Rec*, is to combat polarization with its opposites, "humanism," the belief that people have an obligation to live ethical lives without relying on religion, and "contractualism," a philosophical framework developed in T. M. Scanlon's *What We Owe to Each Other* (which would feature prominently in Schur's follow-up show, *The Good Place*).

"The title, meaningfully, is not, 'Do we owe things to each other?'" he said of that book. "The title is 'What We Owe to Each Other.' It is saying we do owe things to each other, and now our job is to figure out what those things are." He continued: "Scanlon's theory is basically like, you've got to sit around a table and actually hash this out with each other. These are the people we live with, they're the people that we have to survive with and exist with, and the rules need to be worked out in conjunction with other people, even when those other people are irritating or annoying or seemingly unreasonable."

Newsweek cited *Parks and Rec*'s optimism as a radical statement in itself: "It's a rare thing in television these days to see an optimistic character, whose very buoyancy is typically the stuff of mockery. Perhaps indicative of the need the audience has in the uncertain times that we live in, *Parks and Recreation*'s Leslie Knope—played by

Emmy nominee Amy Poehler—has been embraced by both critics and viewers."

The show's holistic view of Pawnee supports its theme of community, and specifically of working with those who are different from you in ways that go beyond politics. We meet the media (newspaper reporter Shauna Malwae-Tweep, dim TV anchor Perd Hapley, diva talk show host Joan Callamezzo), other politicians (philandering city councilman Bill Dexhart), activists, cult members, and myriad other eccentric, bordering on deranged, characters. It's the story of an entire town, with one optimist at its center. As *Newsweek* said, "The show has imbued the fictional town with immense possibility, similar to *The Simpsons*' Springfield." Or to go back further, *Middlemarch*, George Eliot's sprawling nineteenth-century novel subtitled *A Study of Provincial Life*.

And each of these recurring characters, who could have faded into the background or been treated as "minor," feels so distinct that they could be starring in their own show. Shauna's penchant for dating every man in town, for instance: "She is so naive and so earnest," says Alison Becker, who played her. "She really wants to find love. She's just clueless." And instead of a femme fatale, she comes across as quite sympathetic.

"She's not a man-eater who's coming in and maniacally sleeping with people," Becker says. "She's just like, 'Are you my person?' 'Are you my person?' And you just can't help but be like, *Girl*. We slowly started to discover that she is so broken and desperate. What an amazing gift to give an actor."

Actor Jason Mantzoukas is impressed by the detail given to every single character. "Not just the side characters, but the tertiary characters," he says. "Like, I'm in *four* episodes of the show." And yet his character, entrepreneur Dennis Feinstein, is memorable and beloved. "It's shocking to me how many people not just come up to me to say they love *Parks* but that they know that Dennis Feinstein's [real] name is Dante Fiero," he says. "They know the lore. For a character who's only appeared a couple of times, that's incredible."

Most of these characters sprang at least in part from the improvisations of the actors who played them. "I would stick to the script," says Mo Collins, who played Joan. "But the thing about me is that until they call 'cut,' I just keep going. And I think that they realized who I am as a performer. So when I would be there, one of the things I loved *so* much was that Amy would say, 'Mo's here. Just keep the camera rolling.' God, that felt good, but it's also the way in which I think I influenced the writers to go forward with Joan, and see that there was this potential for her."

For instance, Joan's tendency to end up drunk. "Most of my characters somehow go there," Collins says. "It's very strange. I haven't had a drink for five months. I do well playing broken people; that's pulling from the truth. I suppose through the improv, they could see those cracks in me. And I would certainly, in going toward funny, tend to draw from those broken parts."

The drunken moments reveal the pain of a woman who fancies herself to be a glamorous, powerful star of Pawnee television. "It's just like, 'How do you keep up that facade?'" Collins says. "Joan felt like a fraud. Impostor syndrome all the way through, pretending to be greater than she knew she was." Collins believes Joan knows the truth: "She just didn't want to break the dream. She wanted to be bigger than she was. A bit of 'fake it till you make it' was in play."

The eccentric citizenry of Pawnee contrasts with the competence, earnestness, and commitment to service that Leslie embodies. Nearly everyone she encounters in the wider public comes off as, at minimum, crazy, and sometimes evil: the dad who chains himself to a chair in her office to get *Twilight* into the Pawnee time capsule, the Zorp end-of-the-world cult members, everyone who works for Sweetums.

As Lefebvre writes in *Liberalism as a Way of Life*: "Perhaps the show and its writers believe in democracy and 'the people' in the abstract, but its contempt for the citizens of Pawnee is boundless (and given that they created those citizens, the contempt is downright Calvinist). From the first episode to the last, *Parks and Recreation* never wavered."

Lefebvre refers to one of Leslie's few true breaking points in the series, when she's up for recall from the city council and wildly unpopular after stopping a Paunch Burger from being built and implementing a soda tax to fight obesity. She drives her popularity down even further by helping to save the neighboring town of Eagleton by merging it with Pawnee. Such is the tension between the two towns that many Pawneeans are outraged, even though Leslie did what she believed to be the right thing. The storyline is perhaps the wonkiest *Parks and Rec* gets: The nefarious councilman Jeremy Jamm, played to smarmy perfection by Jon Glaser, calls a special session to propose that only someone with an official Pawnee address can vote in the upcoming election, which will determine Leslie's fate. He's clearly doing this to try to swing the election against Leslie, since Eagletonians are more likely to support her. (This is also an obvious riff on voter suppression laws.)

Leslie decides to filibuster the meeting, even though she's already dressed in skates, overalls, and a baseball cap for the nineties-themed roller rink party she's throwing for Ben's birthday. As she talks and talks, it's a heroic effort that appears to be bolstered by the arrival of many Eagletonians, though we soon discover that they're hoping to support a candidate of their own to replace her. Thus her filibuster transforms, in real time, from a self-preservation effort to a self-sacrificing effort as she continues to talk, knowing she's sealing her own fate. Later, Alexis Soloski wrote in *The New York Times*, "That scene felt like a vindication for principled, chatty ladies everywhere."

When Leslie is indeed recalled, in her kiss-off speech, she says, "I love Pawnee, but sometimes it sucks. The people can be very mean and ungrateful, and they cling to their fried dough and their big sodas, and they get mad at me when their pants don't fit. I'm sick of it. Pawnee is filled with a bunch of pee-pee heads."

This speech, in fact, parodies ideas promoted by New York City mayor Michael Bloomberg, policing trans fats and large soft drinks. And it also mimics remarks made by Barack Obama five years earlier when he was a senator. At a San Francisco fundraising event, he said that it was because of unsuccessful Clinton and Bush policies that white, working-class Americans "cling to guns or religion or antipathy to people who aren't like them, or anti-immigrant sentiment, or anti-trade sentiment as a way to explain their frustrations." Smartly, he did not call them pee-pee heads, though that would have been funnier. An incident involving Hillary Clinton and baskets of deplorables a few years later would call this to mind yet again.

While Leslie and Ron represented America's opposing political philosophies, and the minor characters represented the mass of voters, Aziz Ansari's Tom stood in for another key factor in American civic life: capitalism. From the beginning, Tom is an operator who says outright that he pursued government service to make connections that would help boost his entrepreneurial ambitions. He likes nice clothes, cool shoes, and beautiful home decor, and he prides himself on his grooming habits. He wants his own cologne line. He manages to launch a successful nightclub—the Snakehole Lounge—and a signature (if dangerous) drink, Snake Juice. His production company, Entertainment 720, founded with his obnoxious best friend Jean-Ralphio Saperstein (Ben Schwartz), has a surprisingly good run, and he finds success, ultimately, with his store Rent-A-Swag and his restaurant, Tom's Bistro.

With his officemate Donna, who shares his penchant for luxury goods, he invents "Treat Yo' Self" Day, when they allow themselves whatever they want in the name of self-care: cakes, massages, leather goods, mimosas, clothes. Once, they try to cheer Ben up by teaching him about it; he uses it to purchase a full Batman suit for himself. "Treat Yo' Self" would become one of the series' signature catch-phrases and an internet meme favorite.

And like Leslie and Ron, Tom's personality springs from some of Ansari's natural qualities. "It's funny to think about where Tom ends and Aziz begins," writer Alan Yang told *Rolling Stone*. "Tom's like the douchiest version of Aziz."

Ansari and Yang collaborated often to make Tom into a distinctively contemporary guy, a very online, in-the-know, trend-chasing *Maxim* magazine subscriber. If you recall Bill Hader's *Saturday Night Live* character Stefon ("New York's hottest club is . . ."), Tom was the kind of guy who wanted in on those clubs. One of Tom's signature lines is, "Zerts are what I call desserts. Tray-trays are what I call entrées. I call sandwiches sammies, sandoozles, or Adam Sandlers." This is the kind of thing we all agree is not okay to say, and yet he does it anyway.

The part made Ansari a breakout star. *Rolling Stone* followed him for a major profile in 2011, trailing him to a hip Thai restaurant called Jitlada, where he demonstrated his similarities with Tom: "When we sit, people look up from their plates and murmur excitedly," the article says. "The waitress knows Ansari, and she's unsurprised when he maneuvers the extensive menu like a pro, ordering dishes with names like Green Curry Dragon Eggs and Crying Tiger Beef."

He worked hard to take advantage of his newfound fame, writing scripts with former *Human Giant* director Jason Woliner. They had sold three of them to comedy-film impresario Judd Apatow, with Ansari attached to star. Though he was one of very few prominent Indian

Americans on television, he didn't emphasize his ethnicity in his work, and he rejected the Muslim religion of his upbringing. "It's not like my parents investigated every religion and were like, 'OK, this one,'" he told *Rolling Stone*. "It's also so much work. You have to pray five times a day? Come on, man. Let's chill out." He occasionally acknowledged his race: In his comedy routine, for instance, he told a story about a white guy asking him if he was happy about *Slumdog Millionaire*'s success. But, as *Rolling Stone* said, "he won't stoop to make a 7-Eleven joke."

Instead, he embraced a persona that is very American, one who thinks nearly every aspect of the cheapest pop culture is "awesome," and you're never sure whether he's being ironic or earnest. Soulja Boy, Vin Diesel Blu-rays, and Quiznos were all "awesome" to him, as *Rolling Stone* pointed out. He made so many jokes about the awesomeness of Quiznos that he eventually had to change his stand-up routine to overpraise Panera Bread instead. When Ansari and Yang saw a light-up shirt at a gift kiosk in Universal City, they agreed that Tom had to wear it.

Perhaps because of this persona, he would snag roles that were originally written as white, as in the heist comedy film *30 Minutes or Less*, alongside Jesse Eisenberg and Danny McBride. "He's been incredibly smart about what he says no to," Poehler said at the time, "forcing people to consider him in roles they may not have at first."

Parks and Rec remained behind in the ratings. On the other hand, NBC had begun to struggle across the board, so having a sure thing outweighed the risk of a new series. After the show took back its Thursday-night slot from the interloper *Outsourced*, the cast and crew started to feel almost . . . comfortable.

The series had a dedicated enough fan base that, in October 2011,

Hyperion Books published Leslie's fictional book *Pawnee: The Greatest Town in America*, with Leslie Knope credited on the cover as the author. Schur and the writers had come up with the idea during the shortened third season. Poehler did a publicity tour for the book, speaking on behalf of author Leslie Knope. "She thinks Pawnee represents the best of America. Look, she's not deluded. It goes like this: New York, Paris, London, Chicago, maybe Istanbul, and then Pawnee," she told *USA Today*. "The book is a celebration of one great small town and all the good things that are found there."

The detailed and thorough book is typical of Leslie's straight-A-student ways. It begins by citing quotes from a famous liberal and a famous conservative, both of which perfectly encapsulate the *Parks and Rec* spirit. Here's Bill Clinton: "There is nothing wrong with America that cannot be cured by what is right with America." And here's Margaret Thatcher: "It's passionately interesting for me that the things that I learned in a small town, in a very modest home, are just the things that I believe won the election." The book details Pawnee's business community, entertainment and leisure, history, heroes, government, local media, demographics, worst disasters, and many other tidbits. For example, we learn that the gentlemen's clubs in Pawnee include Talent & Poise and the Glitter Factory, *and* that there's also an actual glitter factory in Pawnee.

Timed with the book's release in the real world, the fourth-season episode "Born & Raised" shows Leslie promoting the book, much like real politicians publish books to lay out their own philosophies and platforms. In real life, the book would go on to sell more than eighty-five thousand copies, a solid performance for a book by a fictional author.

In the sixth season, Leslie finds out that she's pregnant, tripling down on the show's message that women *can* have it all—a satisfying career, a soulmate husband, and, now, kids. In fact, she finds out she is having triplets. As Engstrom writes in her GenderWatch paper: "The version of feminism offered by the series clearly advances the liberal version of feminist theory, one in which societal change and attainment of gender equality depend on getting more women into positions of power, such as city government. . . . The palatable feminism and almost heroic portrayal of Leslie Knope combines with the camaraderie evidenced by her female and male friends to create a vision of a gender-equitable feminism, one that promotes cooperation between men and women."

Parks and Rec had found its place in the world, politically and in the television business. Now the creative forces behind the show were facing a problem they'd never encountered before: keeping the show fresh and exciting even as it entered its elder stateswoman era.

CHAPTER 10

"This Guy Deserves Happiness, Too"

Seasons 5 and 6

Writer Joe Mande was new to the writing staff in its fifth season when he faced a unique dilemma. In the second episode he wrote, Tom Haverford's business Rent-A-Swag, which loans his stylish clothing out to children for special events, is thriving. The intended plotline had a middle-aged woman who owned the space next door complaining that Tom was playing music too loud. By the end, the two not only make up but start dating. An older woman seemed plausible for Tom; he had always been great at flirting with Joan Callamezzo.

However, when casting began, Mande says, "We could not get an actress in her fifties to play fifties, to admit her own age in real life." The producers made lists of actresses to approach, but they all refused. Finally, Mike Schur determined that they'd have to change the script.

The writers room brainstormed an alternative: Instead, Tom

would meet his obnoxious friend Jean-Ralphio's sister, Mona-Lisa Saperstein, who matches her twin brother in awfulness. She also vibes with Tom, and he hires her as his assistant, which she is, naturally, terrible at.

Mande, who started out as a comedian in New York, knew Jenny Slate, who was best known for her time on *Saturday Night Live* and from a voice role on the animated series *Bob's Burgers*. After the *Parks and Rec* team created Mona-Lisa that night in the writers' room, amid the worn brown leather sofas and note card–covered corkboards, he immediately texted her and asked if she was available in two days. And thus she became the latest insane addition to the Pawnee-verse, one who would appear on the series several more times before it ended. There was always room for one more in Pawnee.

As *Parks and Rec* carried on into its fifth season and beyond, after several of its lead characters married each other and advanced their careers, the writers had to expand their world to keep storylines fresh. The show's ratings remained middling, with its twenty-two-episode fifth season coming in at No. 111 on the Nielsen charts, averaging 4.1 million viewers. But it fit with NBC's acclaimed Thursday-night comedy lineup and had achieved widespread adulation, with the fifth season scoring a 96 percent fresh on Rotten Tomatoes.

To keep moving forward, it had to grow. We would meet not only Mona-Lisa but also cool single-mom Diane Lewis (Lucy Lawless), snooty Eagleton councilwoman Ingrid de Forest (Kristen Bell), tightly wound Eagleton parks employee Craig Middlebrooks (Billy Eichner), and Councilman Jeremy Jamm (Jon Glaser), among others.

"What I love about the show is it keeps expanding," Amy Poehler says. "So, suddenly in season five, you're like, 'Here comes Jeremy Jamm!' Characters came in just when you were getting sick of everybody. And we gave them so much real estate; it was fun to play with them."

* * *

When Mande joined the show, he was awestruck to witness the smoothly running, but constant, treadmill of an operation churning out twenty-plus episodes per season deep into its run. He and his fellow writers would be breaking stories upstairs for episode 11 while the cast shot episode 8 two floors below. "It's such a machine," Mande says.

Mande had gone to Emerson College, which has a prestigious media arts program, with writer Harris Wittels, who had been with *Parks and Rec* since the second season. Mande met Wittels on his first day of college, and they have remained friends ever since. "He was also one of the most competitive, frustrating people I'll ever know," Mande says.

Instead of moving to Los Angeles after graduating, like Wittels, Mande had moved to New York to do stand-up; he eventually opened for Aziz Ansari. Mande, in his modest mindset, believed that Schur had called him in to interview for *Parks and Rec* just to pump him for embarrassing stories about Wittels.

After Mande left on the day of his interview, Wittels came into Schur's office and asked, "What was that about?" When Schur said he was considering hiring Mande, Wittels said, "I just want you to know Joe and I went to college together. We're kind of competitive."

Schur asked, "Well, do you think he's funny?"

Wittels said yes.

"Well, did he sleep with your girlfriend or anything?"

"No," Wittels said, "nothing like that."

In Mande's mind, he thought Wittels would *like* having another Emerson person around to counteract so much *Harvard Lampoon* energy in the room; Mike Schur, Dave King, Greg Daniels, Alan Yang, Matt Murray, and Aisha Muharrar had all gone to Harvard. "But actually, it was the opposite," Mande says. "I think in his mind, he was like, 'I'm the Emerson person. You can't add another one of me.'"

Despite Wittels's friendly objection, for the fifth season of *Parks and Rec*, Schur hired Mande alongside Megan Amram and Jen Statsky. Mande, who had never written for a sitcom before, sat back and observed for his first few weeks on the job before he started pitching ideas. "But once I got a handle on it, I felt like I was in a safe space," he says. "I felt at home." Soon he wrote "Emergency Response," the lead-up to Ben and Leslie's wedding, and the episode that introduced Mona-Lisa, "Bailout."

Then he confronted the biggest challenge of his sitcom writing career thus far. About halfway through the season, NBC "gifted" the series an extra episode, taking the order from twenty-one to twenty-two total. The writers had already plotted the season, with carefully crafted character arcs. Mande and Yang would take the bullet, writing a random episode that had no storyline tethers to anything that came before or after it.

They did it, but with mixed results. In "Swing Vote," Leslie and Ron disagree over funding a new miniature golf course. They compete for the deciding vote of the always-good-for-a-laugh Jeremy Jamm—naturally, by playing miniature golf. "It was frustrating, because we couldn't interfere with any of the ongoing episodes," Mande says. "It was like, 'What is this weird episode?'" Unfortunately for Mande and Yang, the Golden Age of TV recap culture had dawned online, and *The Onion*'s AV Club was watching, and judging, and literally grading, their every move.

"It was really hard work for us to fit this particular episode in," Mande says. "And then all the reviews of that episode were like: D!" Their main criticism: The episode didn't feel like a seamless part of the season. Mande says, "We were just like, 'Well, it's not.'"

For the record, Mande's memory is grading on a negative curve. AV Club actually gave the episode a C+ and said: "What does *Parks And Recreation* look like when nothing really happens? Well, given the fact that it's almost an inevitability that it'll get renewed, it's a valid question, because there are only so many weeks when things can be advanced to such a degree that the plot becomes central to the episode. 'Swing Vote' is an example of an episode where its outcome isn't contingent on the larger story, and its execution is enough to label it a *Parks* episode, but not enough to make it memorable." In fact, this signified how far sitcoms had come in the years that *Parks* had been on, and a change it had pioneered in the format: the expectation of propulsive serialization.

Still, he and Yang would always joke that they wrote the show's "worst-rated episode," which is an indicator of how high standards had become for *Parks and Rec.*

Despite the challenges, Mande felt that working on the show grounded and focused him in life-changing ways. "It taught me how to write for a large audience and to channel my thoughts in a constructive way," he says. "I learned how to write TV properly there. And it was good for me to work on a show that was positive. Mike is very smart in that he hires people that don't agree with him, to have differing voices in the room. It's funny to have myself, or Dave King, or Harris Wittels, some real dark minds, in that room." In fact, Schur would joke that he sometimes worried about the person Mande could have become if he didn't get that job.

Mande felt it was a dream of a first writing gig. "Especially for me and the people who showed up later in the life of the show, we weren't even there for the growing pains," he says. "By the time we showed up, it was like bowling with bumpers. Like: Writing for TV is easy!"

* * *

Fellow new writer Jen Statsky, who was twenty-seven at the time, had been writing for *Late Night with Jimmy Fallon*, crafting monologues. "It was a great training ground," she says. "You have to write a bunch of jokes every day by a very early time in the morning to tape at five p.m." But she had grown up watching sitcoms, particularly *The Mary Tyler Moore Show*, on Nick at Nite, and dreamed of writing for one someday. She had hit the jackpot on her first try, landing at her favorite series, *Parks and Rec*; *30 Rock* came a close second, which made sense, given both shows' obvious similarities to *The Mary Tyler Moore Show*.

Statsky admired Leslie Knope as a character. "As funny as she is, there's a tremendous amount of dignity and integrity with Leslie Knope," she says. "One of my favorite qualities in a person is caring deeply about a cause or about their friends, and moving through life really knowing that. She cares about her town, she cares about her friends, she cares about everything. That in a comedy is so revolutionary, because it's really hard to do. It's way easier to do comedy about characters who are apathetic or mean and don't care about things. But to do a comedy where the main character's trait is that they care so much, it's unique."

She got the job thanks to Twitter. She and Schur had followed each other for a while and began joking back and forth ("back when Twitter wasn't a hellscape," Statsky says). She tweeted something "about Mitt Romney's wife and throw pillows," she says, that caught Schur's eye and made him think he liked her comedy writing style. When she quit *Fallon* and went to Los Angeles for TV staffing season in 2013, she met with Schur and landed the job.

Megan Amram, too, ended up on *Parks and Rec* via Twitter. She had been tweeting since 2010, throwing out jokes to practice her comedy and possibly get noticed. It worked. When she got a meeting with Schur in 2012, she couldn't believe it. "I did not think it would happen," she says of getting hired on the show. "I was so prepared to move back home and work at Nordstrom in Tigard, Oregon. It did feel like being in *A Star Is Born* or something."

It impressed Statsky that Schur had hired two young women off Twitter. "It's a testament to Mike and what Twitter used to be," she says. "It really democratized the process of comedy writing, because it allowed people who were just funny to have their jokes seen on the internet in the same way making sketch videos and now making a TikTok comedy does."

Schur's appreciation for the form showed, Statsky says, that "he believes a good idea can come from anywhere and anyone. A good comedy writer doesn't have to come from the same three agencies who are going to send you scripts from people. You always want to be conscious of trying to find people who are outside of the system, because there are really wonderful, unique voices out there." Beyond, that is, the Emerson and *Lampoon* pipelines.

Having grown up in a suburb of Portland called Beaverton, Amram felt a connection to Pawnee. "One of the things I think is so amazing about *Parks and Rec* is how people in small ponds or medium ponds, not in a derogatory sense, find so much meaning and importance in the level of work that they are doing," she says. She also drew inspiration from the "absolute weirdos in Oregon. Not just in the *Portlandia* hipsters kind of way. There are people living in the woods. There are people selling raw granola and meat out of the back of their cars. It was very helpful for writing *Parks and Rec*."

Like Statsky, she also saw Leslie as a role model. "I've been really ambitious my whole life," she says. "And I think ambition is something that often, especially in the context of a woman, is seen as a derogatory thing. It's seen as meaning you're not maternal, or you don't have your priorities straight. This was a beautiful, optimistic view of a woman who manages to get power and then also to bring up all her friends with her."

Amram came to the show at twenty-four years old, terrified. She thought, "These are all the real writers and I'm writing fan fiction of a show that I love." That said, she also felt welcomed, and could sense that the writers were still inventing: "We were always trying out new, weird stuff."

The room scared Statsky, too. She rewatched the entire series to prepare and thought, "This show is so smart and funny and good, and . . . *oh my god*." When she got to the room, she saw how much she had to learn, given that it was her first narrative, half-hour writing job. "I went through it that year in terms of trying to fit in and find my place and not freak myself out," she says. "So many people in that room are really smart *Harvard Lampoon* people, and I think I had a complex about being an outside-of-Boston public-school kid." She did go to New York University, which isn't exactly down-market, but her self-effacement is a product not only of her insecurity but also of Harvard's choke hold on the TV comedy writing business at the time.

The writers would play a game called Sporcle at lunch, an online trivia quiz based on naming every country in the world, and Statsky would blanch, thinking, *I'm not smart enough. I don't know all the countries.* She found herself studying world maps in her off time just to write for *Parks and Rec*. "I needed to trust that I was there because of my own voice and because of what Mike saw," she says. "I needed to find my own lane. And credit to Mike, because sometimes that takes a little bit, and some showrunners aren't as patient."

Statsky was also startled by what the job really looked like, day-to-day. "A writers' room is just an eight-hour-plus-long meeting," she says. "I wasn't prepared for how it was just one long daily conversation, and learning to listen and pick your spots where you talked." She would have days when she'd be driving home and would think to herself, "Did I talk today?"

The new and old writers together further expanded the world of Pawnee by dreaming up new romances. By the fifth season, they decided it was time for Ron to have a sane relationship, unlike his disastrous marriages to the two Tammys. "Once we had played those two romances for comedy, with Megan Mullally and Patricia Clarkson, it was like, 'Well, this guy deserves happiness, too,'" Schur says. They began to ponder what kind of woman would make Ron happy. "We designed a character who's a single mom and educator, tough as nails, doesn't take shit from anyone, just a grown-up woman who is every bit his equal in terms of her self-possession," Schur says. That was Diane, played by Lucy Lawless.

Amram loved the match, particularly because Diane also came with two young, chaotic daughters. "It takes a little getting used to, the idea of Ron as a family man, because he is portraying this hypermasculine lone-wolf thing," she says. "But the people in my life who are most like Ron Swanson, I do think there's a gooey core to them. They really just want a domestic life and to be taken care of and to be able to take care of other people. So it fit for the character to me."

Guest stars provided another way to expand the *Parks and Rec* world, even those who weren't romantic possibilities for the main characters.

And while the show had welcomed many recognizable actors over the years, like Paul Rudd and Kathryn Hahn, in 2012 it landed a true dream guest star, if only for Nick Offerman: Maine furniture maker Chris Becksvoort.

Perhaps this didn't make headlines in *The Hollywood Reporter*, but it was a big deal in woodworking circles. An expert in Shaker furniture, he was known across the world for his exceptional work and had made, for instance, a music stand for cellist Yo-Yo Ma. Offerman had read Becksvoort's articles in *Fine Woodworking* magazine and invited him to appear on the show.

Becksvoort's cameo appearance happens in an episode set at the Indiana Fine Woodworking Awards. At first, the script called for him to simply walk through the scene, but Offerman asked the writers to add a few lines so that he got a shout-out. In Ron's most excited on-screen moment since the introduction of Li'l Sebastian, he exclaims, between nervous giggles, "Mary Mother of God, that's Christian Becksvoort! He's the modern master of the Shaker style. I never dreamed that I would see him in the flesh."

It caused quite a stir in Becksvoort's hometown of New Gloucester. "They pick you up at the airport in a limo and it's unbelievable," he told the *Bangor Daily News* in an article on his TV debut. "The money they throw at those shows for a half hour [of finished video] is amazing." But he did not relish the filming process, which he described as alternating periods of "intense activity" and "waiting around." He earned $8 per hour, the standard rate for what was essentially a background role, though he was fine with that since he'd been flown out and fed on set.

A very different cameo came as a surprise, on another trip Morgan Sackett finagled from their modest budget, this time to Indianapolis.

In December 2012, recent GOP primary presidential candidate Newt Gingrich was on a trip to visit Indiana governor Mike Pence when he stopped by the St. Elmo Steak House in Indianapolis for lunch, not realizing it was a dinner-only establishment. He'd seen several trucks and cars in the parking lot, so he assumed it was open for business—but those vehicles belonged to the cast and crew from *Parks and Rec* who were filming there on location for the episode "Two Parties," when Chris Traeger throws a bachelor party in the city for all the male characters on the show after discovering none of them had had one.

This Indianapolis location shoot started with Andy's love for the Indianapolis Colts, who had previously given the series permission to use their jersey for Andy to wear. The production had subsequently tried to work with the NFL to get a player as a guest star, but scheduling had never lined up. The NFL told them there was no chance at a name player like quarterback Andrew Luck or receiver Reggie Wayne.

Then Rob Lowe mentioned that among the many famous and connected people he knew was Jim Irsay, the owner of the Colts. The producers decided to ditch the NFL and go the direct route, making a pitch to Irsay to get some players and offering to put him in the show as well.

Suddenly a few producers, writers, and crew, along with the main male cast members, were going to Indianapolis for a few days of what felt almost like a real bachelor-party weekend. They went to a Colts game. The guys got to play on the field with some of the Colts, including new quarterback and first-overall draft pick Luck.

"The guys were so funny together," writer Dave King recalls. "Rob Lowe I remember being so in the moment for every take. He loved it."

Then they hit St. Elmo Steak House, a real Indianapolis institution that has no relationship to the iconic Rob Lowe film *St. Elmo's Fire* but was meant to appeal to Ron. The production was shooting there during the day, when the restaurant was closed for business.

They were taken aback when Republican presidential candidate Newt Gingrich walked in. The restaurant staff was in the process of telling Gingrich that they were closed but that he could go to their sister restaurant nearby, when Sackett, who was producing on location, heard the interaction and recognized the politician. He offered to walk Gingrich over to the other establishment. As they walked, they passed by the motor home where the cast was waiting while the crew set up the lighting inside the restaurant. Sackett brought Gingrich in to introduce him to the stars. After some pleasantries, Lowe suggested Gingrich appear in the scene.

"I guess I could," Sackett remembers Gingrich saying.

Sackett called Schur and the episode's writer, King, from the motor home; the two were on set in the restaurant. Was there something Gingrich could do?

King felt a moment of hesitation. Did he want to be responsible for putting this guy in the show? While in the US House, Gingrich, a major Republican player, had coauthored the 1994 "Contract with America" that proposed reducing the size of government, cutting taxes, and axing welfare reform, and helped Republicans sweep the midterm elections that year.

"But we had a policy of real-world leaders are welcome," King says. So the team ducked into the trailer with the actors to pitch ideas.

The way King remembers it, Ansari pitched a bit about the similarity between Gingrich and Gergich, Jerry's last name. The scene would go like this: Jerry is sitting at a table that turns out to be Gingrich's, and when Jerry suggests that they might be related, Gingrich scoffs. King appreciated the simplicity and brevity: "Great. Done. He can say one line and we're out of there."

"It was great fun," Gingrich told ABC News when word got out about the run-in. "Always fun to do something like that!" He added modestly, "I had a small role on a Candice Bergen show many years back."

He was referring to the time when he quite famously appeared on the CBS sitcom *Murphy Brown* after Bergen's title character became a political flashpoint in the 1992 presidential election. Vice President Dan Quayle singled her out as a bad example because she had a child out of wedlock. In a bit of stunt casting, Gingrich appeared on a 1996 episode when he was the Speaker of the House, encountering Murphy backstage just after she criticized him during the show's "Presscapade" dinner.

It was hyped as a sitcom showdown, but the exchange erred on the side of affable. "That was quite a speech," and "I can take a little ribbing" he said in his major lines. During on-set interviews, Gingrich and Bergen engaged in a full-on lovefest.

"Ever since I saw *The Wind and the Lion,* I said I'd go to any length to be in the same room" with Bergen, Gingrich said.

Bergen countered: "He did it so quickly, he's a natural talent." When they finished, Bergen gifted Gingrich with a *Murphy Brown* baseball cap and T-shirt. Afterward, *The Washington Post*'s Sharon Waxman wrote, "They promised viewers a rumble, but it was more like a romp."

When word got out about Gingrich on *Parks and Rec*, some speculation ensued that he had purposely tried to get on the show. "But that doesn't seem like it would be worth his time," King says. Having transformed Congress in the nineties and lost a recent presidential bid, perhaps his main goal was now to be on an NBC sitcom with middling ratings? "Like he had been previously spotted around Silvercup Studios trying to get a cameo on *30 Rock* and it didn't work," King jokes. "I don't think that was it." Sackett, however, figures there's a slight chance that Gingrich's young staffers were fans and were responsible for sending him over to the steak house, hoping for exactly what happened—a spontaneous cameo.

Model Christie Brinkley, who was among the more traditional high-profile guest stars, showed up during a long-awaited glimpse at Jerry's home life. "I was one of many who were like, he *has* to have a great home life," writer Katie Dippold says. "There cannot be a joke about his home life ever." We meet his often-mentioned wife, at last, in the Christmas 2012 episode: Gayle was played by Brinkley, to the shock of Jerry's bullying colleagues, and his home life looks idyllic, filled with loving children and piano sing-alongs. The joke, for once, was on everyone *but* Jerry.

Recurring guest stars continued to steal moments, expanding on their characters. In "Emergency Response," Joan Callamezzo appears on the set of *Pawnee Today* hungover, and likely still drunk, from a booze cruise, when she's supposed to interview Ron about the upcoming fundraiser for a new park. While Joan remains colorfully incapacitated, Ron takes viewer calls on his own. Mo Collins loved working with Dean Holland, who, as the episode's director, encouraged her to keep finding different ways of being passed out, "so I just got crazier and crazier," she says. Dressed in a leopard-print dress, Joan lies face-down on the floor. Then she's splayed across two chairs, then she's lying face-up across them, then face-down, almost as if doing a version of plank pose suspended on the arm rests. She ends up underneath the coffee table, only her bare feet visible as they reach to pick up a carton of coconut water on top of the table.

In the moment, she thought, "This is well beyond the reality of what that world could be. It's not real anymore. I'm *planking.* But that's the miracle of Dean as director. He somehow put this montage together, and people bought it. I found it so beautiful, this symbiotic play between director and actors and then just compiling this perfect piece of television comedy." She adds, "I have always loved physical comedy, so anytime anybody gives me room to play like that, I'm in heaven."

Jason Mantzoukas's Dennis Feinstein also grew in screen presence. In one improv-heavy scene, when Ben, Tom, and Andy visit him to ask for a donation to the Sweetums Foundation, the fragrance mogul says, in all sincerity, "I don't like charity. I don't get it. It feels to me like I'm giving money away and getting nothing in return." Still, he sees the chance to make them grovel, so he proposes "goin' out." But first, they have to "scent up," he says, referring to the multitude of fragrance bottles on the table in front of them.

"I call dibs on Ooze!" Tom says in one take.

"I've got Insert," Ben says.

When he asks why it's called that, Mantzoukas as Dennis says offhandedly, "Oh, because it's been in someone." At this, all the actors broke character and dissolved into uncontrollable laughter. The scene would make the DVD blooper reel. "The blooper reel, to me, says it all," Mantzoukas says. "You are watching people delight in the work. And that is what I think they've done incredibly well, is create an environment that is really fun, not just for the show, but with each other."

They had run that scene many times while shooting, with writers shouting out cologne names from the sidelines. "That is what made working on that set so fun and special," Mantzoukas says. "It's not just, okay, we got it, moving on. It's like, 'Let's now take fifteen minutes and do it two more times and just see.' And then it becomes a really fun mix of a writers' room and an improv show—and you've got some of the smartest people in the world pitching you some of the funniest jokes. Then you've got some of the funniest actors in the world saying funny stuff."

Mantzoukas was always excited to get the call from *Parks and Rec* asking if he was available. "It's not just funny people being funny for camera, it's funny people being funny for each other," he says. "I think what people really respond to in *Parks* is that they are accurately capturing not just impeccably written jokes and beautifully performed characters, but you're also watching people genuinely like and be delighted by each other."

Even as the broadcast TV business was growing more cutthroat, *Parks and Rec* had become a fixture of the NBC lineup, against all odds, no longer an underdog.

The major broadcast networks were now freaking out about the incursion of original cable programming and the effects of digital video recorders on their live ratings. In those early days of DVRs, the time-delayed viewers weren't counted at all; they were counted in a special measure called "Live+7" ratings, i.e., the live viewers combined with time-delayed viewers over the following seven days. But advertisers cared most about the live viewers who had to watch their commercials. Occasional new hits emerged, like *Modern Family* and *Once Upon a Time*, but network ratings were shrinking overall. In May 2013, broadcasters responded with some bold programming strategies as they announced their plans for the following fall. ABC, CBS, Fox, and NBC would run thirteen new comedies, more than they had in at least ten years.

But *Parks and Rec* stayed in NBC's crown-jewel Thursday comedy lineup, becoming the opener in the 8 p.m. Eastern time slot, and, in fact, the anchor of the night now that *30 Rock* and *The Office* had finished their runs. It would go up against CBS's mass hit *The Big Bang Theory*, which averaged nineteen million viewers per week, six times as many as *Parks and Rec*.

Parks and Rec now led into *Welcome to the Family*, about a cross-cultural teen couple facing unexpected pregnancy; *Sean Saves the World*, starring *Will & Grace*'s Sean Hayes as a single dad; and *The Michael J. Fox Show*, featuring Fox as a version of himself, a family man with Parkinson's. The network ran ads on the sides of Los Angeles buses touting "NBC's New Family of Comedies" to hype the season, hoping to evoke the spirit of its past victories, such as *Cheers* and *The Cosby Show*, *Seinfeld* and *Friends*.

Parks and Rec had arrived, after several mighty battles, at a sixth season. "After a precarious start," the *Los Angeles Times* said, "the show once thought of as little more than a knockoff of 'The Office' managed to form an identity with its style of humor—a mix of silly funny (e.g. those tastefully tasteless murals) and charmingly sweet; a fitting recruit to stand alongside the network's other faster-paced, niche comedies, 'The Office' and '30 Rock.'"

But not all the major characters would last. Rob Lowe got a call from Rashida Jones, who had just starred in and cowritten the film *Celeste and Jesse Forever.* She was gaining traction around her writing career, and, she explained to Lowe, she was about to write a new *Toy Story* movie, her dream job. She had asked Schur to be released from her contract to do it, and he agreed.

Lowe, hearing about all this, thought, "Oh, well, this will be the end of Chris Traeger as well." He proved right. The writers felt like Chris would be hard to write without her. "And I was okay with Chris being a casualty of Rashida's writing career," Lowe says.

Their characters, Ann and Chris, had begun dating back in season 3 after Ann drunkenly kissed him at April's twenty-first birthday party. But after a few months, Chris broke up with her—so nicely that she didn't realize at first that he'd broken up with her. (Or she's so unused to being broken up with that it doesn't register; probably a bit of both.) Over the following seasons, she'd had a notoriously bad dating life, often taking on the personalities of whomever she was seeing at the time. This culminated in her attempting a relationship with Tom, then finally deciding she wanted to have a child—on her own. After she asked Chris to be her sperm donor—who wouldn't want those genetics?—the two ultimately reunited in romance.

Lowe and Jones announced their impending departure from the series in July 2013. Schur issued a statement saying, "Heading into this year, with the two of them contemplating parenthood, it felt like the natural time to move them into the next phase." Their characters would say goodbye to Pawnee together, moving to Michigan to raise their child.

Some writers also left in the 2013–2014 TV season to launch a new show, *Brooklyn Nine-Nine*, cocreated by Schur and Dan Goor. It shot on the same lot, despite the show's setting in Brooklyn, so Schur could be involved in both; Goor would often still stop by the *Parks and Rec* set and pitch a few jokes (like the seed for Patton Oswalt's *Star Wars* monologue). Norm Hiscock joined Goor in dedicating most of his time to the new show. Goor served as showrunner at the new series, a position he felt confident in after learning from Daniels and Schur.

Goor and Schur had been meeting regularly for a while to talk about ideas they could develop into a show together, just as Daniels and Schur had once developed *Parks and Rec*. "Very early on I pitched the idea of a police station, and we coalesced around it almost immediately," Goor recalls. "I felt like we could do a show that was like *Parks* in a lot of ways, but without the barrier to entry. People don't know about local government; they don't know about environmental impact reports and stuff."

He had gotten frustrated with having to insert talking heads into *Parks* episodes in which a character explains an aspect of local government. So, he thought, if a show starts by establishing that it's at a police station, then one character says to another, "We've got a murder to solve," audiences would know what was happening in mere seconds. There hadn't been a network TV comedy about police officers since the 1970s' *Barney Miller*.

Parks and Rec had now spawned its own non-spin-off spin-off, just as *The Office* had done before it.

The show also expanded beyond the United States. Having traveled to the Grand Canyon, Indianapolis, and Washington, DC, the producers now finagled a deal to go to Europe—not so much because it was necessary, or because it was cool, but because they wanted to help keep Chris Pratt on the show as much as possible despite his burgeoning film career.

In the spring of 2013, the producers heard from Pratt's manager that the actor was up for a Marvel movie, and NBC Universal didn't want to let him out of his *Parks and Rec* contract to do it. Technically, his contract kept the show in "first position," meaning that his first obligation had to be to *Parks and Rec*. If a film wanted him enough, *Parks and Rec* could force that production to work around them. Even when it was Marvel.

On the other hand, NBC hadn't officially picked up *Parks and Rec* for another season yet. And the producers didn't want to stop any of their cast from doing something they wanted to do, especially when the show wasn't a sure thing. Despite the show's newfound security with the network, as usual, their renewal remained a question, and the producers understood this as well as the actors did—they sometimes took jobs in between seasons just in case. Sackett, for instance, had worked on the 2011 pilot for the comedy *Suburgatory*, starring Jeremy Sisto and Jane Levy as a single dad and daughter who move from the big city to the suburbs. He had to quit when *Parks and Rec* came back.

Despite the network's misgivings, the producers gave Pratt their blessing. He landed the role, and they made a deal with Marvel: Pratt would miss the first several episodes of the season, then he'd fly back to Los Angeles and shoot on a long weekend from Thursday to Tuesday to get him into some episodes. Filming on the movie would begin in July 2013 in England.

"Pratt's the nicest guy on the planet," Holland says. "He never asks for anything. Obviously, we're going to let him do whatever he needs to do."

Holland was working on the fifth-season finale in the editing room with Schur when Schur told him, "We're going to lose Pratt for ten episodes." (The producers' recollections of the exact number vary from eight to twelve, so we'll go with ten here.) Pratt had been cast as

Peter Quill, who leads a group of extraterrestrial criminals on the run after stealing a valuable artifact in Marvel's *Guardians of the Galaxy*.

"Ten episodes?" Holland remembers saying. "He's the funniest fucking guy on the show. What are we going to do?" When Schur responded that he didn't know, Holland asked, "Where are they shooting?"

"They're shooting in London."

"Well, let's go to London!" Holland said.

From the editing bay, Schur yelled, "Morgan!"

When Sackett materialized, Holland and Schur told him they wanted to go to London for the sixth-season premiere. Could he work some of his magic?

Coincidentally, Sackett told them, he had just gotten a call from the British spirits company Diageo. Offerman and Schur had discovered a while back that they shared a love for Diageo's Lagavulin whiskey. The producers didn't want to put a generic whiskey bottle in a scene where Ron drinks, so they used a bottle of Lagavulin. "Nick thought we just had the best props department in the world because they knew that he liked Lagavulin," Sackett explains, "but it's really Mike Schur's favorite whiskey." A Diageo product placement rep had called Sackett to thank the show for putting Lagavulin in that episode. He asked if there was anything the company could do for them.

Now, Sackett had the answer: Diageo could help foot the bill to bring *Parks and Rec* to London.

Once the show was picked up for the new season, Sackett got to work making a string of deals. First, he asked Marvel to give up their star for two days *if* the show came to London. Sackett figured that the company assumed there was no chance some sitcom was really going to make it to London.

He got Diageo to agree to fly them out for a location shoot. Then he told the studio where they normally shot, CBS Radford, that they weren't going to pay for the first episode of the new season since they wouldn't be there. This saved substantial money, *and* now they'd have their star part-time, *plus* they'd be flown out for free. This appeared to be Sackett's greatest production miracle yet.

But at the last minute, NBC Universal balked when it realized what a large company Diageo is; the Lagavulin distillery is just a tiny part of it. NBC demanded a $10 million ad buy in exchange for the product placement. Diageo refused, and NBC told *Parks and Rec* it couldn't go. Having made all the arrangements, the producers decided to go anyway, scraping together enough money from the budget. "We kind of figured out all these other ways to pay for it," Sackett says.

And so the production ended up in the UK. "Among the team of heroes responsible for this beautiful piece of work, perhaps second after Mike is Morgan Sackett," Offerman intones with awe. "He quietly is the wizard of this entire production, where Mike is the creative dad. Morgan is the technical dad. Morgan gets the money from the company. And he does things like take us to London without getting extra money."

Poehler agrees, and offers her own metaphor: "Morgan, probably more than anyone, is the reason why we stayed on the air. Morgan kept the ship afloat. You know how there's the captain that's out on the deck with the hat, and then there's the person down below who's making sure that the ship actually gets to where it needs to be? That's Morgan."

The first two episodes of season 6 took place in and around London. And not only did the cast and crew get to shoot in London for about a week and go to "the Lagavulin goddamn distillery," as Offerman says, they also snuck off to Paris to do an even less authorized shoot of Ben and Leslie on a romantic trip.

Sackett planned the logistics with precision to get the most out of the trip. Offerman and a small crew went to Lagavulin to shoot Ron's dream tour. Pratt and Scott shot a scene in front of Buckingham Palace, which Andy mistakes for Hogwarts, the school where the *Harry Potter* series is set. "No, that's Buckingham Palace," Ben says. "Hogwarts is fictional. Do you know that? It's important to me that you know that."

Pratt appeared in another *Parks and Rec* scene with his *Guardians of the Galaxy* costar Peter Serafinowicz playing Lord Edgar Covington, while Sackett was orchestrating a sequence where Leslie and Ron go on a Jack the Ripper tour of London. Then the producers and Poehler and Scott got into cabs and raced to the Chunnel train to get to Paris, where Schur appeared in a cameo sitting next to Leslie and Ben at a sidewalk café.

The Paris episode would run many weeks after the London episode, but they had to bank it while they had the chance. This was an even stealthier mission on a trip that was already a stealth mission. No one at NBC knew it was happening. "The network didn't really know we went to France until we cut that into an episode five months later," Sackett says. "They were like, 'How are you in Paris?' And we were like, 'Oh, we went when we were in London.' They were all very surprised."

Season 6 also brought a major addition to *Parks and Rec* lore, the complicated game that Ben invents, Cones of Dunshire—a Settlers of Catan–meets–Dungeons & Dragons parody. After his congressional campaign job ended, Ben had been reluctantly working for Sweetums candy company, helping to improve their public image with charity outreach. But he'd been fired after Leslie criticized the company publicly, leaving him out of work once again, and feeling adrift. The last time he was unemployed, he made his epic, four-second Claymation film. The writers considered going back to Claymation but felt like the joke was done. Amram suggested Ben invent a new board game this time.

Schur told episode writer Dave King to "just go crazy, make it as intricate and ridiculous" as possible. King loved it: "The idea is Ben Wyatt has lost his mind again. So it was catnip for a writer. You didn't have to worry too much about the logic, but you wanted it to be clear that *he* was very concerned about the logic."

In the episode that introduces it, we do get a brief shot of the rules—printed on a paper meant to look like fake, aged parchment. King, who still gets excited talking about the game, wrote extensive rules. He admits, "It's kind of nonsensical, but I tried to make them at least not contradictory with each other." A blog post on the site of real-life game-maker Cephalofair tries to create a more complete version of the rules based on a screenshot of King's creation, and finds his work a bit wanting: "There's no way around it—the game as shown is a parody. It's showing a massively complicated board game from the perspective of an outsider to the hobby. This is how all hobby board games look to those uninitiated, blown up to the *n*th degree far into the realm of satire. I mean, 'Roll to see how much you roll?' Silliness!"

Still, the writers knew Cones of Dunshire would be the most memorable aspect of the episode, if not become a key part of *Parks and Rec* lore. In the pre-shoot "tone meeting" with the episode director, Julie Anne Robinson, King remembers Schur saying to her, "I cannot tell you how important the Cones of Dunshire is to us."

They also knew that Poehler and Scott could go wild with this setup. Schur told Robinson to let Scott do whatever he wanted, get B-roll of him playing with all the game pieces and showing them off to the camera. "I have one hundred percent faith that this will be fun and funny and memorable," he said, "so you can't overshoot this."

Poehler couldn't believe the level of detail. "What is wrong with you guys?" King recalls her saying. "You wrote all this stuff down? There's *another* alt you need to get in here?"

Scott instantly got it. "He felt like a guy who had spent two weeks doing nothing but tinkering with this game," King says. "One of the things I love about Adam Scott and the performance of Ben Wyatt is that he's able to play intelligent and nerdy and still feel very human. To me, he's very much like the intelligent people that I know and not the intelligent people that are portrayed on TV regularly. They still exist totally well in society. They're not shut-ins, and they're not awkward. One of the great overall choices that Adam made about that character is that he's a *real* nerd and not, like, a *nerd* nerd."

Surely he couldn't be referring to the show's time-slot rival, *The Big Bang Theory*.

Pawnee also literally expanded by merging with Eagleton. New writer Jen Statsky took on the episode "The Wall," in which Leslie holds a press conference announcing the Unity Concert and arranges for a photo op of two Eagletonians striking the fence between the two towns to "tear down the wall," like the Berlin Wall falling in 1989. It turns into a classic Leslie gaffe when they accidentally hit a beehive, causing an angry swarm. "We were really influenced by a viral video of Oprah where she's screaming, 'Bees!' and someone added VFX bees into it," Statsky says, referring to a bit that originated on *Conan*, which mocked the "Oprah's Favorite Things" segment by combining it with her yelling, "Bees are coming!" as her audience is overcome by the insects.

Overall, however, Statsky also points out the important theme at the center of the storyline: "It's this story about a very divided place," she says, "two factions of people that are at odds and don't understand each other, and Leslie trying to get people to come to the middle and have some understanding."

Since Statsky was relatively new to the show, she was, she says, "freaking out on the inside" as she wrote the script. She had been in the writers' room for fourteen episodes and knew how a story document became an outline, then a script. Still, as she sat in her little bungalow in Silver Lake trying to write, she thought, *Can I do this?* "I felt a tremendous pressure to deliver," she says, "because I knew I was handing a script over to this person who was really a mentor to me."

Then it came time for her to cover the set—be present for the filming of her episode to answer any questions or pitch needed substitute jokes—which she had never done before. She hadn't spent much time on a set at all. When she got there for the first time, Poehler put her at ease, laughing at a joke she made in conversation. "She has such a good, big, warm laugh," Statsky says. "That was a career highlight, making Amy laugh, because she is such an important part of what I love about comedy."

Later, when Statsky became a showrunner herself, she would realize that she hadn't needed to be so nervous about it all. "The stakes felt really, really high," she says, "and they weren't. They were personally high for me, but looking back, I'm like, 'You had zero responsibility.'" But she loved the show and its people so much that she wanted badly to do right by them.

The show's sixth season held steady, ratings-wise, and received a 96 percent rating on Rotten Tomatoes, similar to the high marks the show had received since its second season (compared with 68 percent for the first). And Poehler won a Golden Globe for her performance as Leslie in January 2014. "Any kind of recognition was always a huge boost," she says. "For me, the fear of keeping the show on was always creeping in, and I thought, 'This will be good for everybody.'"

With the loss of two major characters, the cast had room for someone new. The producers decided to bring back Craig Middlebrooks, an anxious and loud-mouthed administrator who had joined the Pawnee parks department after the city's merger with Eagleton. He was played by Billy Eichner, who couldn't believe his luck at becoming a regular cast member. "They would laugh so hard at what I was doing during the table read," he says, "and they just made me feel like I belonged there, even though I didn't, necessarily."

It was, in fact, the first scripted show he'd ever been a part of. He had done some acting on camera as a child, but that was it. He had gone to theater school at Northwestern, and everything he did after that was live in New York. He had starred on his own TV series, *Billy on the Street*, in 2011, a game show–like format in which he asks random people on the streets of New York pop culture trivia questions. Ansari and Jones had appeared on Eichner's show, and Poehler, Pratt, and Offerman would follow.

"They were such a well-oiled machine at that point, so I really wanted to not embarrass myself and seem like I knew what I was doing, even though I didn't really, from a technical standpoint," Eichner says of joining *Parks and Rec*.

Schur first offered Eichner the role as an extension of his *Billy on the Street* persona in just one episode as one of the "doppelgängers," the equivalent staffers from the parks and recreation department in Eagleton who show up in the Pawnee office after the merger. He served, improbably, as Donna's doppelgänger, loud and anxious to her nonchalant. The twist: They love each other. "That was a really big deal for me, just to do the one episode," Eichner says.

The producers mentioned that they might want him to return for one more episode, which he was happy to do. But soon he heard from his manager that they might want him for even more since Jones and Lowe were leaving. He was flabbergasted when Schur asked him to join the cast as a regular for the seventh season. His character, he knew, "had such a different energy than the rest of the show, which was known for being this rather sophisticated, gentle, elegantly written and performed show."

Eichner admits that Craig was "a shrill, over-the-top guy. I think it was fun for them to have this wild guy who was the opposite of the world they created. I imagine, having worked on a show for a long period of time, it is fun to throw in a wild card like that, even if it's divisive. You don't care at that point, because it's fun to have a new toy."

But he worried that his character was "upsetting the tone of the show," even though the writers had made a conscious decision to bring him on. "All of Craig's lines were written with five exclamation points at the end, or written in all caps," he says. One of Eichner's favorite Craig lines happens when he's come to proudly report to the team that he's sold everything on the list to raise money for the upcoming Unity Concert. He finds, however, that Ben and Leslie have just announced that they're having triplets. "FIRST MY COUSIN WINONA GETS INTO A CAR ACCIDENT THE NIGHT MY ONE-MAN SHOW OPENS AND NOW THIS? WHY ARE MY ACCOMPLISHMENTS ALWAYS OVERSHADOWED?" he bellows, before muttering a congratulations and storming out.

"Not many of us would say that out loud in the moment, but a lot of us feel that way," Eichner says. "So that's how I rationalize Craig's behavior. It's everyone's id brought to the surface."

And indeed, fans did find him to be . . . an acquired taste. "Certain fans online thought that Craig was the funniest thing on the show, and then certain fans thought he ruined the show," Eichner says. "I completely understood that. It is a little hard to imagine that character existing that way in real life."

Billy on the Street had gotten him used to being a divisive figure on television. But he understood why it was harder to bring that persona to a well-established sitcom that wasn't about him. "It's always a bit jarring to read negative things about yourself," he says, "but sometimes I agreed with them, is the truth of the matter."

When the producers told him they wanted to bring him back for the next season as a series regular, he wanted the job, but he did call Schur to discuss the character. After thanking Schur for the opportunity and emphasizing that he wanted to do it, he said, "The character is really out of control, and the rest of the show is so grounded and beautiful. And if I'm going to come back, we need to bring him down to earth a little bit. Maybe it's my limitations as an actor, but I don't know how to play him at this level and have it feel real."

Eichner remembers Schur responding, "I knew you were calling me about this before I even picked up the phone. Let's brainstorm ways to bring him back down to earth in a way that keeps him funny but makes him a little more human and more relatable."

Schur invited Eichner, who also wrote his own material in other contexts, to visit the writers' room to hash out how Craig could progress for the next season. They came up with the idea that Craig goes to anger-management class between seasons. He could still have occasional outbursts, but they could show him struggling to control them.

Unfortunately for Eichner, the seventh season would indeed end the series. Poehler and Schur decided in season 6 to close with the next season, presuming they got picked up again. Schur said at the time: "We both felt like all we really cared about was that we wanted to be the people who ended the show when we wanted to end it, ideally, if that were possible, and it felt like the time to do that would be at the end of season seven. . . . For whatever reason, our gut was saying: One more season."

There were also more practical business considerations. *Parks and Rec* had not, in the end, matched the popularity of *The Office*, which is why it was always in danger of cancellation—and why ending with the seventh season made sense. *The Office* sold easily into syndication, which allowed for higher salaries for the cast and more seasons on the air. It had lasted for nine seasons this way, losing only Steve Carell before it was through. With its sixth season, *Parks* had only just made it over the hundred-episode benchmark considered standard for syndication sales, and had recently begun airing off-network on WGN America—a bit too little, too late to make a difference. *The Office* was successful enough to sell into syndication when it was still airing new episodes on NBC, debuting in reruns on Fox-owned stations in September 2009, when the series was in its sixth season. On *Parks*, Daniels says, "We didn't have that pot of gold to pay the actors with to extend their contracts. So their contracts were just up at the end of season seven, and then that was the end." In other words, making it past season 7 is a milestone for any show, and trying to push past that would be pushing luck that *Parks* didn't quite have to spare.

The cast, producers, and crew regretted only one thing about this decision: that they wouldn't get to hang out together all the time anymore.

However, they didn't know for sure that NBC would allow them a seventh season, so Schur plotted out a sixth-season finale that *could* be a series finale. He had done this four times previously, with the season 3 finale ("Li'l Sebastian"), the season 4 finale ("Win, Lose, or Draw"), and twice in season 5 ("Leslie and Ben," "Are You Better Off?"). This time, Leslie would take a job with the National Parks Service.

The network agreed to a seventh and final season. "We were like,

'We know it's not up to us entirely because you guys own the show, but in our perfect world, here's how it would go,'" Schur said, "and we laid out the whole plan, and they were like, 'Sounds great!' It kind of dovetailed very nicely with what they were imagining the future of the show was. I mean, we were preparing for an hourlong discussion and it was like three minutes. . . . It was just this wonderful thing. I don't know if I'll ever be that lucky again, that the creative team got together over the course of many months, picked a plan for how to end the show, and then the network was just like: Thumbs-up."

With this decision settled, the writers tweaked the script for the season 6 finale. In the two-parter, the *Parks and Rec* gang plans the Unity Concert to bring together citizens of Pawnee and Eagleton after the two merge. Another rousing *Parks and Rec* event production, this one would feature real-life musical guests such as the Decemberists, Ginuwine (long mentioned as Donna's cousin), Letters to Cleo (of Ben's T-shirt fame), Yo La Tengo as the fictional Bobby Knight Ranger, and Jeff Tweedy as the fictional lead singer of the band Land Ho! Meanwhile, Tom has a successful opening for his bistro. And, most important, Leslie accepts a job as the National Parks Service's Midwest regional director, with the blessing of a cameo from First Lady Michelle Obama.

The Unity Concert came together with such star power partly because of Mark Rivers, the show's resident songwriter, who was well-connected in indie music as a former member of the well-respected power pop band Cavedogs in the late eighties and early nineties. He helped to assemble the Unity Concert episode's lineup, and personally recruited Letters to Cleo.

Letters to Cleo lead singer Kay Hanley was charmed by the cast's friendliness. In the script, Hanley winked at Ben Wyatt as she played and he watched offstage, in a life-changing moment for him. During breaks from shooting that scene, Hanley was standing by the side of the stage, talking to Scott. Suddenly, she saw Poehler running toward her. Though Hanley assumed Poehler was running toward Scott, instead the actress stopped right in front of them and said, breathlessly, "Kay, I'm Amy." (This tracks. When I got on a Zoom with Poehler to talk about this book, she introduced herself, as if I didn't know who she was.)

Poehler continued, "I'm from Burlington, and I heard that you were from Dorchester, and we're both New Englanders. Thank you so much for being here." Hanley thought, "Are you fucking kidding me?"

After they shot that scene, someone from the production approached Hanley and said, "All right, so we'll see you at six a.m. tomorrow." She had no idea what he was talking about. "You're in two scenes tomorrow," he said. He showed her the call sheet, and she blanched. She knew she was a terrible actor, awful at delivering lines. But it turned out there were, in fact, lines. Two lines. The first came when she gets to Tom's restaurant for the after-party; Tom announces the arrival of a rock star, and she thanks him for having her.

She shared the scene with actor Henry Winkler, who played the Sapersteins' father. Every time the production cut and reset, she went back out the door with Winkler, and they hung out together for a few minutes. "Are you having fun?" he asked her at some point.

"Well, kind of," she remembers saying, "but I'm not an actor and I feel really self-conscious about saying this line."

"Oh my gosh, don't even worry about it," he said, proceeding to give her explicit advice about how to enter the scene and deliver her line.

Every time they reset and exited again, he'd ask how it had felt, and he'd rehearse with her again.

"He was the sweetest guy," she says, echoing a known fact in Hollywood. "Just a darling man who loves what he does."

Her fears about her acting skills intensified when she found that her other line in the episode had been cut. She was signing Ben's Letters to Cleo shirt at the bar, and Tom came over to ask if she was having a good time. She said something like, "Yeah, but can you keep this guy from asking me questions?" referring to Ben. At least they had kept her improvised hair flip, a move she was proud of.

The Unity Concert and Leslie landing a new job could have served as the series' end, but with the seventh-season order, the writers added a final scene, and it was daring.

It jumped ahead three years, to 2017. Leslie, now a mother of triplets, is running the National Parks' regional office from the revamped third floor of Pawnee City Hall. We see her confidently firing a problematic employee named Ed. Plenty of shows had done time jumps, and Schur loved the idea of skipping over a bunch of "common tropes in late-season sitcoms like new babies or new jobs," he said.

This one could prove risky, however, given the show's political milieu—and a looming real-life 2016 presidential election. But, in fact, they knowingly jumped ahead to 2017, beyond the Obama era that had defined the series. "We didn't want to deal with an election year," Schur says. They felt this in a general sense; they didn't yet know that Donald Trump would run and upend politics as we knew them. "We wanted to send the characters off into an unknown world," Schur says, "past the point where Obama was president."

The concept impressed the actors.

"It's a baller move," Aubrey Plaza said at the time.

Ansari said, "We need that B12 shot in the butt."

It scared Poehler a little, but she trusted Schur. Poehler, for her part, was happy not to be pregnant again on television; her new babies would show up as toddlers in the following season. Scott liked that it mimicked a scene from *Battlestar Galactica*. As Schur describes it: "They did a thing on *Battlestar Galactica* where they landed on a new planet. And they were starting a new society. The guy who was the sort of president of the colony sat down and put his head down in exhaustion on the desk, and [the camera] pushed into him. When [it] pulled out, it was a year later." This came as part of the settlement of New Caprica, led by newly elected president Dr. Gaius Baltar. The jump forward happens in the second-season episode "Lay Down Your Burdens." When the camera pulls back out from his head, we see that his office has been decorated in the ensuing time, and a staffer is currently before him, pestering him to make a decision.

Schur had done this on purpose, swiping *Battlestar*'s technique—or, put another way, paying homage to a very different kind of show about politics. In the scene, Leslie hangs a picture on the wall of her new office, and the camera pushes in. Then they "match cut"—cut to the same shot in a way that obviously means time has passed—and the camera pulls out, with text on the screen announcing "three years later." Now, the previously empty office is bustling. She asks for a file, and loses her temper with Ed, the worker who has failed to bring it to her.

In a fun surprise, *Mad Men* star Jon Hamm appears in the briefest of cameos as Ed. She fires him, and he leaves. "I just love the idea that we were telling the audience we just intentionally denied you three years of having Jon Hamm on the show," Schur says with a laugh.

Poehler had known Hamm for some time, so the stunt seemed plausible when the writers thought of it. Schur called Hamm and pitched the idea; Hamm agreed, often game for puncturing his suave Don Draper image. Schur wanted to keep it supersecret, though, because if word got out that Hamm was guest-starring, it would make news and blow the surprise.

Hamm's solution: "Oh, then I just won't tell anyone." He didn't inform his agents or his manager. He didn't sign a contract. He drove himself to the lot and walked in alone. He waited until it aired before he told his people anything. Then he filed the proper paperwork.

Parks and Rec was ending on its own terms. But as the unconventional Hamm cameo indicated, it still had plenty of surprises in store.

CHAPTER 11

"The Fruits of the Knope Agenda"

The Final Season

Amy Poehler felt more stress than she ever had in the previous six seasons of *Parks and Recreation*. Though her show was once counted on as a savior for the struggling NBC network, though the first season had been a critical disappointment, though every season had been threatened with cancellation, the seventh and final season was weighing most on her. "The last season, in many ways, was where I was most concerned about taking tender care of everything that we had built," she says, "and delivering for the audience because suddenly we felt like we had one that was watching." She worried about, she says, "saying goodbye in a proper way, like George Washington–style. I really, really cared. That kept me up at night a lot more than at the beginning of the show."

The creative team had determined that it was time to end with the 2015 season, with the radical idea of fast-forwarding the characters to 2017. Though the show's survival had never been certain, now the producers had the luxury to plan its conclusion. The final run would be quick, almost insultingly so: thirteen episodes from January to February 2015, with two installments airing each week. But at least they got to do it their way. Though the network didn't say so, it was an obvious compromise: allowing one of its most critically beloved shows with a relatively small, passionate fandom to go out on its own terms without messing with network ratings too much. Critic James Poniewozik wrote in *Time*: "If you recall the lengthy, loving sendoffs the network gave *The Office*, *Friends*, *Seinfeld*, even the low-rated *30 Rock*, this is . . . not that. This is an effort to give closure to a critically acclaimed, low-rated show, but as fast as possible short of tying it to a brick and throwing it through your window while peeling off in its Dad's Camaro."

The show had failed to achieve cultural domination in its time on the air, but it had survived some difficult headwinds. During its run, network TV comedy had begun to unravel, and American politics had begun to fray due to increasingly vicious partisanship, the antithesis of the ethos behind *Parks and Rec*. The ultimate anti–Leslie Knope, reality TV star Donald Trump, was threatening to run for president. His candidacy was largely treated as a joke, though it would be anything but. *Parks and Rec*, however, had endured, and now it had a chance to do its small part in nudging the nation toward the light, rather than the darkness.

"We're like Hoosiers, in that we stuck to our fundamentals, we put our head down and played our game," Poehler told *Entertainment Weekly* as the clock wound down. "We didn't get distracted by the noise. We had a team filled with clutch players that everybody underestimated. And Michael Schur is the Gene Hackman of television. At least that's how he introduced himself to me when we first met."

During the hiatus between the sixth and seventh seasons, Poehler started doubting the wisdom of the time-jump concept, which they'd committed themselves to with the sixth season's finale. She thought, "Oh no, is this going to be jokes about the future?" But she and Schur had a ritual: Every summer, Schur would call her to talk about what the next season would be like. This time, the call particularly reassured her.

"I don't think I'll ever have that feeling again," she says. "I guess the best way to describe it is if someone was able to tell you your child's future, and it was wonderful."

The final season's premiere, on January 13, 2015, introduces us to a newly hip and thriving Pawnee. We meet yet again Mo Collins's Joan Callamezzo, Jon Glaser's Councilman Jamm, and Megan Mullally's Tammy, in addition to all the main characters. We learn of perhaps the riskiest creative decision the producers made, riskier, even, than a time jump: A rift has developed between Leslie and Ron. During the previous three years, we come to realize, they had a falling out over an apartment building that Ron's new venture, Very Good Building Company, constructed on the site of Ann's old house. When we join them in 2017, they're still fighting. Leslie has set her sights on a parcel of land that she wants to turn into a national park, while Ron is working with tech giant Gryzzl to build a campus there.

It makes sense that Gryzzl wants to locate in Pawnee, given the changes we see. The town, in season 7, is "finally seeing the fruits of the Knope agenda," as *Dissent* magazine pointed out. "Leslie's hometown, which she had once described as 'overrun with raccoons and obese toddlers,' had become a miniature Brooklyn dotted with yoga studios, juice bars, and chic restaurants."

While the show avoided predicting future national politics, it couldn't resist some jokes about the future. Gryzzl is using Pawnee to beta test its drones, phones, and tablets, which Ron hates despite his professional relationship with the company. This plotline feels more prescient every day from the vantage point of 2025. "Our special-effects budget has gone up 15,000 percent, from $1 to $15,000," Schur joked to *Entertainment Weekly*. In other future news, the Bourne franchise has been rebooted with unlikely star Kevin James, Morgan Freeman is feuding with Shailene Woodley, and the Cubs won the World Series. (Imagine!)

The entire season was shot before it began airing, so in some ways, reaction from critics and fans didn't matter—like the first season, the last had no way to respond to public opinion. But the critical response skewed positive, even deferential. Critic Kevin Fallon, writing for the *Daily Beast*, called the time jump "both a creatively genius and a cruel move. . . . As awesome, surprising, and heartwarming as the two-part *Parks and Rec* season premiere was, that unshakable bit of cruelty underlied it. Watching Amy Poehler's Leslie Knope, Aubrey Plaza's April, Chris Pratt's Andy, and the rest of the *Parks* crew living their lives in 2017 was a tease. When 2017 comes around in our real lives, this batty, sweet, close-as-it-comes-to-perfectly-written sitcom will be gone—as will an entire comedy era."

The show had acquired both critical boosters and enthusiastic fans, while some in the cast were experiencing new levels of fame. The crew began to notice something interesting when they traveled to other places, like Chicago and Washington, DC, to shoot during this season. (This trip to DC was at least as star-studded as the last one, with Barbara Boxer and John McCain, again, as well as Madeleine Albright and Cory Booker.) In Chicago, while they filmed at Michigan Avenue near the Chicago River, in the shadow of the NBC building and the *Chicago Tribune* tower, a crowd had formed before they arrived. Fans were following them around and posting the locations on Twitter. Morgan Sackett remembers thinking, "Oh my god, this show is really beloved."

There was also the Chris Pratt factor. *Guardians of the Galaxy* had come out, and now two sets of fans greeted them wherever they went with him: "There were the *Parks and Rec* fans, which were a mellow, fun group and giddy to see us," Sackett says. "And then the Marvel fans are like a different level of autograph-seeker. Some of them, I think it's more of a business."

When Aziz Ansari and Pratt were shooting together, Ansari would give Pratt tips on dealing with fans: Always ask them their name and sign your autograph with a "to" so that it's not valuable to sell. That way, the person won't ask you to sign a bunch of things at once.

The writers knew this season was their last, so they went for every reveal and every guest star they'd ever dreamed of.

Legendary German filmmaker Werner Herzog, of all people, made a cameo in the first episode as Keg Jeggings, a man selling a haunted house that had been a holding cell for people who went insane on the assembly line at the local doll factory, complete with amenities such as three bomb shelters and a staircase to nowhere. "After forty-seven years living here, I decided to move to Orlando to be closer to Disney World," he deadpans in his dour German accent. In September 2014, just after filming it, Herzog made the casting announcement himself while speaking to a crowd at the Brooklyn Academy of Music. After explaining his role and his Disney World line, he added, "I've never seen the show, but I hope they kept some of it."

While it felt surprising to see him in the sunny world of *Parks and Rec*, Herzog frequently turned in cameos puncturing his serious image. He appeared on *The Boondocks* and *American Dad!*, and in the film *Penguins of Madagascar*, in similar capacities. "The joke around the room was that we got Werner Herzog, and Aubrey fully freaked him out," writer Joe Mande says.

The penultimate episode, "Two Funerals," reveals the oft-mentioned, but never seen, Mayor Walter Gunderson—when he dies. And he's played by Bill Murray, a twist similar to introducing Jon Hamm as a character, only to fire him. We see Murray in the casket and in a prerecorded video played at his funeral.

The producers had, back in season 3, considered casting then-California governor Arnold Schwarzenegger, who was friendly with Rob Lowe, as the mayor. But the former actor declined, saying he couldn't take the role while in office. Soon after, the cast and producers began joking that the only other person they'd consider for the role would be Bill Murray. Otherwise, they determined, it would be funnier to never show him.

Then, in commitment to a bit reminiscent of *Philly Justice,* they began what amounted to a campaign to get Murray on. In 2011, Poehler put out a public plea on *Late Night with Jimmy Fallon* to the actor, who was known for not having an agent, manager, or publicist: "Bill Murray, if you're listening, I will pay you $250 to do one episode of my show." Aubrey Plaza met him and encouraged him to come on. Then Poehler saw him and said the same thing. Then Murray and Plaza appeared in a film together, Roman Coppola's *A Glimpse Inside the Mind of Charles Swan III*, and she began lobbying him harder.

As the final season took shape, Plaza and Poehler both reached out to Murray, telling him the mayor was going to die and this was his final chance. Soon, Schur got a voicemail: "Hey, this is Bill Murray. I hear you might have some dead work for me." Still, no one truly believed it would happen until Murray showed up on set that day. In fact, the memorial scene had already been shot without him, just in case.

"Once he had agreed to do it, we thought: The coolest possible thing is just to have him lying in the coffin. That's the artistic choice," Schur told *Entertainment Weekly*. "*But* if you've got that guy around, you might as well try to get him to say something out loud, right?" So the writers came up with about thirty options for his video message. He did every one of them, then improvised two more. One of his improvs ended up as the final choice.

Afterward, he hung out on the set for three hours, observing the shoot and telling each of the actors his favorite moments of theirs in the show. They were all thrilled—he had been watching all along!

Everyone involved in the series knew their time doing this work they loved, with people they loved, to the greatest extreme, was growing short, so they savored every moment.

The episode "Save JJ's" has Leslie organizing a protest when fragrance mogul Dennis Feinstein buys JJ's Diner, her favorite place for waffles, and forces it to shut down. Actor Jason Mantzoukas says wistfully, "The scene when the protesters are protesting and I'm just screaming at them . . . The show gave me an opportunity to really be an industrialist, a villain, which I thought was absolutely delightful. I couldn't be more grateful for them letting me be as mustache-twirling as I could be." His one regret: "I play drums, and I was always pitching to somehow get into the show that Dennis Feinstein played drums for Duke Silver."

"William Henry Harrison" features an enormous visual joke, based on real history: the ten-foot-wide paper ball that US president William Henry Harrison's successful 1840 campaign scrawled slogans on and took from town to town, "keeping the ball rolling," as Harrison's supporters said. (Leslie discovers that Harrison may have had a hunting lodge on the land that she's trying to make into a National Park; the historical connection could strengthen her case for preservation.) "I love that shit," writer Megan Amram says. "The idea of making a trenchant comedy story out of that was a challenge, but then I also found it to be extremely fun."

In the same episode, Jerry—who's now going by Terry, in the running joke about confusion over what his name really is—fulfills his lifelong dream of becoming a notary public. An illness, he explains, made him realize he had to chase his dreams before it was too late. Amram, not one to take her work lightly, began the process of becoming a notary herself. "I kept doing the bit in the room that I wanted to make sure that the notary storyline—which was so small, there were like three scenes of it—was taken seriously," she says.

Then she reached the point where a background check was required to complete her notary certification, she says, "because you will become an employee of the United States government." Her lawyer begged her not to do it, since she'd have to file her taxes differently. She had arrived at the end of the bit. "For any of you out there trying to do it as a joke," she says of becoming a notary, "it's not worth it."

But, Amram adds seriously, "Not to be too highfalutin about it, but the show is about finding the meaning and pride in the most boring-seeming things that exist in our American life." And Terry, she says, "takes so much pride in being a public servant." In the end, Terry may in fact be the best the Pawnee government has to offer, aside from Ben and Leslie, who have their sights set on state and national office.

The next episode provides the biggest emotional relief of the final season. In "Leslie and Ron," a favorite of many of the cast and writers, the gang lures the two feuding characters into the Parks and Rec office and locks them in, with only a baby monitor to communicate with Ben, until they talk things out. Under various time stamps, we see the progression: At 10:04 p.m., they consider lying and telling Ben they reconciled, but then they fight over how to explain the reconciliation, and Leslie breaks the baby monitor. At 11:01 p.m., Leslie draws a timeline of important moments in their relationship, insisting on talking through each one of them. When Leslie concludes that their rivalry began when his company announced plans to tear down Ann's old house, Ron mutters, "That's not the whole story," then locks himself in his office.

Ron emerges at 1:57 a.m., and they start talking about more benign moments in their past, but then Ron, to avoid real confrontation, pulls the fire alarm, which sets off the sprinklers but is not, it turns out, connected to the fire department. (Their friends foresaw their tactics.) So they're drenched and still stuck.

Finally, at 3:37 a.m., wearing ridiculous spare clothing from around the office, they start to really talk over a bottle of Scotch. It emerges that Ron felt abandoned in the parks department when Terry and April left to work for Leslie, and Tom and Donna left to run their own businesses, Tom's Bistro and Reagle Meagle Realty. So he decided to ask Leslie for a job, and the two made plans for lunch. "Like I was coming to a whorehouse, like I was coming to debase myself with the ultimate indignity" is how Nick Offerman explains Ron's mental state in that moment. But Leslie forgot their plans and stood him up; he resentfully started his own business and held a grudge against Leslie ever since.

The team unlocks the door at 8 a.m. the following day to find Leslie and Ron drunk, Ron playing the saxophone to "We Didn't Start the Fire."

Poehler loved it. "We both were characters that often didn't get to technically misbehave," she says. "We were the characters you could push off of a lot. So the fact that we got to be ridiculous and misbehave and trash shit, and the silliness of that and the bonding of that, was so nice."

Offerman appreciated being part of an episode that carried the heft of so many years of relationship building. "All of the pipe that the writers had laid to make that pay off, in the way I hope it did, is one of the joys of this job," he says. "I don't know if it worked on the audience like it worked on me, but I suspect it did." He still gets choked up talking about it.

Soon it came time to marry Donna off to sensitive music teacher Joe, played by Keegan-Michael Key. That allowed for another showy guest star, Questlove as Donna's wedding-crashing estranged brother, Lavondrius. It also made way for Billy Eichner's favorite moment as Craig, when he sings Ritchie Valens's song "Donna" to her at her reception. When he'd talked to the writers about bringing Craig "down to earth," this was what he'd had in mind. He could actually *sing*. "I have a legitimate singing voice," Eichner says, "and at Northwestern I did a lot of musical theater."

He thought it was particularly funny to make Craig not only a good singer but a soft crooner instead of the belter you'd expect. He also liked that he got to sit on Christie Brinkley's lap since she was there as Gayle Gergich. "As a kid who grew up in the '80s," Eichner says, "it was really fun to be with her."

Kathryn Hahn's ruthless political adviser Jen Barkley shows up again, too, to persuade Ben to run for Congress in 2018. Hahn scored a fan favorite moment when she wears a poncho to Ben and Leslie's house because "every surface in your house is sticky." As she gets up to leave, one of the triplets runs by and smears the back of her poncho with blue paint, and she barks, in an improvisation that the editors kept in the final cut, "PONCHO!" to show that she was right. She would miss this set: "There was such a safety to just try whatever the hell," she says, "and if it stuck, it stuck. If it didn't, it didn't. But it was so playful."

Then again, she'd loved the simplest scenes on *Parks and Rec*. "Every time I sat across from the two of them at that diner," she says of Poehler and Scott, "I hold all those scenes so close to my heart. Just Ben and Knope, and Jen."

* * *

When Offerman first read the finale script, written by Poehler and Schur, he got weepy. He thought he was keeping it together, but then his wife, Megan Mullally, popped into the room and asked, "Are you okay?"

"Yeah, yeah . . . the script is really good," he answered. Then, he says, "I had a great purging, racking series of sobs."

The finale shows the next several decades, checking in on characters major and minor.

We learn that Garry Gergich—his final, presumably "real," name—dies peacefully on his one hundredth birthday, honored with a 21-stamp salute by the Indiana Notary Society.

Craig gets married, which meant a lot to Eichner, who has long been an outspoken advocate for LGBTQ+ representation. "You didn't have as many gay characters on TV then as you do now," he says. "I also like that there's no coming out for Craig. We just know he's gay, and that's inherent. But we didn't make heavy weather out of it." Craig marries Typhoon, Donna's hairstylist, played by Rodney To. "There's a time for political statements, and there's a time to just throw it in there, like every other storyline," he says. "I liked that they did that, and it was also just really sweet and funny."

To him, the most shocking part of the finale was seeing himself aged up, because he looked just like his dad.

In Leslie's fast-forward moments, we see her delivering a commencement speech after serving two terms as Indiana governor (and perhaps about to run for president?), having only just now, in the finale, confirmed off-handedly that she's a Democrat. ("Janet from the DNC" first encourages her to run.) In the speech, she states the series' thesis, arguing that doing the work you love can make your relationships with friends and family stronger, and quoting one of the most prominent progressives in US history: "Teddy Roosevelt once said, 'Far and away the best prize that life has to offer is a chance to work hard at work worth doing.' And I would add that what makes work worth doing is getting to do it with people that you love." Something, incidentally, that the *Parks and Rec* cast and crew had gotten to do, too.

The final moments on the set included a hodgepodge of cleanup work, partying, and mourning, with extra onlookers like Greg Daniels and Poehler's sons, now five and seven years old. When the cast members weren't shooting, they'd go up on top of their trailers, sitting together, reminiscing and drinking as the sun went down.

Plaza filmed a scene in zombie makeup. (April, naturally, gives birth in full zombie makeup.) The entire main cast shot the final group scene in the parks and recreation department office, firing off jokes between takes to distract themselves from sadness. "Want me to blast one down the barrel?" Scott said to Schur, referring to his trademark practice of looking directly at the camera, usually with skepticism or disbelief. (Scott as Ben would do this 177 times over the course of the series' aired footage, according to a tally by the dedicated fan @junedug, who made a YouTube compilation that lasts 11 minutes and 42 seconds.) Poehler and Retta executed a scripted hug, then launched into an unscripted singing of the Broadway classic "Memories."

Offerman and Poehler shot a pickup moment for an earlier episode before everyone began celebrating. "We're really making this ending tantric," Pratt joked to visiting *Entertainment Weekly* reporter Dan Snierson during the finale shoot. "Slowing it down, enjoying every thrust, breathing deeply, looking into our lover's eyes . . ."

Offerman broke off to sit alone in the dark on a bench near the City Hall set. There were hugs upon hugs, of course, as each actor was announced as "wrapped" for the entire series. Eventually, Poehler encouraged her sons—whose births had been such crucial turning points for the show—to say into the camera, "That's a wrap on *Parks and Recreation*!" Then she had to clear out her trailer, where the detritus of the last six years included a newspaper article from the show's beginnings ("From Hillary to Parks Bureaucrat"), a book Hahn gave her called *Power Dressing: First Ladies, Women Politicians & Fashion*, a Pawnee beer cozy, and a roll of Eagleton toilet paper. "Nick and Schur and I know a little more about how rare this experience is, how lucky we are," she told Snierson. "Nick's a real big softy. Schur and I are just kind of pretending it's not ending."

As a keepsake, she took home the foam State of Indiana seal that had hung over Leslie's desk. Later, Offerman presented her, the other regulars, and the producers with a custom-made gift: hand-carved, solid red oak, full-size canoe paddles made from the trim and actual office doors on set. "Those last couple of weeks were, like, presents and tears and parties," Poehler says. "It was like we were in high school."

Poehler's final official act as Leslie Knope turned out to be recording a voiceover line for the William Henry Harrison episode. In the episode, the line played with irony, Leslie overdramatizing the significance of the dilapidated hunting shack she wanted to designate as historic. But it felt poignant when she recorded it: "What great historical moments took place within these hallowed halls?"

In the following weeks, workers tore down the Pawnee City Hall set they'd constructed over 125 episodes, having added hallways and murals and floors over the years. At the wrap party, Poehler gave an appreciative speech about Schur, calling him "a benevolent leader." Poehler had learned from *Parks and Rec* that chaos is not necessary for creativity. "It doesn't have to be a horrible, disruptive grind for it to mean something creatively wonderful."

In February 2015, the *Parks* crew learned devastating news: Writer Harris Wittels was found dead at the age of thirty at his Los Feliz home after a suspected heroin overdose. *The Hollywood Reporter* said, "The beloved, raunchy and much-hugged Parks and Recreation co-exec producer, who died Feb. 19, faced his addiction head-on but couldn't beat it." Comedian Scott Aukerman told *THR* that Wittels's career was the "quickest rise to prominence of anyone I had seen in the industry. It was really annoying, actually, but he was that good at what he did."

The finale garnered wistful reviews from critics. "As the cast of NBC's long-running sitcom 'Parks and Recreation' came together on-screen for a final hug last night, I started to cry in a way I haven't since I was a child and my mother came to the last page of 'These Happy Golden Years,' the final volume in Laura Ingalls Wilder's 'Little House' series," Alyssa Rosenberg wrote in *The Washington Post*. "One of the special things about television is the opportunity to live alongside your favorite characters season after season. And if you're particularly lucky, a series can come along precisely at the moment when you need it, showing you the world and life as it can be."

Modern Family and *The Big Bang Theory* remained popular, but some critics regarded *Parks*' departure as the final gasp of broadcast sitcoms. "The state of network comedy now is depressing," wrote Kevin Fallon for the *Daily Beast*. "The continued existence of *Parks and Recreation* in this, its final season, is important because it represents the last time that network comedy was actually good."

Time's James Poniewozik praised the way that *Parks and Rec* embodied the cliché that all politics is local: "It doesn't mention political parties. (In the current season it's 2017, but we don't know who won the election—no spoilers!) *Parks*' concerns are budgets, zoning, local rivalries. It hasn't pushed hot buttons so much as tickled them, as when Leslie performed a photo-op 'marriage' of two zoo penguins who turned out to be gay."

Nicole Hemmer wrote in *U.S. News & World Report*, "'Parks and Rec' never lost the Obama-like belief in government powered by goodwill and consensus. But the obstructionism of the Obama years made this vision seem fantastical, stoking a desire for hard-headed partisans who would get things done."

Parks and Rec's political legacy would turn out to be, as telegraphed by these reviews, complicated. Its sunny view of government rankled the conservative *National Review*: "Even television shows that are legitimately funny, such as NBC's *Parks and Recreation*, are designed to flatter the sensibilities of those in charge. In *Parks and Rec*, self-proclaimed nerds and wonks have adopted liberal bureaucratic functionary and occasional elected official Leslie Knope (Amy Poehler) as one of their own. Her overeager chirpiness and her constant ability to one-up her hyper-libertarian boss mark her as a role model for those who believe that government is a force for good rather than a necessary evil."

But that was when "those in charge" were still President Barack Obama and his ilk. "Few series in recent memory have been as clearly tied to a moment—and, specifically, a presidential administration—as *Parks and Rec*," critic Alan Sepinwall wrote in *Rolling Stone*. "The show's belief in the power of government to make people's lives better—and, more broadly, in the obligation members of a community (be they friends, family, or, as Ron Swanson once put it, 'workplace proximity associates') have to help one another in times of need—made it the standard-bearer for the hopefulness of the Obama era."

It did this, *Entertainment Weekly* noted, by choosing a different style of comedy: "Perhaps most impressive, in an age of jaded, everything-in-quotes comedy, *Parks* chose optimism over irony, espoused unsexy virtues like community and hard work, and wasn't afraid to double down on heart."

It didn't simply uphold the government as an institution; it also could not get enough of marriage. "The series' most obvious crusade was for the dignity and value of public service, but 'Parks and Recreation' wrote regular mash notes to the institution of marriage," Rosenberg wrote. "It's hard to think of another show that has staged so many weddings without losing character momentum or needing to become a different kind of show, and that has so optimistically embraced all the different ways in which marriage can work for couples (even the Pawnee Zoo's gay penguins)."

Parks offered an alternative to work-life balance, Rosenberg said, arguing "instead that work can feed your life and be the shared project that defines your most intimate relationships. That doesn't mean that problems of workaholism and child care automatically go away. But it does suggest that the battle to have it all, or at least to have a lot, can be a mutual and hugely fulfilling endeavor." Rosenberg took this personally, writing, "As I move forward in my own marriage, work and friendships, I'm so grateful for the lesson [Leslie] leaves with me: that you learn how much you already have when you start giving to everyone else."

Ron Swanson's more conservative values left a strong impression, too. The *Daily Beast* called Ron "the unlikely libertarian hero of the Obama Era." "[Swanson] has done more to persuade my (French) wife about libertarianism than I have," Matt Welch, the editor in chief of *Reason*, told the *Daily Beast*. "Though in fairness we've only been married 17 years."

Luke Kenworthy, the director of policy engagement at the conservative organization Generation Opportunity, told the publication, "I don't agree with everything Ron Swanson did or said—but the man certainly had conviction for liberty. Ron didn't just teach us about taxation through a lunchbox demonstration—he also spoke eloquently on the more important subjects, like craftsmanship and bacon."

David Boaz, president of the Cato Institute, said, "In a media world that can only handle a two-dimensional liberal-conservative spectrum, it's been great to have one TV star who explains property rights and taxes . . . to millions of viewers."

The Daily Caller ran a list of "Ron Swanson's 12 Wisest Quotes About the Government." The Heartland Institute celebrated that "he's a hero of the show, not a heel of all the jokes (as you would expect from Hollywood)." *Reason* cheered for the "lovably awesome libertarian character." The Cato Institute cited him in policy papers.

Schur and his team had anticipated what was to come in American politics. As Schur said, the series was meant to show people of different political persuasions working together and loving one another: "It was: Can we function as a country when we're heading toward these opposite ends of the spectrum?" He distinguished his show's approach from the "liberal fantasy" of its more serious predecessor *The West Wing*. He said *Parks and Rec* was "an American fantasy"—a nonpartisan progressive vision for the country.

But *Parks and Rec* had hoped for the best, and America, in the end, did not deliver.

Two months after the *Parks and Rec* finale in February 2015, the US presidential campaigns for 2016 began to gear up. Secretary of State Hillary Clinton, once vanquished in the primaries by Barack Obama, announced she would run for the Democratic nomination. Twenty months later, in November 2016, reality TV star Donald Trump unexpectedly won the presidency. He beat the hyper-competent Clinton, who had often been compared to Leslie Knope due to their overachieving tendencies (and the fact that Poehler had played both of them).

Schur, for the record, does not believe that Ron Swanson would have voted for Donald Trump. He doesn't think he'd have voted for Hillary Clinton, of course, either. Ron, he says, "hates liars. He hates people who deceive and are self-interested. He's either not voting, or he's writing in Johnny Cash." We'll never know, since Ron would never tell anyone who he voted for, or if he voted at all.

Would any of the characters have voted for Trump? He did, after all, win the state of Indiana by nearly 20 percentage points, with Indiana governor Mike Pence as his running mate. Jeremy Jamm, for sure: "Trump's like his hero, right?" Schur says. He adds, "Tom might have voted for him because he thought he was funny and because he's like a businessman. He flies in a solid gold airplane and whatever. Tom probably thought that was cool. And even April might have voted for him, just as a chaos agent, like, this will be funny, because he's an insane person."

Everyone involved with the show agreed about one thing: They were glad that *Parks and Rec* had signed off before this new era of politics, which seemed to be the antithesis of what the show, and Leslie Knope in particular, stood for—hard work, expertise, and big government were out; carnival barking, willful ignorance, and government-slashing were in.

"I had no idea of the mistaken and immoral ideologues who would come to cling to Ron Swanson merely because he wielded a shotgun on television, or because he said John Wayne–esque, libertarian things about the government, that it should be dismantled," Offerman says. "Clearly it was a narrative device to derive humor from inside a governmental office with opposing belief systems." It was not, he emphasizes, meant to advocate for right-wing politics. "Unbeknownst to us, we were preparing a series that ultimately is about empathy and friendship and citizenship and neighborliness. I'm so grateful that we got all of our work in under the wire without needing to address the sudden sea change in national consciousness when it comes to politics and leanings."

Schur was relieved to end before the 2016 election, even before he knew what was going to happen. *Parks and Rec* was his attempt to capture the mood of the Obama era: "post–economic collapse of 2007, hope and optimism, and also incrementalism, the value of grinding it out and making small improvements in the margins, where you can make the place you're living, like, one percent better."

He acknowledges that it would have been interesting to see Leslie react to Trump's election. "She was a federal employee at the time, so how would she have functioned in such a world?" he says. "I don't know. I just didn't want to write it. It felt like that's a different show. And I was retroactively happy, once again, for the millionth time, that we got out when we did."

Maybe so, but *someone* wrote a "letter to America from Leslie Knope, regarding Donald Trump" that was published on *Vox* and went viral two days after the election, explaining her grief at the result but emphasizing her enduring belief in democracy as the best option for governance, even if it is imperfect. "I acknowledge that Donald Trump is the president," "Leslie" wrote. "I understand, intellectually, that he won the election. But I do not accept that our country has descended into the hatred-swirled slop pile that he lives in. I reject out of hand the notion that we have thrown up our hands and succumbed to racism, xenophobia, misogyny, and crypto-fascism. I do not accept that. I reject that. I fight that."

"Leslie's" letter was written for one specific moment, but the spirit behind it continued beyond. In the next decade, the legacy of *Parks and Rec* became more apparent: "The only thing you can actually count on is that there are other people around you," Schur said in an appearance at Notre Dame.

But not everyone saw the good in this. *Dissent* magazine said, "Ten years after its premiere, we're living in the world *Parks and Rec* helped make. That's not just because it remains a ubiquitous cultural presence, especially among millennials. ('I can't go on Tinder without finding some idiot comparing himself to Ron Swanson,' a friend complained to me the other day.) *Parks and Rec* was animated by a coherent philosophy—a philosophy that was still unusual a decade ago, but is now as widespread as GIFs of Ron Swanson eating bacon. It's a worldview that fits perfectly with what American liberalism has become, a self-satisfied politics so confident in its righteousness that it can't quite believe there's anything left to argue about."

On the other hand, the entire government had devolved into a *Parks and Rec* parody. "The big question we get all the time is: Isn't it so funny when you watch these congressional meetings now? And you see stuff that could be on *Parks and Rec*?" Poehler said to me in March 2024. "And I'm like, 'It makes my stomach hurt. It's not funny, because that's real.'" She added, "It's funny when someone's in charge of whether or not we're going to add a parking space, but when it's 'What are we going to tell women to do with their bodies?' it's like, 'This is fucking dire.'"

Just a few years after it went off the air, *Parks and Rec* felt nostalgic, almost sepia-toned, like "a Frank Capra movie or something," Schur says. "Oh, what an innocent time it was!"

Esquire put it this way: "Before everything went to shit, we had a lone beacon of government-employed optimism: Leslie Knope. Even through its grouchiest character—the mustachioed, steak-shoveling Ron Swanson—*Parks and Recreation* showed what can be won when there's a little heart buried in our windowless government offices."

When things *had* gone to shit, we could cling to Leslie Knope as a role model, as writer Megan Amram does. "My whole life, you'd get teased, or get points dinged or whatever because you cared too much," she says. "I love that this is a character who cares so much, and sometimes that backfires on her, but oftentimes it's just like, you can't ever fault someone for caring that much."

In 2017, fantasy author Alexandra Rowland coined the term "hopepunk," which was meant to describe a subgenre of sci-fi that was the opposite of what was called "grimdark." You can tell from the names what both mean, broadly, but hopepunk, if it went beyond just sci-fi, seems as if it could also apply to *Parks and Rec*, particularly in retrospect as the world at large feels more grimdark. Rowland said hopepunk is "about DEMANDING a better, kinder world, and truly believing that we can get there if we care about each other as hard as we possibly can."

As American politics turned toward the dark side, more viewers turned toward *Parks and Recreation* on streaming platforms. After Trump's election, its viewership on Hulu increased 32 percent in 2017 over the previous year. It was one of the ten most-streamed shows on Netflix in 2018, an astounding fact considering that it never broke the top 100 on network TV during its run, except during its hyped first season, when it was No. 96.

Now that Leslie and the gang were running on a time-frozen loop on streaming services, they were always and forever fighting for a better Pawnee in the early 2010s, at a time when it all seemed possible. Or at least that's how it felt to us bereft liberals. As Alexandre Lefebvre says in *Liberalism as a Way of Life*, "Liberals always saw themselves as fighting for the common good."

We would need the spirit of *Parks and Rec* more than ever in the even more difficult years to come, during the pandemic and beyond. And it would be there for us.

CHAPTER 12

"Rupture and Repair"

Parks and Rec Meets the Modern Moment

In May 2020, *Parks and Recreation* returned to the air, five years after its finale, to do something that would have been risky for any other show: a special reunion episode, in the dead of lockdown, near the start of COVID's siege, on network television. We were all still scared, unsure of what would happen long-term, and no other shows had done something quite like this. The characters addressed the pandemic in real time, constrained in their individual Zoom-like boxes, produced painstakingly for a network-quality broadcast. This could have looked like a crass stunt at a time when it was way too soon to laugh; it could get schmaltzy or cynical.

For *Parks and Rec*, it proved the perfect assignment. *Parks and Rec* had highlighted an optimistic view of the power of community and government, but in the years since its finale, the American experience had been discouraging. Central character Leslie Knope, the sunny deputy parks director of Pawnee, Indiana, and her crew of well-intentioned bureaucrats could not rescue us, given that they were fictional. But they could lift our spirits for thirty minutes. Throughout the half-hour special, they made us laugh *and* reinforced their central message that the best way through any crisis is to work together. With all the turmoil perpetuated by the government at the time, we could find comfort in seeing these kind, well-meaning officials back on the screen when such figures felt scarce in real life.

In the special, Leslie has enacted a phone-tree system via a video-chatting service from the *Parks and Rec* universe's tech giant Gryzzl. When Ron complains to Leslie about this system, she asks if he has a better one: "Yes, we talk far less than that, or we just send each other a photo of ourselves holding up today's newspaper to prove we're okay," he deadpans. We know, however, that Ron appreciates her plan. Leslie and Ron just work that way. In fact, Ron conspires with their fellow *Parks and Rec* friends to thank Leslie with a surprise climactic group call and sing-along to the show's signature song, "5,000 Candles in the Wind." The ode to Pawnee's famous mini horse perfectly embodies the silly and sweet of the series. ("And though we all miss you every day / We know you're up there eating heaven's hay / And here's the part that hurts the most / Humans cannot ride a ghost.")

Loyal *Parks and Rec* viewers already knew the subtext, that Leslie and Ron were opposite not only in personality but also in political beliefs: Leslie a cheerful liberal who believed in nothing more than the power of government to do good, and Ron a libertarian who had taken his parks department job with the aim of hobbling the system from within. But they loved each other anyway, which felt even more significant in 2020 than it had when the show had aired from 2009 to 2015.

Parks and Rec had arrived at this central role in the pandemic because in the five years since it had gone off the air, its profile had only risen. As it became a streaming hit, its stars—including Aziz Ansari, Nick Offerman, Aubrey Plaza, Chris Pratt, and Adam Scott—had become more famous and prolific.

Ansari wrote a book about dating in the electronic age, *Modern Romance*, that became a No. 1 *New York Times* bestseller. With *Parks and Rec* writer Alan Yang, he cocreated the acclaimed Netflix dramedy *Master of None*, loosely based on his own life as an actor in New York City. Despite its comedic undertones, it represented a sharp departure from *Parks and Rec*: it aired on a streaming service; had short and meticulously crafted seasons; and was influenced by French New Wave, Woody Allen, classic Italian film, and Spike Lee, nothing like a traditional network sitcom. Netflix also released Ansari's blockbuster stand-up special, filmed at Madison Square Garden.

His career took a turn in 2018 when he was accused of sexual misconduct in a story posted on a website called Babe.net, in which a pseudonymous woman described feeling "really pressured" and "uncomfortable" on a date with him. The accusation sparked discussions about gray areas, men's expectations of women, and explicit consent. In a follow-up Netflix special in 2019, he said, "I'm sure there's some of you that are curious how I feel about that whole situation. . . . There's times I felt scared, there's times I felt humiliated, there's times I felt embarrassed, and ultimately I just felt terrible that this person felt this way. After a year or so, I just hope it was a step forward. It moved things forward for me, made me think about a lot. I hope I've become a better person."

Pratt, meanwhile, transformed from doofus Andy into a chiseled, superheroic leading man who could star in action films such as *Jurassic World* and *The Tomorrow War*, making him one of the highest-grossing movie stars of all time. "I could bribe him with some photos I have of him when we went to Indiana, when he's shirtless on the football field—like, big belly," costume designer Kirston Mann says with a laugh.

Plaza found that she'd played April too convincingly. "There was a period of time where I realized people literally think I am this character, because they haven't seen me do anything else," she says. "When I was trying to do movies, I was just getting offered the same character." Even weirder, she would hear from fellow actors that they were auditioning for roles that were described as "an Aubrey Plaza–type character." "And I'd be like, 'First of all, that is not me. That is a character that I am doing,'" she says.

This motivated her to play as many other kinds of characters as she could. So she took the roles of the sexy Lenore in the raunchy comedy *Dirty Grandpa*, and the buttoned-up lawyer Harper Spiller in the second season of *The White Lotus*, a performance that got her nominated for an Emmy.

Offerman has written several *New York Times* bestselling books, including 2013's *Paddle Your Own Canoe* and 2021's *Where the Deer and the Antelope Play*. In the show's afterlife, he became what *The Washington Post* called "a progressive in right-wing clothing." He won an Emmy for playing a Ron Swanson–like survivalist who falls in love with a man in an emotional episode of the postapocalyptic drama *The Last of Us*. He played a fascist US leader in the film *Civil War*, which was obviously not an endorsement of authoritarianism but, in fact, its own play on the Ron Swanson character. (What if Ron Swanson was the ultimate version of the guy some conservative bro fans want him to be?) "For whatever reason, the way I was brought up and what Mother Nature made me look and sound like lends itself to getting cast to represent people who can use a shovel," he told the *Post*. As he's proven, people who can use a shovel can still run a wide gamut of motivations and emotions.

With the show's upswing in popularity in the 2020s, Offerman only confused fans more. At his comedy performances, he began singing a song called "I'm Not Ron Swanson," explaining all the ways he differed from his fictional alter ego. Some fans expressed upset that Offerman didn't share Ron's anti-government politics, of course. But they also got agitated when he shaved his mustache, and they wanted him to eat more meat. If he was recognized at a restaurant, a chef might send out his meal with extra bacon. "Extra bacon? Hell yeah," Offerman says. "But then, twenty minutes later, you're like, oh, that was a mistake. That was not healthy."

And thus, some sample lyrics from "I'm Not Ron Swanson": "Now your expectations are a little high, I fear. / 'Cause if I tried to live like him, I'd be dead within a year. / You see, he can eat a big-ass steak for every single meal, / 'cause his colon is fictitious, while mine is all too real. / And his Scotch intake, it would be my liver's doom. / 'Cause mine is controlled by nature, / and his by the whims of the writers' room."

His live show, however, demonstrated to Mark Rivers, who helped Offerman write the songs, just how enduring his compositions for *Parks and Rec* were. Rivers brought his mom to an Offerman performance at Largo in Los Angeles. At the end, Offerman played "5,000 Candles in the Wind." "When he announced it, the audience just gasped," Rivers says. "And everybody sang along with it. I was like, 'What the fuck?' And my mom, likewise, was like, 'Everybody knew that song!' I had no idea."

Though Scott has worked consistently since *Parks*, including a supporting role on the murder-mystery sensation *Big Little Lies* and the lead on the workplace thriller *Severance*, he continues to compare every job to *Parks*. "It's seminal for me, because working on *Parks* is when I started becoming more of a recognizable person out in the world," he says. "It's defined me, and my identity for a long time was wrapped up in the character. So it's the show that everything else gets compared to, no matter what."

* * *

When Donald Trump was elected in 2016, Schur's follow-up to *Parks and Rec*, called *The Good Place*, was just beginning. It starts with Eleanor Shellstrop (Kristen Bell) finding herself in what seems like heaven after her death, but she's sure there's been a mistake—she knows she was a bad person.

Several of the *Parks and Rec* writers and crew joined Schur on this philosophical journey, which expounded upon many of the ideas Schur had established as key to *Parks and Rec*, most of all the importance of community. T. M. Scanlon's *What We Owe to Each Other* serves as a foundational text. "I do think one of the reasons *Parks* and *The Good Place* are so wonderful is that he has the ability to spot people pretty quickly who have the same sensibilities as him, who are also hardworking and caring people like he is, and he prioritizes that," says writer Megan Amram, who also worked on *The Good Place*. "I really, really mean it that I think he's such an amazing role model in how to be decent. Basically I would follow Mike to the end of the earth."

Schur thought his new show dovetailed perfectly, if horrifyingly, with the new political guard, "because that show was about ethics." And because of Trump's lack thereof, "ethics was the thing everyone was talking about all the time," he says with a rueful laugh.

Parks and Rec writers Amram, Dave King, Joe Mande, Aisha Muharrar, Matt Murray, Jen Statsky, and Alan Yang all followed Schur to *The Good Place*. Offerman, Scott, and Jason Mantzoukas showed up in smaller roles. Producer Dean Holland had worried at the end of *Parks and Rec* that he'd never work again. "You know how in every business, you need to move out to move up?" he says. "I thought, 'Well, I only worked for Greg and Mike, so no one's ever going to hire me again.' Little did I know that working for Greg and Mike was pretty awesome." Schur brought him along to *The Good Place*, where Holland would continue to direct.

Statsky experienced no hesitation about joining Schur for his next project, given the precarity of the business and the rarity of finding people in Hollywood who were fun to work with. "What you can bet on is the people that you've worked with, that they will be good and kind and you will have a good time making things with them," she says. "That's why I've stayed in this family—why I've been lucky to stay in this family—these are all people I love."

Many successful shows branched off from that *Parks and Rec* node on the TV family tree. Dan Goor's *Brooklyn Nine-Nine* ran for eight seasons, until 2021. That year, Statsky cocreated the award-winning HBO series *Hacks*, about an aging comedian played by Jean Smart and her contentious relationship with her Gen Z writer, played by Hannah Einbinder. Schur serves as a producer, and several *Parks and Rec* writers work on the show. Also that year, Schur cocreated *Rutherford Falls*, returning to some themes from *Parks and Rec*. The show depicts a small town's conflicts over celebrating their white settlers versus the history of the Native Americans who were there first. Here, the casino-owning tribe leader feels almost like a further realization of Pawnee's savvy Chief Ken Hotate (Jonathan Joss), this time as a major character.

Many of the *Parks and Rec* writers who went on to become creators and showrunners credit Schur for showing them how it's done. "He taught me how to talk to people," Statsky says. "Showrunner is a really weird thing where, as much as you work your way up the ladder in a writers' room and you go on set, you're not really prepared. All of a sudden, you run this 250-person company, and every decision is run through you, and it is incredibly difficult. You're so lucky to do it because everybody is servicing your vision, and that's a tremendous privilege, but at the same time, it's a lot."

Having experienced this on *Hacks*, Statsky is in awe of the way that Schur never passed the everyday stresses of showrunning on to anyone else on set. "I try to live that in my day-to-day on *Hacks*," she says. "You're the leader, and that means there's a certain amount of stuff you need to take on and make sure you're not pushing it down and letting it affect the people who work for you."

She also sees *Parks and Rec* as a lasting influence on her own work. "*Hacks* is about a relationship between two people who make each other better," she says. "It's not always easy, but it's worth it. And I think that is what *Parks and Rec* is about. It's about the relationships between Leslie and these people she loves, and they make each other better."

Various permutations of *Parks and Rec* folks continued to work together, having been spoiled by their great experience.

Producer Morgan Sackett admired Poehler's leadership as they worked together on the female-bonding comedy *Wine Country*, which Poehler starred in and directed, and coproduced with Sackett. It costarred many of her longtime buddies, including Maya Rudolph, Rachel Dratch, Ana Gasteyer, Paula Pell, and Tina Fey.

"It was fun because it was her friends," Sackett says, "but she was also the director and had to keep it moving when they all just wanted to horse around." Sackett calls her a "sneaky leader." "She can put people in their place without being mean, without being belittling. She's not the loudest person in the room, but you're not in the room very long before you realize she's in charge."

In 2023, Plaza and Poehler posed on the red carpet together at the Screen Actors Guild Awards, Poehler and Jones posted together on TikTok, and Offerman and Scott reunited in a revived *Party Down* episode. When the SAG-AFTRA and WGA strikes hit Hollywood, Plaza, Scott, Offerman, Retta, Jim O'Heir, Ben Schwartz, Alison Becker, and

Joe Mande were among those who posed with Li'l Sebastian on the picket line to draw attention to the cause.

"Mike was an incredible role model in his activism in the WGA," Amram says. "That was the first strike that I was part of, and I was a captain because Mike is a superpowerful showrunner who is also boots-on-the-ground helping to organize the union."

The 2024 Super Bowl brought a prominent Mountain Dew Blast ad featuring Offerman and Plaza. "They pitched me and Nick Offerman riding dragons," Plaza told *People* magazine. "It's like, you just can't say no to that. That's the best April and Ron reunion that could have ever happened." Pratt had his own Super Bowl 2024 ad, for Pringles, and that company hired Offerman the next year for an ad featuring his (Ron's) iconic mustache.

Schur had another hit with the 2024 Netflix comedy *A Man on the Inside*, in which Ted Danson plays a man who infiltrates a retirement home to solve a theft, but, as usual in a Schur production, finds friends, passion, and a renewed sense of purpose. Producers included Amram and Morgan Sackett; Mann did the costume design. Character actor Will McLaughlin appeared as a police officer, having played similar roles on *Rutherford Falls*, *The Good Place*, and *Parks and Rec* (where he was credited as Officer Killnose). "Just because it's like a bit of an Easter egg, but it's also like, when people are funny, we bring them back," Sackett says.

More recently, the entire TV production cycle that began with *The Office* and then *Parks and Rec* seems to have reached a full-circle moment. *The Paper*, an *Office* spin-off about a local newspaper that is *actually* a spin-off—it features Oscar Nuñez reprising his role as accountant Oscar Martinez—premiered in the fall of 2025. And Poehler and Schur signed on to reteam on a show about, well, a big hole: *Dig* adapts Kate Myers's bestseller *Excavations*, about four women working on an archaeological dig in Greece.

★ ★ ★

Subsets of the cast would also often reunite on social media, to fans' great delight, for Galentine's Day—February 13. The date practically became a real holiday, marked across the nation with not only social media posts but also cards, Etsy products, and in-person celebrations. Many people celebrating didn't know it had started on *Parks and Rec.* I was interviewed by a Vancouver radio station in February 2025 about the phenomenon, so it has at least breached the United States' northern border as well.

"Female friendships are the most important thing in your life," Poehler said in a video she posted on TikTok on the date in 2024 as she walked through falling snow. "The best thing about your friends is they know you better than anyone, and they still want to hang out with you. Happy Galentine's Day!"

The show has become a hit on other kinds of social media, likely driven by new audiences finding it via streaming.

Jay Jackson is still best known for his role as vacuous newscaster Perd Hapley, though he continued to play other TV journalists, and a few non-newscasters. On *Criminal Minds*, he played a cybercrimes unit chief; on *The Neighborhood*, he played a preacher. But the role for which he was invited to appearances and conventions would always be Perd. "I know what he means to people," he says. "I know that they love the character."

He learned this in large part from Cameo, the video-sharing website founded in 2017 that allows fans to order personalized video messages from stars. (Celebrities with a following of twenty thousand or more on Instagram are eligible.) "Perd is a huge hit on Cameo," Jackson says. "Perd has a whole life on Cameo." On Cameo, Perd has helped people to propose to each other, to announce the gender of their babies, to reveal that they're getting a doctorate.

He knows some actors disdain Cameo, but he feels it's worth it to make a fan's day. "Once you have those experiences, you start to appreciate what it means to people," he says. "These characters really start to get into people's lives. You see that on Cameo because people open up their lives to you. And they're willing to pay for it—be serious and be sincere, and I think that's why Perd has a great life on Cameo."

Younger audiences cycled through the episodes over and over. Writer Katie Dippold visited her former high school to talk to the kids about her career. Beforehand, one of the teachers gave her some advice: mention some famous actors she's worked with. She didn't say anything, but she recoiled at the thought. She was no name-dropper. Much less was she about to name-drop to get the approval of sixteen-year-olds. "I'm not that sweaty," she remembers thinking.

As she spoke, she could see that she wasn't connecting. It was excruciating. These kids just did not care about what she did. She started dropping those names: Every actor from every movie she worked on, which included *The Heat*, the female *Ghostbusters* reboot, and *The Haunted Mansion*. Still, nothing. Finally, she brought up *Parks and Rec*. She was taken aback to see the room light up with recognition. "Before that, for years, no one watched *Parks and Rec*," she says. "Truly no one. So nowadays, it's nice to hear people talk about it."

Many of the stars have found themselves watching it in full for the first time with their kids. Schur's kids were at the right age to watch during the pandemic, when a lot of their friends were watching it as well. Poehler watched it in 2020, too, having only ever seen it in editing cuts when they were making it. She liked to tell her sons, "One of you was on *SNL*. One of you was on *Parks and Rec*." Abel was the one who not only appeared in utero during the second and third seasons of *Parks* but who also may have helped secure the third season by forcing the network to commit to it early. "They loved it," Poehler says of her sons watching. "No one really likes to watch their mom, but they found a way."

When she watched with them, she says, "It was so great, because I didn't remember any of the story. Every single time an episode would start, I'd be like, 'I forget, what do I do here? How do I get it done?'" Instead, what she would remember was the felt sense of shooting the episode. *Oh, right, we shot it in that church. I remember that day when we had to slide down that hill.* She would recall it, she says, "from the inside, not the outside."

Writer Dan Goor's two kids have each "gone through a *Parks* binge as they've aged into it," he says. He rewatched "Harvest Festival," which he wrote, with one of them. "It *looks* so good," he says. "You have to give credit to Dean, who directed that, and to Morgan for the production element of it, and obviously to Mike for all of it. There's that shot where they look back at the maze, and Li'l Sebastian is glowing in the middle of it. It's so good."

Jackson, too, has found that when it comes to Perd, "young people love the character just as much as people loved him when it was on the air. It's like fourteen- and fifteen-year-olds who love the show." He's learned to detect it the minute someone recognizes him: "You go out to a restaurant and you get what I call 'the googly eyes.' The googly eyes is when they look at you for three seconds too long. It can become uncomfortable." Sometimes he goes to the gym at 5 a.m. to avoid it, if he's not in the mood.

Offerman's experience with young fans has made him (jokingly) concerned for America's youth. They'll tell him, he says, "I'm so excited to meet you. I've seen *Parks and Rec* all the way through seven times." He adds, "To which I would say, 'Okay. (a) Thank you; (b) Read some books, for Christ's sake.'"

More seriously, he's proud to have made such a positive show that has lasted until a time when the world needs it. "We were just at the right place at the right time, even though people are now surprised to hear that we were never a hit," he says. "We created this medicinal package, thanks to Mike."

Poehler loved experiencing her show during the pandemic with all the other nervous viewers seeking comfort. "Young people really want to watch rupture-and-repair," she says. "They want to see stuff get fixed, especially when the world feels so broken. That's what *Parks* does. It keeps showing you: breaking it apart and bringing it back together. It gives you this warm feeling, and you want to go to that place and be with these people and hang out with them. And I did it, too. I just snuggled in and watched *Parks* like everyone else."

As millions of viewers streamed *Parks and Rec*, NBC contacted Schur in April 2020 to ask if he and the cast would be up for doing some kind of pandemic special. It was becoming clear that the lockdown would be lasting more than the two weeks initially announced, and the network needed to figure out how to make some content that felt relevant to viewers whose appetite for programming was now insatiable as they faced hours upon hours to fill at home. Schur liked the idea of doing something, as long as it was for charity. NBC worked with Feeding America, which felt perfect.

Schur then emailed the cast, and within about two hours, everyone had said an enthusiastic yes. The same went for the writers. On Zoom, the writers gathered to develop the basic idea—that the characters would be meeting, of course on the Zoom-like Gryzzl video chat, to check in with one another during lockdown. "It was really lovely to see everybody, especially during that time," Statsky says. "And it was fun to go back and get to write for these characters again."

They decided not to get tangled up in any of the series finale's references to the characters' futures and instead to focus on basics and what everyone was experiencing in lockdown. None of the characters would have COVID, which was very serious and unfunny, especially in those early days. Leslie would talk about the importance of connection during a lonely time. And Chris Traeger, resident health obsessive, would talk about COVID precautions. Ann, a nurse, would be doing outpatient care. They considered having her working on the front lines of emergency response, but they worried that it would feel trivializing. Ben considers making a Claymation version of his Cones of Dunshire game, but soon realizes this is a terrible idea, while Andy and April are separated due to Andy accidentally locking himself in the shed (a clever cover for the fact that Aubrey Plaza and Chris Pratt couldn't be in the same room). The half hour would wrap up with a group rendition of "5,000 Candles in the Wind."

They divided up the scenes among the six returning writers and drafted a script in four days. Sackett arranged for packages with cameras, microphones, and lights to be delivered to each cast member at home. "This is another credit to Morgan Sackett, who, on a production level, was one of the first people to figure out how to make a TV show during the pandemic," writer Dave King says.

Sackett directed this special episode. The logistics, which had always been his specialty, *were* the project. Given the paranoia and confusion of the time—those of us lucky enough not to be facing illness were sewing our own masks and dousing our groceries in bleach—he "made these packages, little Pelican case things," he explains. "We sanitized everything, because everyone was wiping everything down."

Once they had a script, they held a virtual table read. "And those were the early days of Zoom, where connections were terrible, it was a mess," Sackett says. The actors would not be acting together on Zoom for the actual shoot, so the table read was their moment to see each other and hear the entire script.

Sackett had recently worked with Poehler on the Netflix film *Moxie*, and they had an office in West Hollywood, so he went there the day before her shoot, set up the camera, lights, and microphone, wiped it all down, and left. He did tech checks with all the other actors from his home office, with his kids home from school. The actors had to do everything themselves—"makeup and hair and grip and electric," Sackett says. Jim O'Heir, for instance, had to put sheets over his windows because his scenes were supposed to be at night. Plaza shot from her garage. When they sang "5,000 Candles in the Wind," they did it individually to a sync track, with their voices layered together in editing. (If you've ever tried coordinated singing or music-playing on Zoom, you know that a slight delay makes it impossible to make music live with others.)

Rob Lowe's Montecito mansion was a problem. "Rob, you're supposed to be a government administrator," Sackett remembers telling him. "Try to find the shittiest room in your house." Sackett laughed when Lowe appeared on camera and someone was there touching up his makeup. His wife *is* a makeup artist, though, so this was likely a sanctioned interaction.

Rudd grabbed the "Knope 2012" sweatshirt from his closet to wear for his segment as clueless Bobby Newport. He had an iPhone stand that he'd bought for a different charity video, so he took it outside and shot from his yard in New York's Hudson Valley, standing in for the Newport family's private foxhunting estate in Switzerland.

They shot via Zoom in about three days. Schur and the team edited it remotely.

"People have asked me, in this age of reboots, would we ever reboot the show," Schur says. "And the response has always been, 'You never say never.' But there has to be a good reason for it. Rebooting it just because we love each other and want to hang out is not a good enough reason. There has to be a compelling reason for us to go on one last ride together. This was that compelling reason to me. We were all alone in our homes, and the show was about the power of community and how important it was to be with other people. It was a perfect culmination of everything that the show stood for."

The special included the main cast and several fan-favorite guest stars, such as Jason Mantzoukas as Dennis Feinstein. "It was fantastic," he says, "because I was having what I would describe as a miniature nervous breakdown." Suddenly he got to play with lights and work on building his set. "It was a great opportunity to get on a bunch of Zooms and talk to everybody and connect," he says. "It was, at the time, a real lifesaver. I was delighted to be talking about the collective insanity that we'd found ourselves in."

When it aired on April 30, 2020, it attracted 3.7 million viewers and raised $2.8 million for Feeding America's COVID-19 Response Fund by the next day.

Poehler says, "What I saw during that time is that comedy is like a salve."

Plaza says, "It's amazing how many people come up to you, and they're like, 'I was sick, I was in the hospital, and you guys got me through this really hard time.' I hear that all the time. So it's like, man, it's really meaningful to people."

Fans and critics loved it; it has a 100 percent fresh rating on Rotten Tomatoes. I can report crying nearly all the way through, just seeing these people on my screen at that scary time. It was a novelty, and a piece of television history—the first scripted broadcast series to depict the pandemic, showing social distancing and the new hallmark of the time, Zoom meetings. Leslie and her crew of well-intentioned bureaucrats were what we needed. Throughout the half-hour special, they made us laugh *and* reinforced their central message that the best way through any crisis is to work together.

Entertainment reporters excitedly asked Schur if this kind of production was the way of the future. He squashed that idea immediately, telling them that it was, in fact, quite difficult. "It was really slow and laborious," Schur told *USA Today*. "This is not the way TV is supposed to be made. It required a lot of goodwill volunteer work from sound designers, editors, script supervisors and people doing it because it was a fundraiser." Though it was fun, given the circumstances, he said, "I don't think it's any kind of model for what we're doing going forward."

As the pandemic progressed, *Parks and Rec*'s influence on television grew more evident. It had helped to usher in a period of quality single-camera shows that explored contemporary social issues. Ron, for all the willful misunderstanding that surrounded his character, was, in fact, a harbinger of the positive masculinity trend in shows like *Ted Lasso*. In addition to *Lasso*, some of the other big shows of the pandemic year contained shades of *Parks*, including *Schitt's Creek* and *Abbott Elementary*. *Parks and Rec* had changed television, turning up the brightness with its genial cast and sweet relationships. Its mostly cynical contemporaries had favored humor over humanity. Shows like *Arrested Development*, *It's Always Sunny in Philadelphia*, and *30 Rock* had inherited *Seinfeld*'s principle, "no hugging, no learning." That idea had been revolutionary when *Seinfeld* enacted it in the 1990s, rejecting the schmaltz of eighties sitcoms. As time marched on, though, it turned out that we needed a little schmaltz, presented with modern finesse.

When *Parks and Rec* moved to Peacock exclusively in 2020, the deal cost a reported nine figures. Meanwhile, *Parks and Recreation* appeared on lists of the best TV shows of the twenty-first century so far, from *The Guardian*, *BBC Culture*, and *The Hollywood Reporter*. Fan-service products surged. A kids' book called *Parks and*

Recreation: Leslie for Class President! by Robb Pearlman became a *New York Times* bestseller.

Lowe and writer Alan Yang launched a podcast about the show in 2021, *Parks and Recollection*. Like many of the cast, Lowe had noticed how often he was recognized as Chris Traeger by young people, particularly when he visited his kids at college. "I've been lucky enough to be known for a lot of different roles over the course of my career, but there's something about the love that that segment of the world had for the show that I wanted to keep alive," he says. He had never seen the show until he joined it, so part of the podcast was him watching the first and second seasons for the first time and reacting to them.

Though he and Yang have passed the hosting of that show on to Jim O'Heir and writer Greg Levine, Lowe now hosts an interview podcast called *Literally! With Rob Lowe*, a reference to his *Parks and Rec* character's favorite word.

Songwriter Mark Rivers had to scour his old hard drives for Mouse Rat tracks when the series' producer, Universal Television, licensed the songs to folk and indie rock label Dualtone for a full-length album. "Stupidly, I thought, 'Oh, this is some little promo thing,'" he says with a laugh. "And I didn't do much of a deal for that. I don't know if I got any money for that."

Nonetheless, on August 27, 2021, Dualtone (and Tom's fictional Entertainment 720) released *The Awesome Album* in digital, CD, cassette, and vinyl versions, with a fifteen-song track list that included not only "5,000 Candles in the Wind" but also "The Pit," "Sex Hair," and "Catch Your Dream," as well as "Pickled Ginger" by Land Ho! and "Cold Water" by Scott Tanner, featuring Duke Silver. (Offerman's now close friend Jeff Tweedy was part of both.)

Cocreator Greg Daniels credits this surge in popularity to the "nobility of the characters. The characters are very positive. And they got more positive with each other and loving to each other as the show went on. I think people like that." In other words, the further our reality seemed from *Parks and Rec*'s, the *more* we seemed to need it.

Parks and Rec's idealistic view of politics filled a gaping hole in the television landscape. A 2022 study by American University's Center for Media and Social Impact showed that civic themes appeared in only one-third of all TV episodes, and that, in those, civic engagement was usually brief or in the background, not the main storyline. And, it said, "civic conversation is portrayed nearly three times more than civic action," while "law enforcement dominates portrayals of civic leadership." Elected officials showed up in only 11 percent of episodes, while civil servants showed up in 8 percent, compared with law enforcement's 41 percent. Official corruption was twice as prevalent as policymaking among those elected officials portrayed, and white men dominated as those in political positions. A mere 32 percent were women. And, finally, voting was shown in less than 1 percent of the programming.

Parks and Rec bucked every one of those trends.

And our need for *Parks and Rec* only became more evident with the reelection of Donald Trump in 2024, his second triumph over an astronomically more competent woman who upholds basic beliefs in democracy and liberalism. He took his second victory, which included winning the popular vote, as a forceful mandate to remake government, allowing billionaire businessman Elon Musk to cut thousands of government jobs and cripple the US government. Meanwhile, Trump declared himself a "king" on social media and appointed a squad of unqualified, loyalist cronies to major positions.

We did not hear from Leslie Knope this time, but it's safe to assume she was displeased with this direction, and possibly out of a job. But in typical Leslie fashion, she would never be without optimism.

The fact that *Parks and Rec* remains popular reflects Leslie's ever-present sense of hope, and her belief that there is always good in the world, and places to compromise and work together. There are millions of people who appreciate *Parks and Recreation*'s loving characters and its affectionate sendup of the civil servants who keep society running, who help people in trouble, whether it's because their street has a pothole or they're seeking political asylum. Every day, new viewers are discovering it for the first time, and then excitedly (if ill-advisedly) sending Offerman a Scotch when they see him in a restaurant, ordering up a Perd Cameo, or buying *The Awesome Album* on vinyl.

Actress Alison Becker, who played Pawnee newspaper reporter Shauna Malwae-Tweep, has watched the entire series—except for a few episodes. It's a tradition she has with any works she truly loves. "If I really like a book, I won't read the last few pages," she says, "because then I'm always living in the book."

She's never read the last five pages of *Wuthering Heights*. And she has no plans to finish *Parks and Rec*. Like so many of us, she wants to keep living in Pawnee for as long as she can.

ACKNOWLEDGMENTS

I'm so grateful that Mike Schur and Amy Poehler welcomed me into the wonderful *Parks and Rec* world they so carefully built, full of joy, hope, and good people. Thank you to my fellow Chicago suburbanite Nick Offerman, who spoke with me at length early in the process and so generously agreed to support this book with his own words in the foreword, an extra treat given what a beautiful writer he is. Massive thanks, also, to all my warm, funny, smart, and thoughtful interview subjects: Megan Amram, Alison Becker, Mo Collins, Greg Daniels, Katie Dippold, Billy Eichner, Dan Goor, Kathryn Hahn, Kay Hanley, Norm Hiscock, Dean Holland, Jay Jackson, Dave King, Rob Lowe, Joe Mande, Kirston Mann, Jason Mantzoukas, Ian Phillips, Aubrey Plaza, Mark Rivers, Paul Rudd, Morgan Sackett, Adam Scott, Olympia Snowe, and Jen Statsky. To a person, they all exceeded my already high expectations. So many people say they have a "no assholes" policy when hiring; Mike Schur actually does, and he appears to have a supernatural ability to execute such a policy. Honestly, talking to all these people about this show has been nothing short of a spiritual experience.

I feel so privileged to have gotten to do this dream project, and that's in large part because of my editor, Jill Schwartzman, whom I've wanted to work with forever, and who brought her deep knowledge and understanding to this topic. No one could have edited this better, and I'm so glad that my phenomenal agent, Laurie Abkemeier, made this happen.

Special shout-out to the world's greatest transcriber, Patrick Rapa, who also happens to be a *Parks and Rec* superfan, whose extra notes and asides became vital contributions to this book. (People noticing that April and Andy are like a cat and a dog? Patrick. Anything to do with deep appreciation for the great Harris Wittels? Patrick.) The folks at the Peabody Awards have literally supported me through all this with a dream contract gig, and, in fact, inspired this entire thing by giving me the chance to interview multiple Peabody–winner Mike Schur. In a world of shrinking media jobs, I still have the perfect side hustle with an organization doing real good in this space, and that's honestly a miracle. Bailey Dunn at the Park It Substack, it was so fun and genuinely helpful to talk some of this through as I was researching and writing; I'm so glad *Parks* brought us together. Thanks to my reliable support team at the Ministry of Pop Culture (Saul Austerlitz, Erin Carlson, Thea Glassman, Kirthana Ramisetti) and VIP Club Text Chain (you know who you are), as well as to my forever editor (and photographer), A. Jesse Jiryu Davis.

SOURCE NOTES

INTRODUCTION:
"American Normality"

Wallace, David Foster. "E Unibus Pluram: Television and U.S. Fiction." *Review of Contemporary Fiction* 13, no. 2 (Summer 1993): 151–94.

Archival author interview with Michael Schur (2022).

Quote from Max Weber: "Politik als Beruf." Lecture delivered before the Freistudentischen Bund of the University of Munich, 1919.

Author interviews with Steve Noble, Ric Offerman, Amy Poehler, and Michael Schur.

Collinson, Stephen. "Trump Will Win Second Term, CNN Projects, in Historic Comeback After Losing Four Years Ago." CNN, November 6, 2024. https://www.cnn.com/2024/11/06/politics/trump-wins-election.

Quote from Pete Buttigieg: Mao, William C., and Dhruv T. Patel. "Pete Buttigieg '04 Calls Local Government 'Salvation' for Dems Under Trump." *Harvard Crimson*, November 13, 2024. https://www.thecrimson.com/article/2024/11/13/pete-buttigieg-secretary-transportation-iop-president/.

Ryan, Maureen. "'Parks and Recreation,' 'The Wire' and the Politics of Pawnee." *HuffPost*, January 13, 2015. https://www.huffpost.com/entry/parks-and-recreation-final-season_n_6459726.

CHAPTER 1:
"The Nobility of Working Really Hard for Your Little Tiny Slice of America"
(Creating the Show)

Author interviews with Greg Daniels, Dan Goor, Dean Holland, Amy Poehler, and Michael Schur.

Quote from Barack Obama: Mejia, Zameena. "Barack Obama Says You Should Embrace 'Relentless Optimism' to Be Successful." CNBC, September 22, 2017. https://www.cnbc.com/2017/09/22/barack-obama-says-you-should-embrace-relentless-optimism.html.

St. James, Emily. "The 2 Decisions—and 1 Happy Accident—That Made *The Office* a Hit." *Vox*, December 15, 2018. https://www.vox.com/i-think-youre-interesting/2018/12/15/18141338/the-office-michael-schur-beginning-season-1.

Solomon, Matt. "The Judd Apatow Show Starring Loads of Stars That ABC Threw Out." *Cracked*, April 28, 2022. https://www.cracked.com/article_33621_judd-apatows-star-studded-pilot-that-abc-threw-away.html.

Rudin, Ken. "Is 2008 the 'Year of the Woman'?" NPR, October 29, 2008. https://www.npr.org/2008/10/29/96260710/is-2008-the-year-of-the-woman.

Palumbo, Stephanie. "An Interview with Michael Schur." *Believer*, October 1, 2015. https://www.thebeliever.net/an-interview-with-michael-schur/.

Ferriss, Tim. "Michael Schur, Creator of 'The Good Place'—How SNL Trains Writers, His TV University at 'The Office,' Lessons from Lorne Michaels, Wisdom from David Foster Wallace, and Exploring Moral Philosophy with 'How to Be Perfect.'" *The Tim Ferriss Show*, January 22, 2022. https://tim.blog/2022/01/22/michael-schur-transcript/.

McCaffery, Larry. "A Conversation with David Foster Wallace." *Review of Contemporary Fiction* 13, no. 2 (Summer 1993). https://www.dalkeyarchive.com/2013/08/02/a-conversation-with-david-foster-wallace-by-larry-mccaffery/.

Ryan, Maureen. "'Parks and Recreation' Gets Political: Amy Poehler and Mike Schur Talk Pawnee Debate Night." *HuffPost*, April 25, 2012. https://www.huffpost.com/entry/parks-and-recreation-debate_n_1452848.

Quote from Ben Silverman: Greene, Andy. *The Office: The Untold Story of the Greatest Sitcom of the 2000s*. New York: Dutton, 2020, 301.

Mark, Joshua J. "Pawnee." World History Encyclopedia, January 10, 2024. https://www.worldhistory.org/Pawnee/.

Fling, Sarah. "The Myth of the Vanishing Indian." White House Historical Association, accessed July 15, 2025. https://www.whitehousehistory.org/the-myth-of-the-vanishing-indian.

2019 Annual Report: A Report to the People Pawnee Nation of Oklahoma. https://pawneenation.org/wp-content/uploads/2021/04/2019-Annual-Report-web.pdf.

CHAPTER 2:
"That's My Fucking Part"
(Casting the Show)

Author interviews with Greg Daniels, Jason Mantzoukas, Nick Offerman, Aubrey Plaza, Amy Poehler, Michael Schur, Adam Scott, and Matt Walsh.

Poehler, Amy. *Yes Please*. New York: Dey Street, 2014.

Czajkowski, Elise. "The Evolution of Aziz Ansari." *Vulture*, November 6, 2015. https://www.vulture.com/2015/11/aziz-ansari-evolution.html.

Potts, Michel W. "Aziz Ansari Set for NBC's 'Parks and Recreation.'" *India West*, April 10, 2009, C1.

Jung, E. Alex. "Retta Has a Story to Tell." *Vulture*, May 2018. https://www.vulture.com/2018/05/retta-has-a-story-to-tell.html.

Graham, Jane. "Nick Offerman: Amy Poehler Is a 'Legend of Comedy.'" *Big Issue*, July 29, 2019. https://www.bigissue.com/culture/tv/nick-offerman-looks-up-to-amy-poehler-as-a-legend-of-comedy/.

Offerman, Nick. "Obsessed: Woodworking." *HuffPost*, June 5, 2012. https://www.huffpost.com/entry/nick-offerman-woodworking_b_1569650.

Owens, Alexandra. "Nick Offerman Talks Woodworking, the Value of Craftsmanship and Americana." Sotheby's, January 10, 2017. https://www.sothebys.com/en/articles/nick-offerman-talks-woodworking-the-value-of-craftsmanship-and-americana.

Shenk, Timothy. "Already Great." *Dissent*, Spring 2019. https://www.dissentmagazine.org/article/already-great/.

CHAPTER 3:
"Surrounded by Negativity"
(Planning the First Season)

Author interviews with Greg Daniels, Dan Goor, Norm Hiscock, Dean Holland, Kirston Mann, Ian Phillips, Aubrey Plaza, Amy Poehler, Morgan Sackett, and Michael Schur.

Voss, Brandon. "A-List: Amy Poehler." *Advocate*, April 6, 2009. https://www.advocate.com/news/2009/04/06/list-amy-poehler.

Poehler, *Yes Please*.

Potts, "Aziz Ansari Set for NBC's 'Parks and Recreation.'"

Knope, Leslie. *Pawnee: The Greatest Town in America*. New York: Hachette, 2011.

"Leslie Knope–Approved: How to Tour the Real-Life Pawnee of 'Parks and Rec.'" OneTravel, accessed July 15, 2025. https://www.onetravel.com/going-places/7-parks-and-recreation-locations-you-can-visit-in-real-life.

Catlin, Roger. "Small Town Yucks: 'Parks and Recreation,' by West Hartford Native, Parodies Municipal Government; New NBC Comedy." *Hartford Courant*, April 5, 2009, G1.

Finke, Nikki. "Problems with NBC's 'Parks & Recreation.'" *Deadline*, March 23, 2009. https://deadline.com/2009/03/problems-with-nbcs-parks-and-recreation-rough-cut-pilot-and-amy-poehlers-character-8888/.

CHAPTER 4: "Deluded, Vain, and Completely Out of Her Depth" (Season 1)

Author interviews with Alison Becker, Greg Daniels, Dan Goor, Norm Hiscock, Dean Holland, Kirston Mann, Mark Rivers, and Michael Schur.

Graham, Mark. "CBS Wins 2008–2009 TV Ratings Race, While NBC Places Fourth." *Vulture*, May 26, 2009. https://www.vulture.com/2009/05/nbc_4th_place.html.

Rosen, Christopher. "Ben Silverman, the Consummate TV Executive." *Observer*, August 4, 2009. https://observer.com/2009/08/ben-silverman-the-consummate-tv-executive/.

Belloni, Matthew. "It's Ten O'Clock. Do You Know Where Your Network President Is?" *Esquire*, December 1, 2007. https://www.esquire.com/entertainment/tv/interviews/a3846/silverman1207/.

Camunas, Mike. "Cute Show and Funny: Local Parks and Recreation Managers Can Relate to New Comedy." *St. Petersburg Times*, April 14, 2009, 3.

Poniewozik, James. "Parks and Recreation: Shovel Ready." *Time*, April 9, 2009. https://entertainment.time.com/2009/04/09/parks-and-recreation-shovel-ready/.

Stanley, Alessandra. "Misguided, She Yearns to Guide." *New York Times*, April 8, 2009. https://www.nytimes.com/2009/04/09/arts/television/09park.html.

Leitch, Will. "The Poehler Effect." *New York*, April 2, 2009. https://nymag.com/arts/tv/features/55851/.

Sheffield, Rob. "Trapped in the Cubicle." *Rolling Stone*, April 30, 2009, 32–33.

Seidman, Robert. "Top NBC Primetime Shows, May 11–17, 2009." TV by the

Numbers, May 19, 2009. https://web.archive.org/web/20091118060340/http://tvbythenumbers.com:80/2009/05/19/top-nbc-primetime-shows-may-11-17-2009/19091.

Sepinwall, Alan. "Parks and Recreation, 'Rock Show': Mouse-Rat! Mouse-Rat!" *What's Alan Watching?*, May 14, 2009. https://sepinwall.blogspot.com/2009/05/parks-and-recreation-rock-show-mouse.html.

ABC Television Network Press Release: Season Rankings. ABC Medianet, retrieved May 11, 2025. https://web.archive.org/web/20100427072605/http://www.abcmedianet.com/web/dnr/dispDNR.aspx?id=052709_07.

CHAPTER 5:
"That Extra Realness"
(Season 2)

Author interviews with Mo Collins, Greg Daniels, Katie Dippold, Dan Goor, Norm Hiscock, Dean Holland, Jay Jackson, Dave King, Kirston Mann, Nick Offerman, Ian Phillips, Aubrey Plaza, Mark Rivers, and Michael Schur.

Offerman, Nick. *Paddle Your Own Canoe*. New York: Dutton, 2014.

Haglage, Abby. "Parks and Recreation's Aziz Ansari Is 30 Years Old and Writing a Book About Modern Love." *Daily Beast*, November 12, 2013. https://www.thedailybeast.com/parks-and-recreations-aziz-ansari-is-30-years-old-and-writing-a-book-about-modern-love/.

Werts, Diane. "Laffers Seek Flail-Safe: Winning Characters Keep Sitcoms Alive While They Figure Out Funny." *Variety*, June 17, 2009, A1.

Pannett, Rachel. "A Same-Sex Penguin Pair Captured Hearts. After One Died, the Other Sang." *Washington Post*, August 22, 2024. https://www.washingtonpost.com/lifestyle/2024/08/22/gay-penguin-couple-sydney/.

Schur, Mike. "'Parks and Rec' Boss Mike Schur Pens Tribute to Harris Wittels: 'He Was Basically a Human Teddy Bear.'" *Hollywood Reporter*, February 24, 2014. https://www.hollywoodreporter.com/tv/tv-news/parks-rec-boss-mike-schur-777476/.

Knope. *Pawnee: The Greatest Town in America*.

Poehler. *Yes Please*.

CHAPTER 6:
"A Game Changer"
(Seasons 2 and 3)

Author interviews with Mo Collins, Greg Daniels, Dan Goor, Dean Holland, Rob Lowe, Kirston Mann, Jason Mantzoukas, Amy Poehler, Michael Schur, and Adam Scott.

Poehler. *Yes Please.*

Hibberd, James. "Three NBC Rookies Join Pickup Truck." *Hollywood Reporter*, October 26, 2009, 5.

"Final 2009–10 Broadcast Primetime Show Average Viewership." TV by the Numbers, June 16, 2010. https://web.archive.org/web/20190506213621/https://tvbythenumbers.zap2it.com/broadcast/final-2009-10-broadcast-primetime-show-average-viewership/54336/.

"Wealthier People Watch 'Parks & Rec,' 'Modern Family.'" *HuffPost*, November 15, 2013. https://www.huffpost.com/entry/parks-and-rec-audience_n_4283991.

Shenk. "Already Great."

Andreeva, Nellie. "Peacock Gives 'Parks' the Good News Early." *Hollywood Reporter*, February 1, 2010, 5.

Rizzo, Carita. "A Day in the Life of 'Parks and Recreation' Writers." *Hollywood Reporter*, June 7, 2010. https://www.reuters.com/article/lifestyle/a-day-in-the-life-of-parks-and-recreation-writers-idUSTRE6560PO/.

CHAPTER 7:
"You Take a Running Leap and You Learn to Fly"
(Seasons 3 and 4)

Interviews with Katie Dippold, Dan Goor, Norm Hiscock, Dean Holland, Rob Lowe, Kirston Mann, Ian Phillips, Aubrey Plaza, Amy Poehler, Mark Rivers, Michael Schur, and Adam Scott.

Carter, Bill. "A Sitcom Grows Up and Finds Its Identity." *New York Times*, October 5, 2011. https://www.nytimes.com/2011/10/06/arts/television/parks-and-recreation-finds-its-legs-on-nbc.html.

Poehler. *Yes Please.*

Porter, Rick. "'Parks and Recreation': A Tale of Two Cities." Zap2it, May 6, 2011. https://web.archive.org/web/20160202034455/http://zap2it.com/2011/05/parks-and-recreation-a-tale-of-two-cities/.

Paskin, Willa. "Rashida Jones: 'I'm the town slut.'" *Salon*, August 5, 2012. https://www.salon.com/2012/08/05/rashida_jones_im_the_town_slut/.

Goodman, Tim. "Parks and Recreation—TV Review." *Hollywood Reporter*, January 19, 2011. https://www.hollywoodreporter.com/tv/tv-reviews/parks-recreation-tv-review-73599/.

Rizzo. "A Day in the Life."

Carr, David. "After a Year of Ruin, Some Hope." *New York Times*, December 20, 2009. https://www.nytimes.com/2009/12/21/business/media/21carr.html.

"2010–11 Season Broadcast Primetime Show Viewership Averages." TV by the Numbers, June 1, 2011. https://web.archive.org/web/20190828222426/https://tvbythenumbers.zap2it.com/1/2010-11-season-broadcast-primetime-show-viewership-averages/94407/.

Shenk. "Already Great."

CHAPTER 8:
"Prime-Time Television's Most Committed Political Enthusiast"
(Seasons 4 and 5)

Author interviews with Megan Amram, Kathryn Hahn, Kay Hanley, Dean Holland, Dave King, Aubrey Plaza, Paul Rudd, Morgan Sackett, Adam Scott, and Olympia Snowe.

Carter, Bill. "Official from Pawnee, Ind., Buttonholes Senators." *New York Times*, July 25, 2012. https://www.nytimes.com/2012/07/26/arts/television/parks-and-recreation-goes-to-washington.html.

"Parks and Recreation at PaleyFest LA 2012: Full Conversation." Paley Center for Media, YouTube, posted April 27, 2020. https://www.youtube.com/watch?v=Kf97eHa7n9Y&ab_channel=ThePaleyCenterforMedia.

Lindquist, David. "Ron Swanson: The Man and the Mustache." *IndyStar*, February 24, 2015. https://www.indystar.com/story/entertainment/arts/2015/02/24/parks-farewell-pawnee-offerman-swanson-aziz-elmo-steak-indianapolis/23953575/.

CHAPTER 9:
"A Singularly Compelling Representation of the Liberal Spirit"
(Political Philosophy in *Parks and Rec*)

Lacob, Jace. "On the Set of 'Parks.'" *Newsweek*, September 19, 2011, Newsweek Web Exclusives.

Author interviews with Alison Becker, Mo Collins, Kirston Mann, Jason Mantzoukas, Nick Offerman, Amy Poehler, and Adam Scott.

Lefebvre, Alexandre. *Liberalism as a Way of Life*. Princeton: Princeton University Press, 2024.

Engstrom, Erika. "'Knope We Can!' Primetime Feminist Strategies in NBC's Parks and Recreation." GenderWatch, Fall 2013, 6–11, 20–21.

Haring, Bruce. "Patton Oswalt's 'Parks and Recreation' Rant Was Copied by Disney's 'Book of Boba Fett.'" *Deadline*, May 24, 2024. https://deadline.com/2024/05/patton-oswalts-parks-and-recreation-rant-copied-book-of-boba-fett-1235940635/.

Wilson, Joe. "Spending, Ron Swanson–style." *Politico*, May 27, 2010. https://www.politico.com/story/2010/05/spending-ron-swanson-style-037824.

"In an Extraordinary Breach of Congressional Decorum, a Republican Lawmaker Shouted 'You Lie' at President Barack Obama During His Speech to Congress Wednesday. Rep. Joe Wilson, (R) S.C." Associated Press, September 19, 2009. https://newsroom.ap.org/editorial-photos-videos/detail?itemid=10329ea8d2533739ff6eb01d19172684&mediatype=video&source=youtube.

Barr, Andy. "Joe Wilson: Right-Wing Hero." *Politico*, September 16, 2009. https://www.politico.com/story/2009/09/joe-wilson-right-wing-folk-hero-027220.

Sheffield, Rob. "Captain America." *Rolling Stone*, November 24, 2011, 32.

Kleinfeld, Rachel. "Polarization, Democracy, and Political Violence in the United States: What the Research Says." Carnegie Endowment for International Peace, September 5, 2023. https:// carnegieendowment.org/research/2023/09/polarization-democracy-and-political-violence-in-the-united-states-what-the-research-says?lang=en.

Schama, Simon. "Onward Christian Soldiers." *Guardian*, November 5, 2004. https://www.theguardian.com/world/2004/nov/05/usa.uselections2004.

"Political Polarization in the American Public." Pew Research Center, June 12, 2014. https://www.pewresearch.org/politics/2014/06/12/political-polarization-in-the-american-public/.

"As Partisan Hostility Grows, Signs of Frustration with the Two-Party System." Pew Research Center, August 9, 2022. https://www.pewresearch.org/politics/2022/08/09/as-partisan-hostility-grows-signs-of-frustration-with-the-two-party-system/.

Rogers, Sarah. "How to Be a Better Person: The Ethics of Now with Michael Schur." Kenan Institute for Ethics at Duke, October 20, 2022. https://kenan.ethics

.duke.edu/how-to-be-a-better-person-the-ethics-of-now-with-michael-schur/.

Soloski, Alexis. "I'm a Type-A Know-It-All. Leslie Knope Showed Me That's a Good Thing." *New York Times*, August 12, 2020. https://www.nytimes.com/2020/08/12/arts/television/parks-and-recreation-amy-poehler.html.

Pilkington, Ed. "Obama Angers Midwest Voters with Guns and Religion Remark." *Guardian*, April 14, 2008. https://www.theguardian.com/world/2008/apr/14/barackobama.uselections2008.

Weiner, Jonah. "Aziz Ansari." *Rolling Stone*, September 15, 2011, 8–10.

Memmott, Carol. "Hoosier Author?" *USA Today*, October 6, 2011, D2.

Knope. *Pawnee: The Greatest Town in America*.

CHAPTER 10: "This Guy Deserves Happiness, Too" (Seasons 5 and 6)

Author interviews with Megan Amram, Mo Collins, Greg Daniels, Katie Dippold, Billy Eichner, Dan Goor, Kay Hanley, Norm Hiscock, Dean Holland, Dave King, Rob Lowe, Joe Mande, Jason Mantzoukas, Nick Offerman, Amy Poehler, Morgan Sackett, Michael Schur, and Jen Statsky.

Patten, Dominic. "Full 2012–2013 TV Season Series Rankings." *Deadline*, May 23, 2013. https://deadline.com/2013/05/tv-season-series-rankings-2013-full-list-506970/.

Heisler, Steve. "Parks and Recreation: 'Swing Vote.'" AV Club, April 26, 2013. https://www.avclub.com/parks-and-recreation-swing-vote-1798176603.

Koenig, Seth. "New Gloucester Furniture Maker to Appear on NBC's 'Parks and Recreation.'" *Bangor Daily News*, December 3, 2012. https://www.bangordailynews.com/2012/12/04/news/new-gloucester-furniture-maker-to-appear-on-nbcs-parks-and-recreation/.

Haskell, Josh. "Newt Gingrich Calls 'Parks and Rec' Cameo 'Great Fun.'" ABC News, December 4, 2012. https://abcnews.go.com/blogs/entertainment/2012/12/newt-gingrich-stumbles-into-parks-and-rec-cameo.

Waxman, Sharon. "Murphy Brown's Soft Spot Sitcom Goes Easy on Guest Newt Gingrich." *Washington Post*, February 7, 1996. https://www.washingtonpost.com/archive/lifestyle/1996/02/07/murphy-browns-soft-spot-sitcom-goes-easy-on-guest-newt-gingrich/d1f5ff32-6a5a-45f0-81f6-b9d5519dd255/.

"ALL the Bloopers from Parks & Recreation." Comedy Bites, YouTube, posted November 2, 2024. https://www.youtube.com/watch?v=Zre9j6JCdAg&ab_channel=ComedyBites.

Kissell, Rick. "Big Four Nets Embrace Changes in Skedding Patterns This Fall." *Variety*, May 16, 2013. https://variety.com/2013/tv/news/big-four-nets-embrace-changes-in-skedding-patterns-this-fall-1200482672/.

Villareal, Yvonne. "'Parks and Recreation' Facing Changes and Crossroads." *Los Angeles Times*, September 20, 2013. https://www.latimes.com/entertainment/tv/showtracker/la-et-st-ca-parks-and-recreation-20130922-story.html.

Aurthur, Kate. "Rob Lowe and Rashida Jones Will Be Leaving 'Parks and Recreation.'" *BuzzFeed*, July 31, 2013. https://www.buzzfeed.com/kateaurthur/rob-lowe-and-rashida-jones-leaving-parks-and-recreat.

"The Laws of Dunshire." Cephalofair, June 5, 2014. https://cephalofair.com/blogs/blog/cones-dunshire.

"Oprah Favorite Things—Bees!" *Conan*, YouTube, posted August 15, 2020. https://www.youtube.com/watch?v=ImDj57VeaC0&ab_channel=TeamCoco.

Snierson, Dan. "'Parks and Recreation': Michael Schur on the Decision to End the Show." *Entertainment Weekly*, May 21, 2014. https://ew.com/article/2014/05/21/parks-and-recreation-season-7-final-michael-schur/.

Nordyke, Kimberly. "WGN America Nabs 'Parks and Recreation' Reruns." *Hollywood Reporter*, January 23, 2013. https://www.hollywoodreporter.com/tv/tv-news/parks-recreation-reruns-land-at-414988/.

Schneider, Michael. "'Office' Swings into Syndication." *Variety*, September 25, 2009. https://variety.com/2009/tv/features/office-swings-into-syndication-1118009209/.

Snierson, Dan. "Inside the Final Season of 'Parks and Recreation.'" *Entertainment Weekly*, January 13, 2015. https://ew.com/article/2015/01/13/parks-and-recreation-season-7-final/.

CHAPTER 11:
"The Fruits of the Knope Agenda"
(The Final Season)

Author interviews with Megan Amram, Billy Eichner, Kathryn Hahn, Joe Mande, Jason Mantzoukas, Nick Offerman, Amy Poehler, Morgan Sackett, and Michael Schur.

Poniewozik, James. "NBC Announces Plans to Burn Off Final *Parks and*

Recreation Season." *Time*, December 1, 2014. https://time.com/3612697/parks-and-recreation-finale-nbc/.

Snierson. "Inside the Final Season."

Shenk. "Already Great."

Fallon, Kevin. "The Brilliant, Utterly Depressing 'Parks and Rec' Premiere—and the End of a Comedy Era." *Daily Beast*, January 14, 2015. https://www.thedailybeast.com/the-brilliant-utterly-depressing-parks-and-rec-premiere and-the-end-of-a-comedy-era/.

Wright, Megh. "Werner Herzog to Cameo in 'Parks and Rec,' Which He's Never Seen Before." *Vulture*, September 5, 2014. https://www.vulture.com/2014/09/werner-herzog-to-cameo-in-parks-and-rec-which-hes-never-seen-before.html.

Busis, Hillary. "'Parks and Recreation': Amy Poehler Announces That She Wants Bill Murray to Play the Mayor of Pawnee." *Entertainment Weekly*, March 17, 2011. https://ew.com/article/2011/03/17/parks-and-recreation-amy-poehler-bill-murray/.

Snierson, Dan. "'Parks and Recreation' Got Bill Murray to Play Mayor Gunderson?! How They Did It." *Entertainment Weekly*, February 18, 2015. https://ew.com/article/2015/02/18/parks-and-recreation-mayor-gunderson/.

"Every Single Time Ben Looks into the Camera on Parks & Rec." By junedug, YouTube, posted April 22, 2016. https://www.youtube.com/watch?v=CnedYYgg3N0&ab_channel=junedug.

Abramovitch, Seth. "'Parks and Rec' Writer Harris Wittels' Death at 30: Humblebrags and the Specter of Heroin." *Hollywood Reporter*, February 24, 2015. https://www.hollywoodreporter.com/tv/tv-news/parks-rec-writer-harris-wittels-777477/.

Rosenberg, Alyssa. "What 'Parks and Recreation' Taught Me About Life." *Washington Post*, February 25, 2015. https://www.washingtonpost.com/news/act-four/wp/2015/02/25/what-parks-and-recreation-taught-me-about-life/.

Poniewozik, James. "Knope and Change." *Time*, January 22, 2015. https://time.com/3678065/knope-and-change/.

Hemner, Nicole. "Do Liberals Want Parks and Rec or House of Cards?" *U.S. News & World Report*, December 14, 2015. https://www.usnews.com/opinion/blogs/nicole-hemmer/2015/03/03/obama-era-is-parks-and-rec-while-clinton-would-be-house-of-cards.

Bunch, Sonny. "And Now You May Laugh." *National Review*, September 22, 2014. https://www.nationalreview.com/magazine/2014/09/22/and-now-you-may-laugh/.

Sepinwall, Alan. "All the Presidents' TV Shows: Series That Defined Each Era." *Rolling Stone*, January 20, 2021. https://www.rollingstone.com/tv-movies/tv-movie-lists/president-tv-series-defined-era-994869/richard-nixon-first-term-comedy-rowan-martins-laugh-in-nbc-1968-73-997402/.

Suebsaeng, Asawin. "How 'Parks and Rec's' Ron Swanson Became the Unlikely Libertarian Hero of the Obama Era." *Daily Beast*, February 24, 2015. https://www.thedailybeast.com/how-parks-and-recs-ron-swanson-became-the-unlikely-libertarian-hero-of-the-obama-era/.

Bigler, Taylor. "Ron Swanson's 12 Wisest Quotes About the Government." *Daily Caller*, October 3, 2013. https://dailycaller.com/2013/10/03/ron-swansons-12-wisest-quotes-about-the-government-photos/.

Ryan. "'Parks and Recreation.'"

Knope, Leslie. "A Letter to America from Leslie Knope, Regarding Donald Trump." *Vox*, November 10, 2016. https://www.vox.com/first-person/2016/11/10/13580582/leslie-knope-donald-trump.

"A Conversation with Mike Schur." ND College of Arts and Letters, YouTube, posted September 19, 2019. https://www.youtube.com/watch?app=desktop&v=cWCVuml10EI&ab_channel=NDCollegeofArtsandLetters.

Nahman, Haley. "If You Haven't Heard of 'Hopepunk,' Allow Me to Gently Introduce You." *Repeller*, January 23, 2019. https://web.archive.org/web/20230126165711/https://repeller.com/hopepunk-new-optimistic-movement/.

Romano, Aja. "Hopepunk, the Latest Storytelling Trend, Is All About Weaponized Optimism." *Vox*, December 27, 2018. https://www.vox.com/2018/12/27/18137571/what-is-hopepunk-noblebright-grimdark.

Adalian, Josef. "'Parks' and Relocation: Streaming's Musical Chairs Problem." *Vulture*, October 1, 2020. https://www.vulture.com/2020/10/parks-recreation-leaves-netflix-for-peacock.html.

Sharf, Zack. "Netflix Users Are Spending More Time Streaming 'The Office' Than Any Other Show—Report." *IndieWire*, April 24, 2019. https://www.indiewire.com/features/general/the-office-netflix-most-streamed-series-friends-1202127682/.

Lefebvre. *Liberalism as a Way of Life.*

CHAPTER 12:
"Rupture and Repair"
(*Parks and Rec* Meets the Modern Moment)

Way, Katie. "I Went on a Date with Aziz Ansari. It Turned into the Worst Night of My Life." Babe, January 13, 2018. https://babe.net/2018/01/13/aziz-ansari-28355.

Parker, Ryan. "Aziz Ansari Addresses Sexual Misconduct Allegation in Netflix Special: 'I Just Felt Terrible.'" *Hollywood Reporter*, July 9, 2019. https://www.hollywoodreporter.com/tv/tv-news/aziz-ansari-addresses-sexual-misconduct-allegation-netflix-special-i-just-felt-terrible-1223082/.

"Top 100 Stars in Leading Roles at the Domestic Box Office." The Numbers, accessed May 14, 2025. https://www.the-numbers.com/box-office-star-records/domestic/lifetime-acting/top-grossing-leading-stars.

Author interviews with Megan Amram, Alison Becker, Greg Daniels, Katie Dippold, Dan Goor, Dean Holland, Jay Jackson, Dave King, Rob Lowe, Kirston Mann, Jason Mantzoukas, Nick Offerman, Aubrey Plaza, Amy Poehler, Mark Rivers, Paul Rudd, Morgan Sackett, Michael Schur, Adam Scott, and Jen Statsky.

Yuan, Jada. "How Nick Offerman Became a Progressive in Right-Wing Clothing." *Washington Post*, April 25, 2024. https://www.washingtonpost.com/entertainment/movies/2024/04/25/nick-offerman-civil-war-politics/.

DeBianchi, Antonia. "Aubrey Plaza and Nick Offerman Have a *Parks and Rec* Reunion Riding Dragons in Mountain Dew Super Bowl Commercial." *People*, February 6, 2024. https://people.com/super-bowl-2024-aubrey-plaza-nick-offerman-parks-and-recreation-reunion-mountain-dew-super-bowl-commercial-8558247.

Nardozzi, Erica. "People Left Stunned After Only Just Realizing 'Galentine's Day' Was Invented by a Popular Sitcom Character." *Daily Mail*, February 13, 2024. https://www.dailymail.co.uk/femail/article-13079813/galentines-invented-character-popular-sitcom.html.

Poehler, Amy (@amypoehler). February 13, 2024, TikTok. https://www.tiktok.com/@amypoehler/video/7335135963389332782?lang=en.

Snierson, Dan. "*Parks and Recreation* Creator Mike Schur Breaks Down the Uplifting Reunion Special." *Entertainment Weekly*, May 1, 2020. https://ew.com/tv/parks-and-recreation-mike-schur-reunion-special/.

Porter, Rick. "TV Ratings: 'Parks and Recreation' Special Scores for NBC." *Hollywood Reporter*, May 1, 2020. https://www.hollywoodreporter.com/tv/tv

-news/parks-rec-young-sheldon-tv-ratings-thursday-april-30-2020-1292806/.

Ryan, Patrick. "'Parks and Recreation': 5 Questions About NBC's Coronavirus-Themed Special, Answered." *USA Today*, April 28, 2020. https://www.usatoday.com/story/entertainment/tv/2020/04/28/parks-and-recreation-everything-we-know-coronavirus-special/3041901001/.

Abbott, Kate, Hannah J. Davies, Gwilym Mumford, Phil Harrison, and Jack Seale. "The 100 Best TV Shows of the 21st Century." *Guardian*, September 16, 2019. https://www.theguardian.com/tv-and-radio/2019/sep/16/100-best-tv-shows-of-the-21st-century.

"The 100 Greatest TV Series of the 21st Century." *BBC Culture*, October 18, 2021. https://www.bbc.com/culture/article/20211015-the-100-greatest-tv-series-of-the-21st-century.

Fienberg, Daniel, Angie Han, and Robyn Bahr. "Hollywood Reporter Critics Pick the 50 Best TV Shows of the 21st Century (So Far)." *Hollywood Reporter*, October 4, 2023. https://www.hollywoodreporter.com/lists/best-tv-shows-21st-century/sex-and-the-city-hbo-1998-2004/.

Borum, Caty, Paula Weissman, and David Conrad-Perez. "Watching Out for Democracy: How Entertainment TV Portrays Civic Leadership and Civic Engagement in the United States." Center for Media & Social Impact, June 2022. https://cmsimpact.org/report/watching-out-for-democracy/.

INDEX

Index

Index

ABOUT THE AUTHOR

New York Times bestselling author **Jennifer Keishin Armstrong** has written seven pop culture history books, including *Seinfeldia*, *Mary and Lou and Rhoda and Ted*, *"Sex and the City" and Us*, and *When Women Invented Television*. She is the cofounder of the "Ministry of Pop Culture" Substack and a former local newspaper reporter. She lives in New Paltz, New York.